MW01617742

THE SPEAKER'S BLUEPRINT

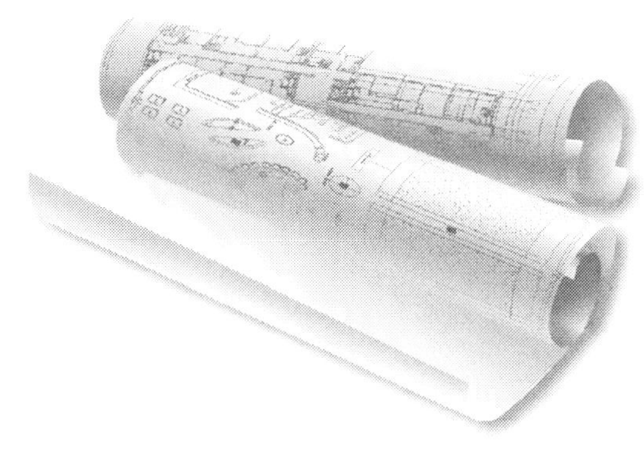

5 Essentials When Building A Great Speech

BRIAN WOOLF

The Speaker's Blueprint:

5 Essentials When Building a Great Speech

ISBN-13: 978-0-9632025-9-8 (paperback)

1. Speech. 2. Public Speaking 3. Communications

Intent: The quotations from all sources used in this book have been chosen to illustrate excellence. In adherence to the "fair use" rule of the US copyright law, this book makes limited use of copyrighted excerpts from the Toastmasters World Championship of Public Speaking® for the purpose of criticism and commentary, and for the purpose of providing a public good by elevating presentation skills of aspiring speakers. As indicated by my association with Toastmasters going back over 50 years, it is my hope that this book increases the number of people exposed to the organization and its mission.

Cover Design: Amy Tedder, atyourdesign.com

Published by Teal Books

brianwoolf@speakers-toolbox.com

ALSO BY BRIAN WOOLF

Shrinking the Corporate Waistline
Measured Marketing: A Tool to Shape Food Store Strategy
Customer Specific Marketing: The New Power in Retailing
Loyalty Marketing: The Second Act
The Speaker's Toolbox: 47 Tools to Build Better Speeches
The Non-Humorist's Handbook: How to Easily Add Humor to Your Speeches

Available at Amazon and leading booksellers

For quantity discounts, please contact: *brianwoolf@speakers-toolbox.com*

First edition October 2019

Printed in the United States of America

To Marie

Contents

Introduction

Great projects are always built from a blueprint... Jim Rohn

The purpose of *The Speaker's Blueprint* is to give you an easy-to-understand framework to help you build great **persuasive** speeches.

You will learn the tools, techniques and tricks of the trade of designing and constructing unforgettable speeches, drawn from decades of observing speakers, studying speeches, and assessing what works best. The framework comprises five inter-related parts:

Point. A clear point or message is essential. Otherwise, why are you speaking? And to achieve an optimal outcome, point out to the audience the first action step to be taken.

Opening. Grabbing your audience's attention at the beginning is essential to optimize your limited time with them. Make every minute matter.

"Konnect." If you don't connect, you have no effect. This is the most essential element in speaking. The stronger your audience connection, the more effective your persuasion.

Emotion. Emotion is essential because it precedes logic when persuading others. If you don't show how you feel about your message, why should your audience feel excited about it?

Remember. As the purpose of most persuasive speeches is to transmit an idea or point, it's essential that you help your audience remember it. For as experienced speakers tell us: *If they can't repeat it, they didn't get it.*

These essentials are readily remembered by the mnemonic **POKER.** And just as a poker is used to stir the coals to bring a fire to life, this POKER will give life to your speeches.

Each of the five POKER essentials has a section devoted to it. Each begins with an explanatory overview followed by details, guidelines, and quotes. *The quotes chosen illustrate speaking techniques, not necessarily the beliefs expressed.* Those obviously belong to the person quoted.

To demonstrate different POKER elements in action, included are actual speeches with explanatory comments. Most have YouTube viewing links listed.

In my experience, too many speeches are mediocre for one simple reason: the speaker is unaware of the key elements of success. It is my hope that the POKER framework, its supporting techniques, and the examples given, will guide you to the excellence you seek.

My special thanks to those permitting publication of their speeches and to Randy Harvey, Gregg Parr, Sindy Martin, and Phoenix Miller for their invaluable help.

Brian Woolf
Greenville, South Carolina
October 9, 2019

SECTION 1

POINT

Let your message launch a thousand lips. [AN]

There is something in the makeup of human beings that makes us dream about building things, doing things, changing things, and making things better. The improvement of our countries and cities, the growth of our companies and organizations, and the betterment of our individual health and attitudes have all come about because of those dreams.

The translation of those dreams, big and small, into reality usually comes when people like you and me persuade others to think, feel or do something differently.

This book introduces you to proven practices that will help you, as a speaker, become more persuasive in translating your ideas and your dreams into reality.

This section helps you clarify what it is that you want to persuade others to think, feel, or do differently.

And should your speech goal be the last mentioned —the ultimate in persuasion — to persuade audience members to do something different about something — which covers anything from exercise to excellence, from giving to personal growth, from better health to more happiness ... the possibilities are limitless — you will be urged in this section to show your audience how to start and **point** them towards the first action step they must take to achieve that something different.

Accordingly, the section is deliberately titled **Point** to emphasize encouraging and **pointing** your audience towards that first action step to achieve what you consider worthy. This emphasis echoes Helen Keller's belief that *Ideas without action are worthless.* In the speaking world, desired action, begun by that first step, is considered the pinnacle of persuasive speeches.

Having said that, understand that not all persuasive speeches involve action. Some simply seek to persuade you to a different way of thinking about an issue. Also understand that not all action-oriented persuasive speeches demand instant action. Sometimes they are conditional, such as "Whenever X happen, respond with Y." In these cases, you point to the first step to be taken after that specific trigger event takes place.

In other words, there are gradations of persuasive speeches with gradations of outcomes. This section explains the differences and steps to take so that you will be successful in influencing your audiences to think, feel or do something differently about the ideas and values you care about.

1.1 Your Message and Your Point

The most important part of a speech is not the message, but rather what the audience does with the message hours, days, weeks, months, or even years after they hear it. [LM^]

Introduction

A persuasive speech delivers a message that seeks to influence the audience to **think, feel**, or **do (or act)** something differently. You have two options:

- **Change their Attitude** (i.e., how they think and feel about the issue.) Changing attitudes shows the effect of your **message** on their hearts and minds.
- **Change how they Act** (i.e., inviting them to take the first step in altering their habits or behavior.) This means taking the next step beyond changing their Attitude and starting a path of action.

Where the Two Options Are Used

The Attitude Option (think or feel differently) is common in these situations:
- The message is broad rather than specific, conceptual rather than concrete
- The speaker wants to influence only the audience's thinking on an issue
- The speaker leaves it to the audience to decide and act in their own way
- Action on the message in the short term may not be appropriate
- The speech length is insufficient to explain action details
- The speaker is not fully confident of his message

The Action Option (pointing to the next step) is common in these situations:
- The speaker believes the sooner a listener acts, the greater the chance of adoption
- The speaker lives his message, knows its benefits, and wants others to gain
- The audience needs an encouraging invitation to take the first step
- The speaker believes in the adage: *Strike while the iron is hot*
- The speaker has a deep belief in his or her message
- An invitation to act flows naturally from the speech
- The message is clear and specific

Simple Examples of the Two Options

Achieve better health with yoga.
Achieve better health with yoga — start tomorrow with 10 Cobra poses.

People ache for applause.
People ache for applause — every Friday recognize an excellent performer.

School bullying is a big problem.
School bullying is a big problem — call your kid's teacher and ask how you can help.

The first lines, above, are important messages, but are general and non-directional. They may change how a listener thinks or feels on those subjects but whether or when they result in action is questionable due to their lack of next-step specificity.

The second lines are the same messages coupled with a suggested specific starting **point** to translate the message into action.

Which Option to Use?

Both can be successful. But the latter, the Action option, is typically more successful because when audience members take an active step towards adopting your message, it indicates they have bought into it. Therefore, it makes sense to point to and invite the audience to take that first step.

More Than One Possible Action

Note that inviting an audience to take this step may comprise more than one action. For example, a North Carolina speaker, Gregg Parr, recently spoke to a group of professional women on the power of speaking. He concluded his 45-minute presentation encouraging those wishing to become better speakers to begin their journey with three simple steps in the next 30 days:

- Watch one of three TED talks by women (which he named)
- Speak once where you haven't spoken before (e.g., at work, church, or an organization you belong to)
- Invest in yourself by joining Toastmasters (he mentioned a specific local club and its next meeting time, location, and website)

Specificity of what to do next makes taking that first action step so much easier.

Point Towards Action

Action is the desired ultimate outcome of most persuasive speeches even when the immediate goal is to alter how the audience thinks or feels. Why? Because speakers hope those thoughts and feelings will, eventually, be translated into action.

The term Point in this section is highlighted because it reminds us to point the way to the specific first step that will transform your message into reality. It points the audience towards action and implementation.

Delivering a message without pointing to the first step means the audience must decide if, how, and when they should act. You have probably already experienced human nature's law of diminishing intent—the longer listeners wait to act on what they hear, the less likely they will. Increasing the probability of your message being adopted comes by pointing to the first action step. If you really care about your message being adopted, a point-less speech is pointless.

1.2 Differences: Message vs Point

Not every message has a point. But every point is part of a message.

What is a Message?

- The general theme of your speech
- Your one-line answer to a problem
- The idea you want your audience to embrace and act upon in some way
- What you want the audience remember even if they forget everything else [~LE]
- What you want your audience thinking about when your presentation concludes [DH^]
- The heart, soul, and center of your speech—the one essential thing you want your audience to remember [~JK>]

What is a Point?

- It points to action
- It asks for the sale
- The encouraging push
- The message's call to action
- Seeks acceptance and action
- Presses the audience's action button
- The first specific step the audience is encouraged to take
- The part of your message where your words are converted into action steps
- Answers the audience's *What do you want me to do after you walk off the stage?*
- The sharp point at the end of your message that shows the first step to be taken

Phrases That Point Your Message Towards Action

Think of any great motivational speaker you have heard. Most likely the speaker used the connect-persuade-action format: he connected with you, then persuaded you, and ended with a specific action step for you to start becoming that better person he promised. And his point-to-action phrase was something like this: *I invite you to …*

Here are some suggestions for your own point-towards-action closing phrases. Personalize any of the following that resonate with you:

Are you ready to get started?

Are you ready to make a difference?

Are you ready to take the next step?

Before leaving tonight, please consider …

Consider trying X each morning this week …

Do it now. You have nothing to lose and everything to gain…

Friends, I invite you to take the next step …

Friends, your life can be better by taking this one step …

I assure you, you will never regret …

I believe that …

I invite you to join (give specific names) who are seeking the same outcome …

I strongly urge …

I submit to you that …

I truly hope …

I unequivocally believe that if …

I'm excited about this because … and I want you to be excited about it too—

If this is something that will benefit others who you care about …

If you do this … then …

If you take only one thing away from here today, I want it to be this …

If you want more from life, then …

If you want to … then …

If you want to help others, I invite you to …

If you would like more … I urge you to ….

In one year's time, what decision will you wish you had made today …

It's not just about you, it's about those you care about, too …

It's up to you to make things better, to …

Leave your fingerprints on life. Start by …

Let's commit to making this a better place. Let's commit to …

Let's take the first step to make ours a better world. Let's …

My challenge to you is …

Once a month is not a high price to pay for …

Please don't waste your life, start today …

Starting this moment, for the next 24 hours …

Take a chance. Don't be afraid to …

Take control of your life. Start by …

The next time we meet, I hope you'll tell me you took this step …

The next time you experience X, respond this way …

The next time you hear X then …

You have nothing to lose if …

For 30 days, starting tomorrow, the first time you sit behind your steering wheel I invite you to say out loud… RM>

1.3 Highlights of a Persuasive Masterpiece

The Strangest Secret is described as "the seedling from which the entire personal development industry grew." This still-available audio classic, recorded in 1956, has influenced millions of people world-wide for over six decades. Its simple message speaks directly to each listener about the secret of success and it ends with an invitation to begin a 30-day test to achieve it.

This recording by Earl Nightingale is an example of a brilliantly-crafted, persuasive speech. It begins with an intriguing title, has a curiosity-arousing opening question, provides an explanation of the secret, and ends by pointing to a test to take.

To elaborate: *The Strangest Secret* opens with a question—*Why do so many fail today?* Only 5% of people succeed—and 95% fail. And what is success? *Success is the progressive realization of a worthy ideal.* And from his research Nightingale explains how he discovered the key to success and the key to failure—*We become what we think about*—which he elaborates upon in detail.

Then, calling back to the title, comes his great attention-catching question: *Why do I call it strange and why do I call it a secret?* Nightingale follows with an explanation why and how we can use this knowledge to become a success in our own lives.

After laying out his thinking he addresses us directly—*Now I want to explain how you can apply the secrets you have just heard in your own lives, by undertaking a 30-day test. It's not going to be easy, but if you give it a good try it will completely change your life for the better. You have nothing to lose by taking this test—and everything to gain.* He then goes on to explain his 30-day test.

In summary, Earl Nightingale, a communicator with a quiet persuasive style, awakens our imagination about becoming more successful and explains the elements involved. But he doesn't stop there. He invites us to take the next step by undertaking a 30-day test which he then lays out. He points us to a path that will give us personal success. His message? *We become what we think about.* His point? *The 30-day test.* No wonder this speech is still persuading people today to change their thoughts and actions. It's a wonderful example of a perfect speech and is recommended for your learning pleasure. A google search should find you an available book or audio copy.

Examples from the World Around Us

We see specificity (and urgency) of action every day on television. We see commercials whose message offers "irresistible" benefits followed by an invitation to take an immediate step. Many are like this: *Call the number on the screen in the next 30 minutes and you'll get our New Amazing Product for 30% off.* Advertisers have learned that the message alone is not enough. The call to action—the pointing towards action—is essential to make the sale. Ever wonder how much their sales would drop without this action invitation? Such commercials make one wonder how many "persuasive" speeches are soon forgotten when a point-towards-action is not offered to the audience.

Global charities have taught a parallel lesson: specificity trumps generality. Persuasion based on a single person is more effective than based on a crowd. These masters of separating us from those precious dollars in our bank accounts have found that when seeking money for, say, helping the underfed and underprivileged, the response is much stronger when they invite us to support a specific child or family than contribute to helping a group or country. Helping one specific person is more emotive than helping an anonymous crowd because being able to picture the object of persuasion helps significantly. The lesson? The greater the specificity, the more likely a response. A closer-to-home example is: "Start each day at 4:00AM" trumps "Get up earlier each day." Specificity trumps generality.

1.4 Examples from World Champions

An exemplary demonstration of Pointing is seen in **Craig Valentine**'s World Champion of Public Speaking winning speech. His concluding lines ...

> <u>If you take 5 minutes of silence each day</u> *[The invitational "if"]*
> <u>I guarantee you</u> that the other 23 hours and 55 minutes of your day
> Will be filled with a tranquility, a serenity, a peacefulness
> You never knew even existed. *[Benefit 1]*
> Five minutes of silence will give you confidence
> Exuding from every pore in your being. *[Benefit 2]*
> And five minutes of silence
> Will lead you to feel fulfilled ... *[Benefit 3]*
> No longer do I wake up to my life and fear it.
> All because I had the courage to listen to my spirit. *[Reinforcement 1]*
> Ladies and gentlemen
> I want to leave you with one thing today.
> This one thing
> Is more powerful than anything I could ever say as a speaker.
> More meaningful than anything I can ever say as a Toastmaster.
> I want to leave you with this
> [Stands silent for 12 seconds]— *[Reinforcement 2]*
> Madam Contest Master.

Early in this speech, *The Key to Fulfillment, Craig* tells us how he once contemplated suicide. He goes on to explain how, in our noisy, busy world, he regained wholeness by drawing upon the tranquility of silence. Craig wants his audience in their personal hectic worlds to similarly gain, so he begins his close by pointing out how they can.

He uses the non-aggressive, think-about-this "if" word which is then smothered with a reassuring guarantee and three attractive benefits followed by an amazing, completely unexpected, 12 seconds of silence—a dramatic reminder of his message. His point-to-action—5 minutes of silence daily—suggests it is easy to do and yields benefits that make it completely worthwhile.

Jim Key used the same invitational "if" to close his World Championship speech:

> If you forget everything else I've said
> It would thrill me
> If you remember this—
> It's never, too late to follow your dreams! JK^
> [Ends speech in silence, using sign language]

Otis William Jr, another World Champion Speaker, inspired his audience not to join the "experts of negativity" who say that our dreams and plans cannot be achieved. Instead, he urges joining those who believe accomplishment comes to those who say *It's Possible* (the speech's title.) Otis shares his own DAP success formula, where D=Desire. A=Action. P=Persistence. His encouraging close opens with credibility (*I can do it—so you can do it, too*) and the invitational "if." His point-towards-action comes in his final words:

> I learned that your mind can—and will—
> Amaze your body
> If you just keep saying to yourself:
> It's possible — It's possible— It's possible.

Some speeches seek a change in mental outlook rather than a change in physical behavior. **Vikas Jhingran's** winning WCPS semifinal speech, *Postcard*, is such a speech (view YouTube.com, *Vikas Jhingran Postcard.*) It's an invitation to think differently about life, to be more aware of the beautiful reality around us, of being in the present, rather than going through life viewing surroundings as if they are lifeless postcards.

Vikas ends his speech by describing how he has just been to the Taj Mahal where he was so worried about pickpockets he overlooked enjoying the magnificence in front of him. It was a lifeless experience. Then he creates an image we'll never forget—the Taj Mahal versus a lifeless postcard of it. His message: don't live like a postcard. It's one of my favorite speeches and one of my favorite closing lines.

> Friends, there are too many of us
> Who live our lives worrying about our wallet
> And forget to enjoy the magnificence of the Taj Mahal in front of us—
> Not realizing that if we fail to capture the moment—
> The sound, the smell, the touch, and the feeling —
> What remains is a picture without a soul—
> A memory without emotion—
> Just a postcard——
> Your life is much more than a simple——postcard.

The speech offers another valuable lesson. Should you have an abstract message such as *Adopt an attitude of gratitude* if you use a related vivid image or metaphor you will make it more concrete, more relatable, and more memorable, for your audience.

1.5 Choosing Your Message

Never separate the life you lead from the words you speak. PW+

Introduction

Isn't it strange how we have no problem discussing, sometimes passionately, diverse topics in different conversations over the course of a week, yet when asked to give a speech we often become flustered as we wonder what we should talk about?

Persuasive speeches are best when they involve you. No, I don't mean that you should stand in front of an audience and brag about yourself. I mean talking from your heart about things that have happened to you, or things that didn't happen to you but you show how they influenced or affected you.

Why are persuasive speeches best when given about things you have felt, thought, or experienced? Because details readily bubble to the surface making them easy to write. They are you, talking from within.

Further, when delivering them you are re-living them, giving you authenticity and credibility, perhaps a sparkle. When you talk about things you know or have experienced, your delivery is more animated, your connection is more natural.

What Message Do You Want to Deliver?

Which part of your past do you delve into? Which part of your mind, body or soul; which part of your past, present, or future; which part of your successes, fears, or failures; which part of your beliefs, values, or interests? The possibilities are endless. Your goal is to choose just one issue, one thing, one idea.

One of the best pieces of advice on quickly choosing a message I learned from David Brooks [www.DavidBrooksTexas.com], the 1990 World Champion of Public Speaking. He called it the *Business Card Test.* This is what David wrote;

> *Before you speak or write a single word, ask yourself: "What do I want my audience to think, feel, or do as a result of this presentation?" You may think this is common sense. It is, but it's not common practice. Most speakers skip this step, assuming "I know my material. I'll say it and the audience will hear it; if they hear it, they'll figure out the message." Wrong. Your purpose will never be clearer to a listener than it is to you. Clarity is king. That's why I recommend you apply the Business Card Test.*
>
> *Write on the back of your business card exactly what you want the audience to think, feel, or do, as a result of your presentation. Why use the back of a business card? It's big enough to hold only one handwritten sentence—and if you can't define your purpose in one sentence, you're not ready to speak.*

One sentence. It's that simple—but not that easy. It can take a lot of focused thinking to come up with one sentence of up to a dozen words that is clear, understandable, and memorable. Albert Einstein pithily summed up this concept: *If you can't explain it simply, you don't understand it well enough.*

Mark Brown [WCPS-95] embraced the Business Card challenge and expressed his winning message with great clarity in just five words: *Everyone deserves a second chance.*

Six years later, when coaching Darren LaCroix for his World Championship speech, he gave advice that Darren says made all the difference: *Imagine you are dying and want to share a special lesson you've learned with a favorite young relative. What would it be?* Over the following three days Darren filled three single-lined sheets with possibilities aimed at his young nephew. Reviewing what he wrote, he found four words, part of one line, that exactly captured the essence of what he was aiming at: *Be willing to fail.* Darren won.

"Doc" Blakely, a popular platform speaker, tells new speakers: *If you can't write your message in one sentence, you won't be able to give it in an hour.*

The good news is that you are not married to that one sentence from its conception. As one speaker suggested, it's more like a going-steady arrangement where there's a lot of give and take before you get to the altar. The intention is clear and you still finish up with a refined business-card size message.

Searching for Your Message

If you wish to persuade others to think, feel, or do something different, choose a message you are passionate about. To paraphrase John Wesley, the founder of the Methodist Church: *Be ignited by fire and the crowds will come for miles to see you burn.* An equally appropriate thought comes from Wesley's contemporary, Benjamin Franklin: *Your audience will be no more passionate about your message than you are.* If you want to persuade, choose a message that, first of all, matters—to you.

What issues, topics, subjects are you most passionate about? Do you keep a story file? Can you recall mistakes you've made? Judy Carter, author of *The Message of You*, helpfully suggests *Make your mess your message.* Draw on topics that let your authority, authenticity, and emotion shine through. The important word here is *you*—what moves you? Even if it's an obscure topic, the key ingredient is why it's important to you because only you can re-live it, only you can make it unique.

If you don't already keep a list of such possible topics and issues, the following methods will help you create one that suits you…

The TED Method

Ideas worth spreading has been TED's slogan since its first annual conference in 1990. It's the criteria TED uses to choose their speeches and speakers. It's also a simple but effective way for you to learn what you care about most. Here's the method. Imagine you want to speak at your nearest TEDx next year. Think of 3-5 ideas that you think worthy of spreading to a large TEDx audience—and why. Do that and you are on your way!

The Jeremy Donovan Ask/Drill Down Method

Jeremy has authored several excellent books covering TED and the Toastmasters World Championship of Public Speaking. To find a subject or message he suggests beginning by asking yourself:

- What is the greatest lesson I have ever learned?
- What is the greatest joy I have ever had?
- What is my current life's mission?
  [You may add similar questions.]

Then, to discover more about each choice, drill down:

- How did I learn it?
- When did I learn it?
- Who did I learn it from?

Record your answers, reflect on them, add them to your potential speech file. This ask/drill down approach is common to many search methods as you'll now see.

The Emotions Method

As emotions are a powerful connector to your audience you can search for stories (and therefore messages) through them. Using Paul Ekman's six basic emotions and the ask/drill down approach, ask yourself these emotion-based questions:

- The happiest time of my life was …
- The biggest surprise I've ever had was …
- My saddest moment was when…
- I have never been so angry as when …
- I felt absolutely disgusted when …
- My most fearful (scared) moment was when …

After each response, ask what it meant to you. Result—you'll have more personal stories and message material to incorporate in new speeches.

The Brett Rutledge Method

Rather than choosing his message first and building a speech, Brett Rutledge [WCPS-96] now says he often chooses his core story first, one that he really likes, seeks an appropriate message to fit it, and then builds the speech. This is an excellent short-cut method if you like using stories and have easy access to a variety of them.

The Lessons Learned Method

Patricia Fripp offers this approach. Take a sheet of paper. On the left-hand side, list those people who have influenced you in your life. On the right-hand side, under the heading, What I Learned From this Person (good and/or bad), jot down your memories.
Stories, speeches, messages, and points will appear.

The WWW Method

Randy Harvey [WCPS-04] goes deeper with his WWW approach. He invites us to ask ourselves three questions:

Who are the 4 most important influences in my life?

What was the most important lesson each taught me?

Why do I remember it (and what was the occasion when I learned it)?

This provides a shortcut to your principles and values—your core drivers. Because they involve values, they bring to the surface your authenticity and credibility. They unearth deep-felt elements that will unconsciously play out when you speak.

Why is this important? Here's how Randy, a true connection meister, explains:

> The reason a personal story is stronger when speaking to an audience is that it is already pre-recorded three-dimensionally in your psyche. When you tell a story based on a personal event in your life, or about an individual person in your life, you tell it multidimensionally. While you are telling your story, you have the memories that enfold the tactile and psychological senses: sights, sounds, tastes, touch, smell; and, the six basic emotions including happiness, sadness, surprise, anger, disgust, and fear. These six basic emotions are encoded in our facial expressions and are universal across races and cultures. They all connect.

The Who Am I? Method

On your computer you probably use the screensaver feature that randomly shows your favorite photos, reminding you of many diverse people, places, and experiences across the expanse of your life. A parallel idea is creating a computer Word document where you type a just few words describing each of the myriad things in your life that you can recall that register with you for some reason. Plan to keep adding to it for the rest of your speaking life. Title the document file *Who Am I?* It's your personal file of snippets of your life. Whenever a memory occurs, add it. Don't hold back: throw in the good, the bad, and the ugly—you are creating a widely diverse, colorful composite of your life. You'll find you need only a few words to bring back a clear memory of each entry. It acts as an excellent go-to file when contemplating possible speeches as it provides a rich compost heap of unique ideas for stories, topics, and messages.

To give an idea of entries that might appear, below is a small smattering from my Who Am I? file. Some are serious; some are oddities; some are achievements; and some are failures.

Again, why are such reminders important? Because they are about you. As Scott Adams, the creator of *Dilbert*, points out, *Persuasion is strongest when the message is credible*—and you are most credible when talking about your life.

A Selection of Who Am I? Entries

- Ancient Greece and Rome—lifelong fascinations since first visiting region
- Antarctica—racing with whales
- Antarctica—quiet, white stillness—closest I've ever felt to God
- Arriving exactly on time inspired by favorite novel, *The Count of Monte Cristo*

- Boxed (not well) in early teens
- Cancer—malignant—at 20 —made 3 big wishes if I lived—all done
- Cyril Watson – *You don't need a suitcase to carry around a good education*
- David Duggan — met in my 20's—wisest man I have ever known
- Discovered that when my High School friends changed, so did my grades
- Dr James Farr, Greensboro ... Phrase: *Thank you for sharing that with me*
- El Greco—favorite painter — remember the day and place I discovered him
- Fiona — birth — felt that I was but a link in the human chain since Adam
- Fiona — took her to Disney every half-birthday for 12 years
- First car — accident —speeding
- Highly ethical CEO Feargal took a few hours off each week to ride his horse, which he named *Business*. Secretary told callers he was away on "business."
- Ida D — taught me religious tolerance
- Ina Smith–employee—lost note of appreciation given her—asked for another
- Joined Toastmasters at 22 when it began in New Zealand
- Looked across plane aisle and saw a stranger reading a book I had written
- Loveable Rosie, our Lhasa Apso with her ever-wagging tail
- Major business mentors: THAC, BHP, DSR, NK; later RWK & TES
- Met Norman Rockwell; Peter Drucker; John A. Lee
- Mike, first year University roommate, taught me how to study effectively
- Nearly drowned — saved by sharks
- On tram going home (Cleveland 1979). It stopped. Then started. Man fell under tram. Decapitated as it restarted. Reminder — life is fragile; enjoy each day
- Paper route as kid—biggest lesson—when collecting the fortnightly dues, seeing the diversity of how people act, live, and maintain their homes
- Squibby—age 6—mouth washed out with soap by nun for swearing—big lesson
- Sunsets in Indonesia and Santorini
- The death of my older brother
- Travels around Ireland. Father-in-law and I graded towns by their Irish Coffee
- Very best birthday celebration of my life was my 40th. It was a bitterly cold January night and Marie surprised me at the door as I returned home from work and...
- Visited a Home for the Elderly (at age 8)— a sad memory ever since
- Week-long fast — nothing but water
- Zak Saba (superstitious) stayed in bed every Friday 13th— died there on that day

I highly recommend keeping your own *Who Am I?* set of snippets. They are extremely useful when preparing speeches and can be used in conjunction with the other methods described above. Some snippets become part of entertaining speeches; some of informative speeches; some of persuasive speeches; and some fit all three categories. Best of all, some become the inspiration for new speech messages.

1.6 Frameworks and Filters

Once you know your destination, you have to figure out your route. [JH]

Introduction

Once you have your message, the hardest part is behind you. Your next step is to choose your speech's framework (or skeleton) and filter (a checklist of characteristics you would like to see in the speech.)

Frameworks

Three of the most common frameworks for a persuasive speech are:

The single story—where the whole speech revolves around a day or event. A favorite example of the single-story framework is Ed Tate's [WCPS-00] winning speech, *One of Those Days*. Covering about six hours, Ed recalls the ups and downs of the day he wanted to fly from Chicago to Phoenix. It begins with a speeding ticket and ends boarding the plane with a complimentary first-class ticket—but with plenty of excitement in-between.

The three-part speech—with each of the three parts supporting its core message. Ramona Smith [WCPS-18] [view YouTube, *Ramona Smith Toastmasters*] is a recent excellent example. She talks of college, marriage, and speaking, explaining how she failed in all three. Then, using a 3-round boxing analogy, she relates how she fought back in each round, tying the rounds together with a memorable, repetitive phrase, *I'm still standing*, her speech's inspirational message.

Speech framework—these are typically mnemonics, with the letter (word) order indicating their speech sequence. AIDAA, the second framework below, illustrates this perfectly. Such provide you, the speaker, a framework to organize your thoughts and marshal your arguments in a way that leads to a logical conclusion.

AIDA Attention. Interest. Desire. Action.

AIDAA Arrest Attention; Arouse Interest; Create Desire; Convince Audience; Get Action. *... Millard Bennett's variation of AIDA*

EASE Exemplify. Amplify. Specify. Electrify. [Formula of James C Humes]
... Meaning: Exemplify the issue with a human story. Amplify with broader picture, etc. Specify a solution. Electrify audience into action.

EASY Exemplify. Amplify. Specify. Yousify.
... Richard Spencer's variation. Yousify means getting You, the audience, to act.

CHOS Connect. Hook. Obstacle. Solution.
... Steve Jobs' annual presentations had this framework—connect, hook audience with benefit, present the obstacle, show the solution and call for action.

Filters

Filters are a set of questions some speakers ask themselves about their speeches after one or more drafts have been written. They are assessing how relatable the speech is to the audience? They seek to know what might add more life, connection, and enjoyment to it?

Some speakers create filters to reflect their own style preferences and use them as a checklist when the draft is completed. Here are several to consider:

HHHH

Head – Does it make you think?

Heart – Does it touch your soul?

Humor – Does it make you laugh?

Heavy-Duty – Is message significant/important? [ET^]

HCT

H Make them high.

C Make them cry.

T Make them try. [DN^]

Steve Jobs' Filter

His 60+ minute speeches were noted for certain common characteristics: A memorable phrase. A memorable moment. Continuous audience dialogue. Passion. Fun. Continual changing of pace—mixing together speech, stories, videos, slides, surprise, laughter, props, metaphors, analogies, and inviting others to participate. And Steve often ended with *Oh, and one more thing…*

1.7 Gandhi, Randy, and Selfie Filters

These are three over-arching filters to make your speeches even better. They help you with authenticity, differentiation, and keeping your audience uppermost in mind.

The Gandhi Filter

[Story sourced from habitsforwellbeing.com and wordpress.com]

One often-recounted encounter in Gandhi's life is known as the *Sugar Story*. The event reflects Gandhi's values although not necessarily his absolutism for truth as the story is not found in his autobiography. Regardless of its veracity, the story is very Gandhian and is repeated here because the lesson is critical for all speakers.

> *During the 1930's, in India, a mother became very concerned with the amount of sugar her son was eating. No matter what she said, he continued satisfying his sweet tooth. Frustrated, she decides to take her son to see his great hero, Mahatma Gandhi.*

After walking many miles in the hot sun to Gandhi's ashram, they approach the great leader most respectfully. She explains:

"Bapu ("father"), my son is eating too much sugar. It is very bad for his health. Would you please advise him to stop eating it?"

Gandhi, after silently listening to the woman, turns to her son:

"Go home and come back in two weeks."

The woman, obviously perplexed, wonders why Gandhi does not ask the boy to stop eating sugar. Puzzled, she takes her son's hand and, slowly, they walk back home.

Two weeks later they return and Gandhi motions them to come forward. He looks directly at the boy and says:

"Boy, you should stop eating sugar. It is not good for your health."

The boy nods to Gandhi and says he will do his best to stop.

The boy's mother is pleased with Gandhi but is understandably curious why he needed two weeks to tell her son that. With great respect, she asks him.

Gandhi smiles and says:

"Two weeks ago, I too, was still eating sugar. I needed that time to cut back myself."

Moral for speakers: Gandhi lived with such integrity he would not give advice unless he was living by it himself. The lesson? Authenticity. Preach only what you practice.

The Randy Filter

Dr Randy J. Harvey Ph.D. is a great storyteller as well as the 2004 World Champion of Public Speaking®. For many years, he was in Education where his skills were constantly called upon. The following is how he closed his presentations to incoming teachers:

How many of you remember a teacher who made a difference in your life? — On the count of three, say his or her name out loud.

How many of you remember a teacher that you disliked so much you would have slashed their tires if you could have gotten away with it? — On the count of three, say the name out loud.

Now, there are three kinds of teachers in the world, the two I have just mentioned are immortal, and will likely be remembered by you the rest of your life and you will tell your children about them. I know I have.

But the third kind is a pitiful and sorry state of affairs, a blight on our profession.

How many of you can remember a year you were in school—but cannot remember the name of the teacher?

It is an unforgivable indictment of this teacher who had you in their class for an entire year, and they made so little impact on your life that you cannot remember their name. They made so little investment in you that you cannot even honor them with a memory.

Every teacher has the opportunity to be immortal either for the good or evil they do in the life of a child. But a forgotten teacher's anonymity? — That is a sin against the profession, an indictment of their career.

Moral for speakers: What's your message? Will it — will you — be unforgettable? Or will it and you be forever forgotten like that third teacher? You make that choice.

The Selfie Filter

Mankind appears hard-wired with a WIIFM (*What's in It For Me?)* mindset. Audiences certainly think this way and are quick to press their mental "off" switch if they don't see a compelling benefit to continue giving you their full attention. Never forget that a speech is largely a one-way vocal, two-way mental, conversation — that can be easily cut-off (rightly or wrongly) by the audience tuning out. It's even been compared to dating: *A good speech is like a good date—a dialogue between two interested parties!* [PF]

Moral for speakers: Why should your audience members listen to you? What are you planning to say and do that will grab and hold their attention? What benefit will they gain by staying tuned in? When and how will that be shared? What *mental speed bumps* do you plan to build into your speeches to reawaken any minds that might have started to wander or nod off?

Closing Comments

A persuasive speech seeks to change an audience's mind and/or feeling about an idea through its message. Many times, but not always, it seeks a change in the audience's behavior (i.e., doing something different.) The best way to achieve the change in behavior is by pointing the audience towards the first action step.

Persuasive speeches include motivational, inspirational, and patriotic speeches. Their common characteristic is its message. Persuading listeners to actually act upon your message is one of the most satisfying joys as a speaker. So, go all out to turn your message into action—and point the way.

Entertaining and Informational speeches typically don't carry a message.

Does that mean that if you are in a speech contest you must have a persuasive speech to win? Not necessarily. Speech styles reflect the times. For example, in the 80-year history of Toastmasters World Championship of Public Speaking, for many years the winning speeches were primarily the motivational-inspirational-patriotic-persuasive type. Over the past few decades that has changed. Speeches with a high entertainment element, with less emphasis on a memorable message, now frequently win. This, in my opinion, is because we have evolved into a television-internet-saturated society. To hold viewers' attention in our fast-paced, high-distraction, visual-medium society requires attention-getting-and-holding entertainment content. This focus has flowed over into speech contests. A persuasive speech with entertainment (humor, surprise, differentiation) often trumps a straight persuasive speech and, also, a highly entertaining speech with an abstract or light message can trump a straight persuasive speech.

As Bob Dylan first sang in 1963: *The times they are a-changin'*

Example of Both Message and Point in a Speech

The following persuasive speech, with accompanying comments, illustrates what we have covered in this section.

In Lieu of Flowers — Or Breaking the Tyranny of Tradition

John Andrews

Winner 2017 Semifinal 8, World Championship of Public Speaking®

www.Last-Writes.com *L = Laughter* *View YouTube: John Andrews Toastmasters*

[Walks onto stage with yellow school backpack on shoulder. Places on floor.]
001. Two widows were grieving at neighboring graves
002. For their departed husbands.
003. The North American woman was laying an arrangement of flowers
004. When she realized the Asian woman over there
005. Was laying out a bowl of soup and some rice.
006. Full of curiosity—
007. And void of tact—
008. She asked
009. When exactly do you expect your husband
010. To come up out of the ground to eat his food?
011. And the Asian woman fired back—
012. Right after yours comes up out of the ground to smell his flowers. [L]

013. Now that story teaches us three things about expressions of sympathy.
014. Number one — they do nothing to practically benefit the deceased.
015. Number two — they exist for us, the living—
016. So we can have a visible expression of our grief.
017. And number three —
018. Just because another expression looks a little odd to you—
019. All that means is —
020. You got used to doing it a different way.

021. If it disturbs you
022. That I have such a keen fascination with gravesite tributes—
023. Let me assure you my interest is purely professional. [L]
024. For the 11 past years
025. I have been a licensed funeral director—
026. Or — as I introduce myself at parties—
027. I'm an underground commodities dealer. [L+]

028. I've helped a number of people make final arrangements in my career.
029. Many of them want the following line in the newspaper notice—
030. In lieu of flowers donate to — something.
031. The reason they ask for that—
032. In their words — not mine — is that
033. They don't want people spending all that money on something
034. That they're going to throw out in a couple of days.

035. When I say all that money—
036. I searched florists in my neighborhood

037. And you can't get a sympathy arrangement for under $50.
038. One I consider typical— is more like $130.
039. Now, that really is a lot of money
040. For something – as I mentioned in point number one –
041. That does nothing to practically benefit the deceased.
042. So these people would prefer
043. If you spent your money helping others instead.

044. Funny thing about death—
045. It makes you re-evaluate what's really important in life –
046. Hashtag # Undertaker Wisdom.
047. But here's the problem with their request—
048. It's almost never honored.
049. Visitors are still bringing thousands of dollars
050. Worth of funeral flowers into my home—
051. Because — as I mentioned in point #2
052. They need a visible expression for their grief—
053. Writing a check is not good enough.

054. So, I thought
055. There must be some way I can satisfy both of these parties—
056. And there is.
057. But I face a major hurdle—
058. Our society needs to get over this idea
059. That flowers are the only expression available to us.
060. If we can do that
061. It frees us up to create new symbols
062. That give you the visible expressions
063. That help others in the process
064. And—actually—could be a better way
065. To honor the memory of our loved ones.

066. I'll tell you what I mean—
067. But keep in mind what I said in point #3—
068. Just because another expression looks a little odd to you—
069. All that means is that you got used to doing something different.

070. Imagine for a minute I have to make arrangements for a handyman—
071. You all have someone like that in your life—
072. Unless you are that person for the rest of us. [L]
073. It's usually a man—
074. Always tinkering in his workshop.
075. Every time something breaks in your house
076. You hope he can fix it.
077. What if I said—
078. In lieu of flowers
079. I want you to go to the hardware store
080. Buy a brand-new tool
081. And bring that into my funeral home instead?

082. Because if he was surrounded by tools in life
083. Then let's surround him by tools in death.

084. Now after the service
085. I can take those tools to Habitat for Humanity
086. Who will use them to build new homes for the homeless.
087. Wouldn't that be a legacy
088. That your handyman would love to leave behind?

089. Maybe — talking about a teacher—instead of a handyman
090. I said—
091. In lieu of flowers,
092. Go buy a backpack
093. Fill it with school supplies
094. Let's make that visitation room
095. Look more like a classroom.

096. After the service
097. I'll take the backpacks to the Salvation Army—
098. They'll give them out to poor kids
099. And then those kids
100. Will carry on that teacher's legacy
101. By having a better shot at a good education.

102. One day, I had to bury a man who loved teddy bears.
103. So we said
104. Go down to the toy store and—
105. In lieu of flowers—
106. Buy a brand-new teddy bear.
107. And the people listened—
108. There were over FIFTY teddy bears
109. In that visitation room—
110. Far and away
111. The most adorable funeral I have even run.
112. I would say—
113. It was un-bear-ably cute. [L]

114. But you know the best part?
115. After the service
116. I got to take those teddy bears downtown—
117. To our big Children's Hospital.
118. Hi there, honey *[Kneels on one knee]*
119. Are you here all by yourself? *[Takes a teddy from backpack]*
120. You miss your friends, huh?
121. Well, I have someone who wants to keep you company.
122. *Yeah, yeah — take him — he's yours.* *[Hands teddy to imaginary child]*

123. *Cool out there, buddy.* *[Kneels, facing another imaginary child]*
124. You like T-ball—

125. And you can't play because you're here.
126. Well, as soon as you're feeling better
127. This guy wants to go to one of your games.
128. Yeah, take him — he's yours. *[Hands a teddy to the imaginary child]*

129. And as I walked around that Children's Hospital
130. I watched 50 very sad pairs of eyes —
131. Light up!
132. Some kids were extra happy to meet a man—
133. Who had the same haircut they did.[L] *[Speaker is bald]*
134. But that moment was possible
135. Because one man's family
136. Listened to a new idea.
137. And I challenge you, Toastmasters——
138. Do you listen to new ideas?
139. Or do you insist we always do things the traditional way?
140. Does it bother you that I started back there — *[Indicates back corner stage]*
141. Rather than the more traditional front and center?
142. People have told me it does—
143. But no one can say what's wrong with it.
144. It's just that this is where I expect a speech to start.
145. I expect everyone to do it the same way.

146. No, that is when tradition becomes tyranny
147. And you will get trapped.
148. Because you will always do what you have always done.
149. You can only achieve
150. What you have always achieved.

151. Now, I'm not saying that every new idea is a great one.
152. I'm saying that no idea is worth holding onto—
153. With all your might—
154. If you do it blindly.
155. Because only new ideas
156. Have the power to change the world.

157. Teddy Bear Man's family changed the world—
158. For 50 sick kids.
159. Because when they got the chance
160. They broke the tyranny of tradition
161. And accepted non-traditional expressions of sympathy —
162. *In lieu of flowers.*

163. Mr. Toastmaster...

In Lieu of Flowers — Or Breaking the Tyranny of Tradition Comment

When I heard John Andrews deliver this speech, its message struck deep. Perhaps recent deaths of friends had made my mind more receptive but I found myself absorbed by John's experiences and his creative evolution of an age-old practice, one with which we all are too familiar. As his story unfolds his message clearly emerges and the action step he points each of us towards becomes blindingly obvious — when a similar occasion arises in our life, then do likewise.

In persuasive speaking, there are two common calls to action:

- **Start today (or tomorrow)**— used by motivational speakers when inviting action on a daily or regular basis.
- **When/then** — an invitation to use when a certain event occurs.

In some speeches the action pointed to is delivered towards or at the speech's closing (e.g., Earl Nightingale's *Strangest Secret* and Craig Valentine's *Key to Fulfillment,* discussed earlier); in others, possible action steps are indicated throughout the speech as in this speech and in Manoj Vasudevan's *Pull Less, Bend More (see page 216.)* What is important is that the audience is shown the path to transmogrify the message into reality. That's the value of pointing and John's speech exemplifies this superbly.

Another aspect of this speech was special. Rarely does a 7-minute speech open my eyes and change the way I think about something that is accepted practice. This one did. How did he do it? Let's start with the structure.

Speech Outline

Graveside's cultural differences—lessons?
Why my fascination?
Professional—I'm an undertaker.
Help with final arrangements, e.g., flowers.
What's the purpose of flowers?
What else might meet the same purpose?
Handy man, teacher, teddy bear man?
Are flowers the best option?

Or, In Simple Structural Terms

Opening story (Foreshadows the message)
Establishes credibility (Why me?)
3 stories (about breaking tradition)
(Implied) Invites us to break with tradition

Why was the Speech So Well Received?

The speech touched Aristotle's three bases of a persuasive speech: credible, emotional, and rational

Clear message that pointed the way to action

Speaker did not give but "lived" the speech

Flowed seamlessly from title to opening to credentials to examples to closing

Idea is original, practical, and easy-to-adopt

Speaker owned the stage—expansive and energetic (see video)

Eye-catching props

Melody through pairing, e.g., tools in life, tools in death; visitation room, classroom.

Spoke in a comfortable, well-paced, well-paused style

Speech engaging and conversational—lots of *you's* and questions to the audience

Speech full of vivid, memorable pictures and images

Speech had an emotional undertone (sympathy, teddy bears for cancer children, etc)

Speech related to the whole audience

Speckled with humor

Authentic and highly credible speaker—personal experiences

The speech is a balance of emotion and logic, with emotion heavily trumping logic. The opening story and three "in lieu of" stories persuaded my heart; and the following five interspersed phrases then persuaded my mind—

> *Just because another expression looks a little odd to you – all that means is that you got used to doing it a different way.* [18]
>
> *Just because another expression looks a little odd to you – all that means is that you got used to doing something different.* [68]
>
> *That is when tradition becomes tyranny—and you will get trapped because you will always do what you have always done.* [146]
>
> *No idea is worth holding onto with all your might—if you do it blindly.* [152]
>
> *When they got the chance, they broke the tyranny of tradition* [159]

Many of these characteristics are discussed in detail in the four following sections.

SECTION 2

Opening

If you don't plan to grab your audience at the beginning, when do you plan to?

The two simplest, easiest, and guaranteed ways to immediately grab your audience's attention is to **ask a question** or **create curiosity**. Why? Because a question says *I am talking directly to you* and a curiosity statement says *I have something that you will find interesting*. Both work in every speaking situation. Even after decades of speaking, I find most of my openings are still either questions or curiosity arousers.

Professional speakers tell us there are two dozen ways to open a speech. Which one you choose usually depends upon your audience, your speaking style, and the topic, purpose, and occasion. They are:

- Ask a question
- Create curiosity
- Ask audience to imagine something (a hybrid of a question and curiosity)
- Bold or shocking action or statement
- Bring audience into scene immediately (e.g., take a photo of them)
- Conversational (i.e., using an easy conversational style to address the audience)
- Describe scene (e.g., *Picture this...*)
- Explain your interest in the topic
- Instruction requiring physical participation (e.g., *Hands up if you...)*
- Instruction requiring verbal participation (e.g., *Help me complete this jingle...)*
- Piggyback on something said by a previous speaker
- Point out something unique or important about the audience or event
- Prop or visual image
- Putdown (i.e., putting oneself down, self-deprecation)
- Quotation
- Relate one to others (e.g., *Look at the person on each side of you. One of you is...*)
- Silence
- Singing (or using popular song lyrics)
- Sound effect
- Speech length (e.g., *Gettysburg Address was only 266 words, this speech is...*)
- Spell out why this topic matters to the audience
- Surprise—do something unexpected (e.g., throw away money)
- Tell an anecdote or story
- Tell audience what they are going to learn
- Title integrated into opening

2.1 Why Your Opening Is So Important

Dana LaMon, the 1991 World Champion of Public Speaking®, observed that in his 26 years as an administrative law judge he heard over 6,000 cases. He estimates that, in about 95% of those cases, he knew what he would decide before the hearing was over. After many years as a Toastmaster and professional speaker he says he learned that, similarly, audiences also make their decisions well before the presentation is over. This led him to the belief that the opening is the most important part of the speech—it is where we begin guiding our audience towards the outcome we seek. And the sooner we begin, the greater our likelihood of success.

An effective opening, he believes, answers *yes* to two questions—Does it grab my attention (delivery) and does it grab my mind (interest)? In other words, is this a speech I want to listen to? And that's critical for as Dana stresses to speakers:

If you don't get them in the opening you won't have them at the end.

2.2 How to Use this Section

The intention of this section is to offer you a wide range of openings to stimulate your creativity. Each reflects its speaker's goal of connecting immediately with the audience.

Above each example are its opening characteristics. To provide context and background, an explanatory note often follows. If the speech can be viewed on TED.com or YouTube.com, such is indicated.

The examples let you see how the minds of skillful speakers quickly communicate and plant the seed of their message.

As you review each opening, ask yourself: How well does it grab your attention? Does it indicate a speech that you'd like to hear in full? If not, what changes would you make to create a more interesting opening? (Make allowances for the fact that reading a speech is not as impactful as hearing it.) Later, ask which openings appeal to you most: those with an intriguing title, or are short, or "talk to you," or put yourself down, or those that surprise? Use your answer to influence your openings in upcoming speeches.

Remember this—one of the greatest compliments you will ever receive is to have an audience member come up to you after your speech and echo Renée Zellweger's words in the movie *Jerry Maguire*:

You had me at "hello."

2.3 Speech Opening Examples

question. shock. surprise.

Darren LaCroix — Ouch!

Can you remember a moment
When a brilliant idea flashed into your head?
It was perfect for you.
And then all of a sudden—
From the depths of your brain, another thought
Started forcing its way forward through the enthusiasm
Until finally it shouted
"YEAH—great idea—
But what if you—
[*Falls on face on stage*] Fall—on your face?"
What do you do when you fall on your face?
Do you try to jump right up and hope no one noticed?
Are you more concerned with what other people will think—
Than what you can learn from this? [DLC]

... This is the opening of one of Toastmasters best-known speeches. The audience becomes engaged by the one-to-one questions and receive a shock when Darren unexpectedly falls flat on his face.
View YouTube: Darren LaCroix Toastmasters

question. curiosity.

Simon Sinek — How Great Leaders Inspire Action

How do you explain when things don't go as we assume?
Or better—how do you explain when others are able to achieve things
That seem to defy all of the assumptions?
For example—why is Apple so innovative?
Year after year, after year,
They're more innovative than all their competition.
And yet—they're just a computer company.
They're just like everyone else. [SS>]

... This is the opening of one of TED's most popular speeches. The questions compound our curiosity and we are "all ears" waiting to learn the answers.
View: TED.com

question. curiosity.

Anita Fain Taylor — It Is What It Is; It Ain't What It Ain't

Have you ever discovered a bruise on your body—
And you couldn't remember how it got there? —
Me too.
Imagine striking yourself with such force—
Causing the blood vessels under your skin to burst—
And not remembering how it got there.

But scars? —
Scars are different.
I bet if you examined every scar on your body—
You could tell in great detail how it got there.
Because — beneath every scar — there is a story. [AFT]

... An engaging one-to-one opening which segues into a speech about two emotional scars she carries.
View YouTube: Anita Fain Taylor Toastmasters

curiosity. conversational. question. humor.

Willie Jones — A Warm Boot

I want to come out to the front of the stage
So everyone can get a good look
At this guy. [All smiles]
Last year I got a letter from AARP
Saying I was 50.
You know what I mean—don't you? [WJ^]

... A different way to make an immediate connection with your audience—a warm friendly invitation to "look him over." And it worked!
View YouTube: Willie Jones Toastmasters

question. humor. curiosity. conversational.

Vikas Jhingran — Perfect

Let me ask you a question that may seem a little strange.
How many of you chose your parents? —
How about your kids? —
Some of you probably wish you had.
Or your health problems?
No — they just happened.
My point is that whether we like it or not
Everything in life is arranged. [VJ^]

... The two opening questions and the humorous aside grab us immediately as we wonder where this is going to go. [This was Vikas' winning District speech before he went on to win the 2007 WCPS]

curiosity. shocking. bold.

Craig Valentine — The Key to Fulfillment

Years ago
I had many conversations—
With myself.
Some contemplating my life—
But unfortunately
Many were contemplating my death. [CV^]

... Craig had me at "hello."

conversational. putdown.

Steve Jobs — You've Got to Find What You Love

I am honored to be with you today
At your commencement from one of the finest universities in the world.
I never graduated from college.
Truth be told—
This is the closest I've ever gotten to a college graduation.
Today I want to tell you three stories from my life.
That's it—No big deal—Just three stories. [SJ+]

… This opening of Steve Jobs' Stanford Commencement address (2005) is remarkable because, in a simple conversational style, he puts himself down (never graduated, doesn't put himself above his audience) and says he will tell them just three [simple] stories [note: not "lessons"] from his life. His stories weave into a powerful point.
View YouTube: Steve Jobs Stanford Address

conversational. question. humor.

Sir Ken Robinson — Do Schools Kill Creativity?

Good morning.
How are you?
It's been great, hasn't it?
I've been blown away by the whole thing.
In fact — I'm leaving. [KR+]

… A creative, relaxed opening in a conversational tone, with a highly-amusing surprise Twist.
View: TED.com

question. conversational. humor.

Kwong Yew Yang — Four Words

Have you ever met somebody who just drove you nuts?
Yeah all the married couples are nodding their heads.
But—more often than not—it's the people closest to us—
Our friends—our families—our loved ones.
They're the ones who frustrate us the most. [KYY]

… Opens with a question which most of us can say yes to and allows a humorous reference to many in the audience. His answer surprises and we look forward to hearing more (because it's about us.)

shock.

Jamie Oliver — Teach Every Child About Food

Sadly— in the next 18 minutes when I do our chat
Four Americans that are alive—
Will be dead from the food they eat. [JO]

… Jamie, you had me at "hello!" I'm in. Tell me more … and he does. He tells us that America is "one of the most-unhealthy countries in the world," and goes on to explain how we can change that.
View TED.com

conversational. curiosity. title.

Harry Emerson Fosdick — On Catching the Wrong Bus

Recently the newspapers carried the story of a man who boarded a bus
With the full intention and desire of going to Detroit.
But when at the end of a long trip he alighted at the destination,
He found himself,
Not in Detroit
But in Kansas City.
He had caught the wrong bus.
Something like that goes on habitually in human life. [HEF]

... Yes, I want to hear more because this sermon from *Riverside Sermons (1958)* by a renowned preacher is obviously going to be aimed at, and be relevant to, each person listening to or reading it.

shock. curiosity.

Mohammed Qahtani — The Power of Words

[Puts cigarette in mouth, pulls out a lighter—audience gasps—he looks up—laughter]
What? — All of you all think smoking kills?
Let me tell you something—
Do you know that the amount of people dying from diabetes
Is three times the number of people dying from smoking?
Yet, if I pulled out a snicker bar—nobody would say anything. [MQ^]

... A shock opening—his intent to light a cigarette at the start makes the audience gasp, then laugh as he looks up. Grabs our attention. As did his statement on diabetes (which, he later explained, was a made-up statistic!)
View YouTube: Mohammed Qahtani Toastmasters

curiosity. conversational.

Bill Sands — Who Cares About Me?

I don't speak with notes.
Not that I don't care—
But because I care too much.
If it doesn't come from the heart—
It isn't real. [BS+]

... Sometimes when you hear a speaker for the first time and you don't know his background (Bill Sands was serving three consecutive life terms in San Quentin before age 20 and is the author of *My Shadow Ran Fast*) you don't know what to expect. But when I heard this opening, not knowing his background, I thought, "This guy is the real thing. I want to hear his story."

question. curiosity. shock.

Angus Deaton — Address

Did you know that it will take Indian women 200 years to grow as tall on average as British women? [AD+]

... The 2015 Nobel prize winner in economics engages us directly with a question that shocks.

shock. curiosity. title.

Jane Fonda — Life's Third Act

There have been many revolutions over the last century—
But perhaps none as significant
As the longevity revolution.
We are living on average today
34 years longer than our great-grandparents did.
Think about that—
That's an entire second adult lifetime
That's been added to our lifespan. [JF]

... Wow! I'm hooked already. I want to hear more. The title suggests a third act being added to our lives. Will she give us ideas how we might use these bonus years?
View: TED.com

shock. curiosity. question.

Dr Denis Burkitt — Address to Doctors Conference

How many of you are sufficiently concerned about your wife's health to check a weekly stool specimen? [DB]

... An attention-getting, no-nonsense speech opening to an appropriate audience. The speaker, the plain-spoken author of *Don't Forget Fibre in Your Diet,* was speaking on his research on how insufficient dietary fiber is the cause of many common diseases. To clarify and emphasize his opening statement and his overall beliefs, he later says: *If you pass small stools, you have to have large hospitals.*

shock.

Newt Gingrich — Address to YPO Conference

If you were born today, you would already owe $186,000 to pay off your share of the National Debt. [NG]

... Newt Gingrich, in a speech to the Young Presidents Organization, as related by Patricia Fripp, a speaker at the same conference.

curiosity. conversational. title.

Kathleen Parker — Borat

I went. I watched. I winced.
I felt ashamed. I felt proud. I felt sorry.
I laughed. I didn't laugh.
I hated it. I loved it.
I don't want to think about the wrestling scene.
I can't stop thinking about it.
There's something about "Borat." [KP]

... Engaging opening of thoughts about a movie. The triples and contrasts make it enjoyable listening and increase my interest in hearing more.

quote. curiosity.

William H. Peterson — Brave New Economic World

It was the best of times, it was the worst of times
It was the age of wisdom, it was the age of foolishness...
It was the spring of hope, it was the winter of despair.
1793 or 1977—
France under revolution—
Or America under peace and prosperity?
You recognize of course
The lines from Dickens' *A Tale of Two Cities.*
The lines form one theme for us here
In the shadow of Youngstown's fading steel mills
Where the fires are being banked—perhaps forever. [WHP]

... This quote comparing today with the past is effective as it reminds us that troubled times are not new. France emerged from the French Revolution with hope. Perhaps there's hope for the steel towns of Ohio. The speech was to the American Institute of Economics in Youngstown Ohio, in 1977.

curiosity. question. quote. title integrated.

Brian Woolf — The Greatest Thief

I KNOW YOU'RE NOT ONE. [*Pointing to a member of the audience.*]
You don't look like one. [*Pointing to another.]*
I'm certain you're not one. [*Pointing to another.]* *<Pause>*
And I'm not a thief either—— *<Pause>*
OR ARE WE? — *<Pause>*
Are we all thieves?
For as once hinted
By the great playwright
George Bernard Shaw—
The greatest thief is he who withholds deserved praise. [BW]

surprise.

Jock Elliott — Que Sera

When I was just a little boy
I asked my mother
"What will I be?
Will I be handsome?
Will I be rich?"
Here's what she said to me.
She said——
"No." [JE^]

... At the time this speech was delivered (1994) the song was well known. The audience related to the opening words—and its surprise Twist— which triggered lots of laughter.

curiosity. question.

Patricia Hill — The Unexpected Journey

What do you do
When the Universe buys you a bus ticket
Puts you on the bus
And gives you the voice of a bullfrog? [PH<]

… Patricia has us immediately as we try to connect the Universe, bus tickets, and her bullfrog voice; answer her question; and let our curiosity wonder what's coming next. [The speaker goes on to explain how her voice changed to being like a bullfrog's during her fight with cancer.]

curiosity. prop. humor.

Vikas Jhingran — The Swami's Question

My hands were shaking —
My throat was dry.
[Holding an envelope.]
In my hands was a letter that was going to change my life —
Would it be for better? —
Or worse?
The answer was inside.
I stared at the return address—
Massachusetts Institute of Technology—
The Graduate School of my dreams.
Would it begin with "Congratulations"—
Or
"You've got to be kidding!"?
The answer was inside.
My mind drifted back to when it all began …
Fourteen years ago. [VJ^]

… With curiosity and humor Vikas captures his audience who now want to hear his story and learn what was inside that envelope.
View YouTube: Vikas Jhingran Toastmasters

question. surprise.

John Shepherd — A Legacy of Courage

Will Edmund Ross please come to the lectern?
Mr Ross?
Is there an Edmund G. Ross in the audience?
Apparently Mr Ross isn't with us tonight—
I'd be surprised if he was—
He died in 1907.
But his spirit fills this room. [JS]

… This imaginative opening introduces us to Senator Edmund Ross and the courage he showed with his vote in the Presidential impeachment trial of Andrew Johnson in 1868.

curiosity. conversational. humor. prop.

David Brooks — Silver Bullets

"You can't go home again"—
That's what Thomas Wolfe said.
But, ladies and gentlemen
I was born and raised right here —
In Dallas Texas
So at least for today—
I've come home—
And it feels good.
In case you're wondering—
Yes, some of us really do dress this way down here—
The tuxedo is a symbol of respect.
And the jeans?
Well, the jeans mean we put just a *little* too much of our oil money
Into Texas Savings and Loans. [DB^]

... David personalizes and humanizes his opening by sharing that this is his home town and he is dressed in a local code that reflects recent bad economic times. He arouses curiosity through his dress code and then tells us something we don't know. It's a form of personal putdown and it's something we'll never forget for he wears his Texas Tuxedo throughout.

shock. question.

Joel Weldon — Toastmasters Regional Speech Contest

Walks onto stage wiping brow. With head down and shaky voice, says—
After hearing the previous three speakers
I realize I am not good enough to compete.
I'm sorry if I've caused any problems
but I won't be able to give my speech.
Sits down—audience is shocked.
Contest Chair walks to lectern.
With a quizzical look, says—
"Well, I guess, on with the show ..."
Then, before the next contestant is announced
The speaker leaps from his chair shouting—
Please sit down!
Speaker then turns to puzzled audience, and asks—
How many times
Do we see people ready to quit before they even start—
Just like that previous speaker—
Who was ready to give up?
How often does the fear of failure
Prevent us from doing things we really can do? [JW+]

... This dramatic surprise opening, spoken directly to each attendee, helped Joel Weldon win the contest enabling him to compete at the 1974 WSPC where he placed third. Unforgettable for all attendees.

singing. curiosity. conversational. title.

Randy Harvey — Don't Settle for Greatness, When You Can Be Immortal

[Begins singing]
Hello, Mary Lou—Goodbye heart.
Sweet Mary Lou—I'm so in love with you.
I knew Mary Lou we'd never part.
So hello, Mary Lou, goodbye heart.
Mary Lou was my momma.
And up until the age of nine—
I thought my daddy wrote that song.
When I came to breakfast singing that song
My momma would light up like fireworks on the 4th of July.
It's important that you know my momma was an Immortal.
There are many good people in this world
And there are a few great people—
But there are very few Immortals. [RJH]

... Only time I've ever heard a speaker open by singing a popular song (which he learned from his dad when growing up) and then find out it's about his momma, who turns out to be the story's hero! Interspersed are anecdotes like how his mom would "light up like fireworks on the 4th of July." Put this together with an intriguing title (which punches our curiosity button) and we are captivated, awaiting what follows. This was Randy's winning Semifinal speech before going on to win the WCPS.

shock. motivational.

Gen George Patton — Speech to Troops on June 5, 1944, Eve of D-Day Invasion

Men—
This stuff that some sources sling around
About America
Wanting out of this war
Not wanting to fight—
Is a crock of bullshit.
Americans love to fight, traditionally.
All real Americans love the sting and clash of battle.
You are here today for three reasons.
First, because you are here
To defend your homes and your loved ones.
Second, you are here
For your own self respect
Because you would not want to be anywhere else.
Third, you are here
Because you are real men and all real men like to fight.

... You can read the full speech and more about Patton in Charles M. Province's *The Unknown Patton*. This speech opening is included to offer a peek at a highly motivational speech, in an emotionally taut situation, to a tough, mature audience.

curiosity. shock.

Andrew Dlugan — Example

Booze—— *[long pause]*
Drugs—— *[long pause]*
Guns—— *[long pause]*
Were seized in a search *[slight pause]*
Three months ago
In a school—Near my home
In the locker *[pause]*
Of a sixth-grader! [AD]

... This is adapted from an example of a captivating opening on Andrew Dlugan's outstanding free Speakers website, sixminutes.dlugan.com. It is a curiosity-arousing, triple-pause opening, with a shock Twist. Its structure is adaptable to many different situations.

curiosity. bold. title integrated.

Bill Mintz — It's About Time

It's about time we recognized our Real Enemy!
I would like to talk to you tonight about a subject—
About a situation that should be of concern to every American.
It's a situation that—in my opinion—
Poses a greater threat
To our democracy—
Our way of life—
And the security of our country—
Than all of our economic problems
And all of the nuclear warheads
That have been stockpiled throughout the world. [BM^]

... The ambiguous title followed by the bold opening grabs everyone's attention. It's one reason why I still remember this 1982 speech about the decline in the love and respect for our country.

relate one to others. humor. title integrated.

Pamela Meyer — How to Spot a Liar

Okay, now I don't want to alarm anybody in this room
But it's just come to my attention
That the person to your right is a liar. *(Laughter)*
Also—
The person to your left is a liar.
Also—
The person sitting in your very seat is a liar.
We're all liars!
What I'm going to do today is ... [PM]

The title intrigues us. We think we will learn about other people—but we learn about ourselves, too. Her triple (right-left-you) is a great humorous Twist. Pamela immediately gains our full attention. View: TED.com

speech length.

C. John Tupper, UC Davis School of Medicine — Address

I stand before you today not only as your president-elect
But also as a dean and as a professor.
As a professor—
I am programmed— once started—
To speak for fifty-five minutes.
However, I have been reminded
That the story of the creation of the world is told in Genesis in 400 words.
That the world's greatest moral code — the Ten Commandments—
Contains only 297 words.
That Lincoln's immortal Gettysburg Address is but 266 words in length
And that the Declaration of Independence
Required but 1,321 words to set up for the world a new concept of freedom.
I think I get the point... [CJT]

speech length.

Ralph W Ketner, Founder, Food Lion — Address

As anyone who listens to speeches knows, brevity is an asset.
Twenty minutes are ideal.
An hour is the limit an audience can listen to comfortably.
In mentioning brevity —it is worth mentioning—
The shortest inaugural address was George Washington's second—
Just 135 words—less than two minutes.
The longest was William Henry Harrison's in 1841—
He delivered a two-hour 9,000-word speech
Into the teeth of a freezing northeast wind.
He came down with a cold the following day—
A month later he died of pneumonia.
You'll be relieved to know
That Washington is a hero of mine ... [RWK]

curiosity. putdown. humor.

Dan Pink — The Puzzle of Motivation

I need to make a confession at the outset.
A little over 20 years ago—I did something that I regret.
Something that I am not particularly proud of.
Something that in many ways I wished no one would ever know
But that here I feel kind of obliged to reveal—
In the late 1980s
In a moment of youthful indiscretion—
I went to law school. *[Laughter]* [DP]

... View: TED.com

curiosity. putdown. humor.

Brett Rutledge — My Little World

I was the kind of kid
Your parents told you not to play with.
You probably remember me—
The Detention Hall's only permanent resident. BR^

... Humorously puts himself down while engaging directly with us (using "you," "your.")

imagine. curiosity.

Ric Elias — Three Things I Learned While My Plane Crashed

Imagine a big explosion as you climb through 3,000 ft.
Imagine a plane full of smoke.
Imagine an engine going clack, clack, clack, clack, clack, clack, clack.
It sounds scary.
Well I had a unique seat that day—
I was sitting in 1D.
I was the only one who could speak to the flight attendant. RE

... And now we're ready for the rest of the story.
View: TED.com

imagine. question. curiosity.

Simon Bucknall—To Be Perfectly Honest

Imagine – you're sitting at a job interview
And you're asked the question that nearly every candidate hates–
"What's your greatest weakness?"
How would you answer — honestly?
Or would you think of a strength—
And try to pretend it's a weakness?
When I was asked that question
I was tempted to say... SB^

imagine. curiosity. title.

Ruth Witty — Imagine

Imagine you are a child again—4 or 5 years old.
Pick up your favorite book.
Remember how it felt?
Remember what it was like to be read to?
Now close your eyes
Imagine what it would have been like—
If there had NOT been books in your home as a child? [5-second pause] RW^

... The directly engaging opening of a speech on fighting childhood illiteracy. It's a creative approach adaptable to many speech topics.

questions. imagine.

Kathleen Callendar — What Pharmajet Offers

Did you know there are 1.8 billion vaccinations given every year?
Did you know up to half of those are given with reused needles?
Did you know we are spreading and perpetuating the very diseases we're trying to prevent?
Imagine if there was a painless, one-use needle for a fraction of the current cost.
You don't have to imagine it—
We've created it—It's called PharmaJet … [KC]

… The above is an example of a highly effective business sales presentation opening using Sam Horn's Did You Know? — Imagine If… problem/solution framework, taken from *Got Your Attention?* her ideas-rich book for speakers. Another example from the book, using the same concept, is next…

questions. imagine.

Sean Keener — ex BootsnAll Website

Did you know you used to need a travel agent to book a multi-city trip with 5 stops?
Did you know it used to take up to 48 hours to book a 5-stop trip?
Did you know it used to take up to 5 days to receive a price quote for 5-stop trip?
Imagine if for the first time ever you could plan and book a 5-stop trip yourself?
Imagine if you could get your own price quotes for a multi-stop trip?
Imagine if you could do all that in less than an hour?
You don't have to imagine it—
We've created it—it's called Indie. [SK]

… The above two examples take the audience from problem to solution right from their opening words. The rest of the presentation is about the details. It's an imaginative speaking structure that can be adapted and used in either sales presentations or when delivering a persuasive speech.

silence. shock. prop. putdown.

Darren Tay — Outsmart, Outlast

[Silently stands looking around the audience for 8 seconds.
Then pulls a pair of white underpants from his pocket.
Puts them on over his dark suit trousers.
Arms folded, legs apart, stares at audience a few seconds longer—
Then shouts…]
"Hey, loser—
How do you like your new school uniform?
I think it looks great on you."
Those were the words of my high-school bully. [DT^]

… Darren's opening—his silence and his underwear—was dramatic and had shock effect. He put himself down as he visually demonstrates how he was bullied at school. The opening leads to a speech about bullying and the need to battle it.
View YouTube: Darren Tay Toastmasters

putdown.

Vanessa Van Edwards — You Are Contagious

Hello, I am Vanessa, and I am a recovering awkward person. [VVE]

… These words, with warm natural gestures and a wide smile, opened a TED talk describing how our everyday behavior, from hand gestures to saying hello, influences how others perceive our confidence. They are a humorous putdown of herself as she prepares us for what we expect will be her "recovery process."
View TED.com

humor.

David Nottage — Get Up!

The wind was blowing through my hair
The adrenalin was pulsating through my young body—
The ecstasy! The excitement! The rush of air fills my senses—
I was 6 years old—
On a bicycle—
For the first time in my life. [DN^]

… Speaker cleverly misdirects us thereby creating humor.
View YouTube: David Nottage Toastmasters

participation. question. curiosity.

Brian Woolf — Reach Out

Would you all please help me complete an old AT&T advertising jingle—
Reach out and … [cups ear] … [Audience: *touch someone.*]
Again—Louder this time—
Reach out and … [Audience: *touch someone.*]
Thank you!
Did you know that jingle last aired in 1984?
Yet you remember it—
Why? [BW]

humor. putdown.

Bishop Fulton Sheen — Address

Applause sums up the highest of Christian virtues.
To applaud—as you just did—
At the beginning of my speech—
It is an act of faith.
If you applaud in the middle of my speech—
It is an act of hope.
And if you applaud at the end of my speech—
It is an act of charity. [BFS]

question. putdown.

Simon Scriver — Nuggets of Love

Can a chicken nugget change the world?
My first job—when I was 16—
Was at McDonald's
And my career has pretty much gone downhill since then. [SS^]

curiosity. twist.

A Better You

I have a magic pill to sell you.
It will help you
Make more money
Be happier
Look thinner
And have better relationships.
It's a revolutionary new pharmaceutical product
It's called — Late-No-More.
Just one dose every day... [AN]

question. curiosity. humor. twist.

A Better Future

It's April—the first quarter has vanished. Poof!
So how's progress on your New Year's resolutions?
Can you still remember what they were??!!!
One of mine was to lose 10lb—
And, yes, I'm still working on it—
I 've got 15 to go.
Madame Chair and Friends
Which leads to today's question—
Is there an effective way to achieve what we set out to do? [AN]

question. curiosity. twist.

A Better Speaker

From your High School days
Do you remember the formula to calculate the area of a circle? [$A = pi.r^2$]
Do you remember Einstein's formula for energy? [$e = mc^2$]
Do you really care?
Friends, today you will learn two new formula
That you will care about.
They won't help you with your math—
But they will with your speaking—
They are... [AN]

question. curiosity. twist.

The World's Greatest Architect

A nickel for your thoughts *[pouring a mug of nickels (5c) onto floor]*
What building is usually found on these nickels?
What person is usually found on these nickels?
What's special about this person?
Well, this 6'2" red head is not just our second President
With his blueprints, he was—
An architect of buildings
An architect of our nation
An architect of our freedom. [BW]

curiosity. conversational.

Nancy Duarte: The Secret Structure of Great Talks

You have the power to save the world.
I don't mean that to be a cliché
You really have the power to change the world.
Deep inside of you—
Every single one of you—
Has the most powerful device known to man—
And that's an idea...
But an idea is powerless if it stays inside of you. [ND]
View TED.com

title. conversational. participation.

Aaron Beverly — Leave a Lasting Memory, Using As Few Words As Possible and Strive With Every Fiber of Your Being to Avoid Being the Type of Person Who Rambles on and on With No End in Sight More Likely Than Not Causing More Listeners to Sit and Think to Themselves, Oh My Goodness, Can Somebody Please Make This Stop

Be honest —
You enjoyed that, didn't you?
Now please do me a favor—
Recite that entire title off the top of your head —
Right now — go [waits] — Not all at once.
Wait a minute –
Do you mean to tell me
That you cannot remember all 57 of the words in that title?
Neither can I.
But do you know what that proves?
Just because you say more
Doesn't mean that people will remember what you say. [AB>]

... This 57-word opening was read twice, as required by the rules of the WCPS contest, and brought great laughter before Aaron uttered his first word. It helped him, in 2016, win second place. The title, followed by the interactive conversation (participation), engaged the audience immediately.
View YouTube: Aaron Beverly Toastmasters

title. curiosity.

My Life as An Underground Commodities Dealer

Unemployed and desperate—
Have you ever been there?
Because I have.
Right around the time I started hanging out
With a bunch of people I would describe as purveyors
Of underground commodities and services.
But I was desperate—
And they were recruiting.
It started simply.
I would run some errands—
Drive some people around—
And soon, I was thrust into a world full of pain, suffering, and death. [JA>]

... The title tweaked my attention—what on earth is an underground commodities dealer? The opening heightened my curiosity — I was on full alert as to what would come next. Now, if you want satisfy your curiosity and enjoy this engaging speech, view YouTube: John Andrews Toastmasters.

humor.

And Yes, In the Right Circumstances, An Opening Quip Does Work

Mr Chairman, Guests, and all of you who once believed in Santa ...

[Holds camera.] Big smile please. [Takes photo of audience.] Thank you. I'm going to send that to my kids—they won't believe people actually paid to hear me speak!

On my way here, only God and I knew what I would be presenting today. [Looks around a bit nervously.] — Now, only God knows.

The human brain starts working the moment you are born and never stops—until you stand up to speak in public. [GJ]

There are two types of speakers—those who get nervous and those who are liars. [MT]

The chairman told me your town's secret—one in three people is rated good-looking. So look at the person on your left—and right. If it's not them—it must be you! [~ZZ]

Before we begin, let me apologize for one speech defect that I hope is not too annoying or distracting as you listen—I'm really sorry, but my speech is full of spelling errors.

I'm here to say a few words. — Now, if you believe that, you'll believe anything.

Well, no doubt many of you are wondering why the speaker is so old. — Well, the answer is obvious. He hasn't died yet! [CM] *...Charlie Munger, at age 83, opening his Commencement Address at USC Law School.*

SECTION 3

KONNECT (or CONNECT)

If you don't connect, you have no effect

Whether you spell it Konnect or Connect, this is the book's most important section. If your goal is to persuade your audience to think or act differently but you fail to connect, then all your work is wasted. When you don't connect, your words lie comatose. Connection precedes persuasion. Or as Sam Horn says: *If you can't get their attention, you'll never get their connection.*

We connect mentally and emotionally with audiences. And when we do, they move from passive to active listeners. Connecting mentally engages listeners' minds. Obviously, the greater the engagement, the greater the connection. This section focuses on that mental connection. The following section, *Emotion*, focuses on building audience connection using emotive techniques.

It is our responsibility as speakers to ensure our message is heard and acted upon. We—not the audience—have to do the hard work to connect and communicate. We have to concoct our unique connection chemistry to gain and maintain attention. This section offers you a range of simple-to-understand and easy-to-implement techniques to help you achieve that.

Ask yourself how well you connect. Try this simple test. Think of a recent speech you have given. Think of words you used and how you used them. Did you talk to each audience member (e.g., *you will recall that* ...)? Did you seek agreement as you spoke (e.g., *don't you agree?*) Did you ask for participation in some way (e.g., *repeat after me* ...)?

This section explains the following connection techniques:

3.1A Mind Your U's (You's)

"You" — the word audiences love most

Introduction

I bet you've noticed two things about conversations: people like to be acknowledged and included and, if given a chance, they like to talk about themselves. As speeches today are more like conversations, doesn't it therefore make sense to acknowledge and directly engage your audience when you are speaking?

The simplest way to do that is to "Yousify" your speech. This means peppering it with "you's" so that each listener knows you are talking to him or her individually, and not to everyone as a group. Using "you's" says each audience member is important. The following range of "you" examples emits a conversational flavor reflecting today's speaking style.

Similarly, inclusive words such as We and Us are preferable to I and Me and should be given preference. You'll see examples of these, too.

For many platform speakers, the ratio of You's vs I's (and Me's) is of such concern they measure their speeches' *You-I Ratio*. The higher the ratio, the happier they are.

Examples of U's (You's)

As you can see…

As you know so well…

As you may be aware…

As you sit there in the privacy of your own mind, think of a situation where… [AN]

Can you keep a secret?

Can you imagine that?

Can you remember/imagine/think of …?

Friends, I want to leave you with this thought…

Have you ever wondered…?

How many of you were kids when growing up? [humor]

I asked how she felt about her gift—you know what she said … [HL^]

I bet you noticed that God didn't call them the 10 Suggestions [ZZ]

I bet you're like me…

I bet you've discovered in life that some folks are wise and some—otherwise. [AN]

I bet you've found there's nothing so annoying as having someone go right on talking when you're interrupting. [DB+]

I bet you've noticed that a lot of folks want to serve God—but only as advisors. [ZZ]

I don't know what advice your father gave you, but mine always said...

I don't have all the answers. But you do. You know the people...

I don't know about you but …

I don't know what you learned growing up but I ...

I encourage you to think what this means—

I had some of those things. You probably got some of them, too! Don't tell me you don't — I know you have them [WJ^]

I invite you to consider... [TR]

I sense you are extroverted but at times you find yourself quite shy. [AN]

I submit to you that ...

I think you'll agree...

I think you'll relate to this...

I wish you could have been there when...

I'm sure you've noticed that some minds are like concrete—thoroughly mixed up and permanently set

I'm sure you've noticed that ...

If I was to ask you ....

If you had known me when I was growing up...

If you think of it...

If you were with me when ...

In 45 minutes, you will walk out of this room knowing how to ...

In this room you know there are probably ...

In this very room you know there are lots who care...

Let me share this with you ...

Let me tell you what I learned that day....

Listen, it's in your hearts right now... [DR^]

May I submit to you ...

Maybe you wanted to ...

No matter what zip code you live in...

Now, there's something I've noticed lately—you probably have too—and it's this... [BC]

Perhaps you've discovered...

Right now, you are probably thinking that...

So my invitation to you is...

So what? you might ask. Well, here's what... [BC]

So you see, my friends... [DT^]

The importance of this to you is ...[BC]

Think of a time when you suddenly found ...

Think of the teacher who made a difference in your life...

To challenge my fears even more, like you I joined Toastmasters [JAG]

Well, you know the answer to that...

When you were in this situation, you probably did the same thing ...

You already know this but ...

You and I know... [FDR] [A favorite phrase in FDR's radio messages]

You are not alone...

You can imagine her response...

You can't outrun your destiny... [MA]

You don't need me to explain ...

You have probably already discovered that ...

You know what happens when ...

You know what it's like to...

You may have heard of the Mayo Clinic finding that ...

You might be asking yourself why you should be interested in this. Here's why ... [BC]

You noticed there was a part that wasn't optional... [LSR]

You're all impressed—I can tell! [DLC]

You're probably thinking...

Your next step is ...

Examples of We's and Us's

All of us have a something special...

Here are some of the choices we face...

I—like many of us here—have dreamed impossible dreams. [MH^]

Let's talk about that for a minute ...

Now we all know that ...

Ours is a throwaway society—and we do it with people as well as machines.

These appear to be the options confronting us...

This we must do for our children. [FDR]

We all know...

We already know this but ...

We are surrounded by ...

We can't let that happen. We can't. [BC]

We have to rethink... [KR+]

We know three things about... [KR+]

We really aren't any different, are we?

We've seen this before, haven't we? [JE<]

What we do know is...

Somewhere along the way we learned a painful truth. We learned that failing to achieve our dream hurts. We encounter critics, who ridicule and crush our dream, and it hurts. We hear an inner voice that cries out — *No more!* [JK^2003]

In just the past three years we've seen an Olympic athlete stripped of his gold medals because he used drugs. We've seen not one, but two television ministers fall from grace. We've seen billionaires bankrupted by greed. And we've seen Donald Trump—be Donald Trump. [DB^1990]

How to Talk to Each Member of a Large Audience

Connecting with each attendee, where there may be a thousand or more in the audience, is aided by choosing the right words. The trick is to use the language of one, not all, when addressing the audience as seen in this comparison given by Lance Miller [LM^]

- *How many of you have ever had to tell your dad you'd crashed his car?*
- *Have you ever had to tell your dad you'd crashed his car?*

The latter is better because of its "yousificity" vs the former's general inclusiveness.

Deeply imbedded in the American mind is a First World War poster of Uncle Sam pointing a finger saying "I Want YOU for U.S. Army." There is no doubt that Uncle Sam was talking directly to the reader even though it was aimed at 50 million other Americans as well. It was highly effective. And you, too, can be effective with the right words as the following choice (*You* vs *Many of You*) indicate:

You		**Many of You**
Do you currently feel stressed?	—vs—	How many of you are stressed?
Can you guess what this is?	—vs—	How many of you know what this is?
Have you ever...?	—vs—	How many of you have ever...?
Can you imagine ...?	—vs—	Can you all imagine...?
Raise your hand if...	—vs—	Hands up all of you...
May I ask you a question?	—vs—	May I ask you all a question?
May I talk to you about...?	—vs—	May I talk to you all about...?

In both large and small audiences, the secret of connection is to talk to each attendee (you) rather than to everyone (many—or all—of you.)

3.1B Mind Your Q's (Questions)

To sell them, don't tell them—ask them [AN]

Introduction

The rationale underlying the above sliver of wisdom lies in the fact that when asking your audience questions, you demand more of their minds than when you are just making statements; you unobtrusively move them from a passive to an active state of involvement with a significant positive byproduct—a reduction in their minds' inclination to wander.

Consider the following line of a speaker, followed by his coach's suggestion:

S: The easiest way to be happy is a family drive.

C: What's the easiest way to be happy? —— A family drive. [CV^]

The first statement is passive. The audience sits back with a ho-hum attitude awaiting the next line. However, by switching from a statement to a question, the audience's minds immediately become engaged as each listener considers his or her answer while, at the same time, wonders what the speaker's answer will be.

Tom Hopkins, a professional speaker, once told me (and 1,200 others): *Get the audience's mental engine out of neutral and into gear by asking questions—because questions engage the engine.*

Well-designed and well-positioned questions are powerful connective aids. And when carefully positioned throughout a speech they engage and maintain your connection with your audience.

Questions that involve listeners in the story or the scene you are describing are called **Involving Questions (IQs).** Two other major types of Questions are **Agreement** and **Humorous.** Their goal is the same: to help you build your speaker-audience connection. Examples follow of each type to provide ideas how you might use them.

Involving Questions

An Involving Question (IQ) usually follows a speaker's statement, with the goal of increasing the audience's involvement and engagement. We begin with this excerpt from **David Brooks:**

> But it was home for the first half of my life.
> The place where my two brothers and I learned values and principles—
> Such values and principles as honor, integrity, and self-respect.
> And from whom did we learn these values? (Pause)
> From television! Yes television — because that's where our heroes lived. [DB^]

... David's beginning 3-line statement was a great set-up for his Involving Question — "And from whom did we learn these values?" In turn, this was another great set-up for his surprise answer and what was to follow. [His boyhood heroes, we later discover, were Superman, Roy Rogers, and the Lone Ranger; and they lead to the speech's hero, a current real-life Lone Ranger-type TV hero of David's.]

Arabella Bengson helps us discover what her speech, cryptically titled *Pygmalion*, is about with two Involving Questions (IQs):

> It is said that behind every successful man is a woman and a surprised mother-in-law.
> I say—behind every successful person is a mentor—a Pygmalion.
> What would Helen Keller — totally blind, deaf —
> Have achieved without her teacher, the miracle worker, Anne Sullivan?
> Would Eliza Doolittle —Cockney flower girl—
> Have become My Fair Lady without Professor Higgins?
> The difference between the lady and the Cockney flower girl is, as Eliza puts it—
> "It ain't how she behaves; it's how she is treated." AB^

Note how **Mohammed Qahtani** adroitly changes from an inspiring thought to two IQs that place us right in the middle of his speech:

> You can change a life—
> Inspire a nation—
> Make this world a beautiful place.
> Isn't that what we all want?
> Isn't that why we are all in this hall? MQ^

Veterinarian **Morgan McArthur** has a wonderful way of using IQs to bring his audience right into his scenes. Two of my favorite examples are:

> It's dark. I'm in a barn with no electric power.
> There's a cow strapped to a post with a rope.
> And back here is a cold cowboy aiming his flashlight — poorly.
> Would you like to talk about a bad day at the office? MM^

Followed by:

> I reached for the instrument bucket.
> Forgot my hand was wet.
> Now here's a science quiz — True or false? —
> Wet skin freezes fast to super-cold metal.
> True!
> I was stuck to my bucket! MM^

... Two clever things were done here: Morgan could have made a statement like ... "Oh, no! My hand froze to that ice-cold bucket." Instead, he moves his audience from passive to active involvement by asking a simple question that brings us deeper into his speech. Second, the question's answer, "I was stuck to my bucket," was the speech's first mention of the speech's title, "Stuck to a Bucket." He has now vividly established in our minds the speech's core message.

Dave Sanfacon delivers an unsettling, thought-provoking speech about our lives. Here's how he gets the audience involved:

> Imagine the shock one feels
> When flipping through the back chapters of his life
> And realizing—I didn't write this.
> Imagine the shock one feels
> When he realizes that for most of his life

He has been nothing more than the ink—
The ink inside of a pen—
Being guided by a bunch of
Unknown, Unnamed, Unauthorized biographers.
Ladies and gentlemen,
Have you ever surrendered your pen to satisfy the expectations of others?
Who is writing the script? DS>

... This speech, which won second place in the 2003 WCPS, lays out the position that, for most of us, we live lives scripted by others. Then he challenges us with two of the toughest IQs of all—what about us? This is not a speech about others; it's about us. About our lives. His two IQs do that effectively.

The speeches of **Manoj Vasudevan** are noted for their audience engagement through his frequent use of IQs, as you will see in his WCPS speech *(see page 216.)* The following two examples come from an earlier version of that speech:

Every relationship started with great expectations
And ended in great depression.
Have you had problems in your relationships?
How did you fix it? MV^

I went to the one woman I trust—my mama ...
"Mama, I want a wife."
She said, "No problem. We can fix it."
Ladies and gentlemen—did you hear what my mama said? MV^

For some speakers, such as **Vikas Jhingran,** Involving Questions(IQs) seem to be part of their signature style. Here are three examples from his World Championship Speech:

The year was 1989
I was a teenager and my parents were desperate—
Sounds familiar, doesn't it? VJ^

I really did not believe in this meditation stuff
But one look at my mom *[Gives frightened look]*
And I knew I would have to give it a try—
But then I got hooked.
Did you know that meditation is cool?" VJ^

So mom and I went back to the Swami ...
"Ask yourself question: Who are you?"
Have you ever looked at modern art and wondered — which side is up?
My visit to the Swami was equally confusing ...
I tried to answer the Swami's question
And—miraculously—my grades improved so much
That I was accepted into a good undergraduate program in India.
Freshman year of college — What's not to love about it?
Meditation was out and in came — girls!!! VJ^

Agreement Questions

One speaking trademark of Steve Jobs was repeating **agreement questions** such as: *Wouldn't it be cool? Wouldn't it be great? Pretty cool, huh?* Such phrases get minds (and heads) nodding in agreement, gaining not only your audience's concurrence but actively engaging them in your conversational dialogue.

Two similar types of connectors are **engagement** questions, where you engage your audience directly with a question to set the stage for what follows (e.g., *How many of you chose your parents?* [VJ^]) **and check-in** questions that acknowledge the audience's presence and checks that they are following your thought flow (e.g., *Does that make sense?)*

An excellent, easy-to-access site to see and hear questions in speeches is TED.com. Choose some of their 25 most-visited speakers and see how they connect with their audiences. Recently, when re-watching Sir Ken Robinson's speech, *Do Schools Kill Creativity?* his easy use of questioning phrases popped out. Phrases such as: *Am I right? Are you struck by a new thought? Do you? Don't you? Hasn't it? Haven't there? How amazing would that be? Isn't it? Isn't that true? So why is this? Wasn't she? Why not? Why?* Sir Ken's speech was delivered in 2006. In the first 13 years since, it is TED's most frequently-viewed presentation. Yes, connection counts and questions aid in that connection.

Although seemingly innocuous, all three types of questions—agreement, engagement, and check-in—help keep your audience's minds engaged. The following list, a mix of all three types, are questions to help you strengthen your audience connection. Test drive some in an upcoming speech:

Am I going too fast?

Am I right?

Are you ready for this?

Are you still with me?

Be honest — you enjoyed that, didn't you? [AB>]

But do you know what that proves? [AB>]

But sometimes things don't work out well, do they?

Can you guess what this is?

Did I say the day was hot? (Can repeat this or a similar phrase throughout speech)

Did I tell you that...? (Can repeat this phrase or similar through speech)

Did you ever notice that...?

Did you know?

Do you agree?

Do you ever feel like a person in a catatonic trance—unable to speak or move, but perfectly aware of everything around you?

Do you ever...? (e.g., find yourself singing in the shower)

Do you know what he called her?

Do you remember a time when...?

Do you remember this? — (e.g., hold up a slide rule!)

Do you think...? (e.g., we've missed the boat)

Does that strike a chord with you?

Does that work for you? [MB^]

Don't you find/feel...?

Don't you hate it when...? (e.g., your spouse is right and you are wrong)

Don't you think...?

Ever considered taking a lesson from the weather? It doesn't pay any attention to criticism.[AN]

Ever feel that you're different? I feel I'm diagonally parked in a parallel universe. [AN]

Ever had one of those days that just crumble before your eyes? [DLC]

Ever stop to think, and forget to start again? [AN]

Has that ever happened to you? [PF]

Have you ever been hurt in the game of love? — I mean, really hurt? [CV^]

Have you ever been talking to someone when...?

Have you ever felt insignificant? — Sort of like a zero with the rim rubbed out?

Have you ever felt that way?

Have you ever noticed that...? (e.g., spectators never appear in the record books? [ZZ])

Have you ever wondered...? (e.g., what your next 10 years look like)

Have you ever...?

Have you noticed it's easier to send a man to the moon than win an argument with your wife?

Haven't you found...?

How do you...? (e.g., sort the bills in your wallet)

How many of you have children? [Pause] How many of you are children? [Laughter.] [CV^]

I got out of there quickly—Have you ever seen the space shuttle take off? [AN]

I'll bet that feels pretty good, doesn't it?

Is it wrong that...?

Isn't it amazing? [SJ+] (seeking confirmation)

Isn't it strange that...?

Isn't that unbelievable? [SJ+] (seeking confirmation)

It sounds crazy, doesn't it? [KS]

May I ask you a very personal question?

May I talk to you, one to one?

Now what do you say to that? [MT]

Now, do I exaggerate?

So what does this mean to you? Well, I'll tell you...[BC]

So what explains this?

So who's right? Why?

Tell me this ...have <u>you</u> ever rehearsed a speech in your car? [JAG]

Was it easy? (Vigorously shakes his head) No! [JAG]

We all have heroes in our lives, don't we?
We really aren't any different, are we?
What are the benefits for you?
What do you do when facing a problem like this?
What do you think I was thinking when...? [CV^]
What would you do if...?
What would you have done?
What's the easiest way...? (e.g., to make your spouse happy)
When was the last time you...? (e.g., committed yourself to do something)
Who are you afraid of?
Why do I believe this?
Why do I share my story with you? [PH>]
Why do we call that a Toast? Well, I'm glad I asked me that...
Why should you believe this?
Why should you care? Because ... [BC]
Will you look back on life and say, "I wish I had" or "I'm glad I did"? [ZZ]
With children—it's different, isn't it? [MH^]
Would you admit that...?
Would you care to guess the result?
Would you like to hear what Paul Harvey calls the rest of the story?
Would you stop...? (e.g., a great idea racing around the corridors of your mind)
Wouldn't you agree...?
Wouldn't you say that...?
Wouldn't you...? (e.g., like to start all over again)

Adding Humor to Involvement Questions (IQs)

IQs may also be embellished with humor, as the following four examples show:

> The first time my wife and I had an explosive argument —
> My wife won.
> The second time my wife and I had an explosive argument —
> My wife won.
> The third time my wife and I had an explosive argument —
> Guess what happened? *[Pause]*
> I lost! [PS^]

> There was a study comparing people's estimated work weeks
> With their time diaries.
> They found that people claiming 75-plus-hour work weeks
> Were off by about 25 hours. *[Pause]*
> You can guess in which direction, right? [LV]

A humungous horsefly shot through the window,
In my mouth, and down my throat.
It came back up—lodged in my right nostril.
What would you do with a horsefly buzzing in your nose—
Taking bites the size of Texas? [RJH]

In my life as an underground commodities dealer—
I've seen things you couldn't pay your therapist enough to help you un-see—
And don't get me started on things I've smelled.
Do you know why I'm not curled up in a fetal position every night? [JA>]

Putting U's and Q's Together

Sometimes U's and Qs cascade down together and capture us as did Darren LaCroix's opening to his well-known WCPS speech, *Ouch*! See how smoothly the You's not only infiltrate his Involving Questions (IQs) but also as his connecting sentences.

Can you remember a moment
When a brilliant idea flashed into your head?
It was perfect for you
And then all of a sudden—
From the depths of your brain another thought
Started forcing its way forward through the enthusiasm
Until finally it shouted
"YEAH—great idea—
But what if you— [Falls on face on stage] **—fall on your face?"**
What do you do when you fall on your face?
Do you try to jump right up and hope no one noticed?
Are you more concerned with what other people will think—
Than what you can learn from this?
[Speaker still lying face down on stage while speaking]
Mr. Contest Chair —Friends — And the people way in the back!
[Stands up]   OUCH!
Do you feel I stayed down too long?
Have YOU ever — stayed down — too long? [DLC]

... In the above 121-word (70 seconds) opening there are 7 Involving Questions and 14 You's (or Your's). Darren involved us with his questions and spoke to each to us directly with his many you's. It's no surprise that this speech is among the most-remembered World Championship Speeches. View YouTube: Darren LaCroix Toastmasters

3.1C Mind Your P's

Best served rare or medium, not overdone

Introduction

Inviting your audience to participate in your speech is another easy way to connect. Participation involves talking directly to your audience like U's and Q's but, in addition, invites them to participate in one of myriad ways, such as asking them to raise their hand; stopping and asking them to think about something; shouting out an answer to a question; or inviting them to repeat a key phrase.

Participation helps shape the audience's attitude towards you, your message, and your event. Why does it work? Because as author and speaker Mark Victor Hansen points out: *Having the audience call back to you your key words or phrases keeps them actively involved while increasing their enjoyment; further, when you have the audience touch themselves at chest level while saying an affirmation, it increases their participation level and stimulates their senses thereby anchoring your message at a deeper level.* Another professional speaker, Tom Hopkins, shares a similar discovery: *If I say it, they can doubt me. But if they say it, it is true to them.*

In other words, don't just plant a seed; invite the audience to help you plant it—and, when your audience participates in the planting, there is a sense of co-creation and co-ownership creating a stronger connective thread between them and you.

Participation takes audiences from passive listening to active involvement; they become more engaged.

The following eight examples demonstrate the diverse ways speakers have, with good effect, invited their audiences to participate in their speeches:

1. Invite Audience to Repeat a Phrase

Example

Repeat after me — *When in trouble, ask questions.* [MA^]

Title: The Ride of Life [Message: Get back on the ride]

I have found a secret.
But, first, there is something that we must always do.
Repeat after me — Never give up!
[*Audience*] *Never give up!*
Get back on the ride!
[*Audience*] *Get back on the ride.* [JW^]

Title: Crazy

Our three inmates—
Mother Teresa, Abraham Lincoln, and Nelson Mandela—
Are in here because they did the incredible.
They dedicated their whole lives to their ideals.
They pursued their goals with unparalleled resilience.
They did, in other words, what we all agreed is—
[Waits for audience reply]—*crazy*.
I can't hear you —
It's [*Audience*]— *crazy*. JM^

Title: The Snakebite

How many of you have been hurt by another person?
Put your hand up. [Speaker puts his up]
I know you have.
I want you to repeat after me.
I've been bitten
[Audience] *I've been bitten—*
But it didn't kill me
[Audience] *But it didn't kill me.*
Turn to somebody on your left or right and say
I'm moving on.
[Audience] *I'm moving on.*
But it didn't kill me. ~ CV^

Title: Rematch!

Let's close with some fun!
I want you to sit up in your chairs and when I signal
I want you to shout Rematch! —
If you miss out on that job promotion you desperately want
What will you say?
[Audience] *Rematch!*
If you lock yourself out of your house in your underwear
What will you say?
[Audience] *Rematch!*
If I get rejected on another date
What will I say?
[Audience] *Rematch!* LC^
... Note the clever amusing twist from "you" to "I" at the end

Title: I'm Proud of You

Let's practice that together — *I'm proud of you!*
Now let's say it so others can hear it —
*[***Audience***] I'm proud of you!!*
One more time — shout it so your kids at home can hear it—
[Audience] I'm proud of you!!! RS^

Title: One of Those Days

In his WCPS-winning speech Ed Tate takes us through the ups and downs of a hectic day where, after each up and down, he repeats the title phrase *It's going to be one of those days.* This is how he ends his speech:

And it was like I always said—
I knew—it was going to be—
[Opens arms inviting audience to complete]
[Audience] — *One of those days* [ET^]

2. Invite Audience to Complete a Well-Known Phrase or Expression

Example

It's my way or— *[Wide, one-arm wipe inviting audience to complete] —the highway.*

Title: What We Knew Then

Let's play *Finish the Cliché*—
If I only knew then what I know — [Audience] *Now*
Very good!
How much more successful you'd be
How much more you would've accomplished—
But wait a minute —— What if ——
Help me turn this upside-down
What if we knew now, what we knew — [Audience] *then* [RH^]
... Speaker Rich Hopkins creatively takes a familiar phrase for the audience to complete and then flips it for the audience to complete the reverse. It engaged the audience's minds and they enjoyed it — I know, I was there in the audience, participating.

Title: Reach Out

Would you all please help me complete an old advertising jingle—
Reach out ...
[Audience] ... *and touch someone.*
Louder—I can hardly hear you. *[Speaker cups ear]*
Reach out ...
[Audience] ... *and touch someone*!!!!
Thank you ... [BW]

Title: Silver Bullets

I'm going to start a famous phrase and I want you to finish it
When I give you this cue [hand moves as if twirling a lasso.]
But remember, we do things BIG down here [in Texas]
So I want them to hear you
From Singapore to San Antonio.
Are you ready?
Then return with me now to those thrilling days of yesteryear...
A fiery horse with the speed of light, a cloud of dust and a hearty

[*Audience*] *Hi-yo Silver, away...*
Yes! The Lone Ranger rides again—
Makes you feel good, doesn't it? [DB^]

... David Brooks took the well-known opening line to every episode of the popular Lone Ranger TV series that the audience grew up with and invited them to complete it.

3. Invite Audience to Complete a Well-Known Phrase—Then Twist It

This approach takes a truism that the audience accepts—and then show that it's not so wise after all. It mentally engages your audience before you surprise them which strengthens the connection. Here are two examples from Lance Miller and Zig Ziglar:

Lance's speech was titled, *If At First You Don't Succeed*. He opens by inviting us to remember the sweet feeling of success when we accomplish something we wanted. He then asks us to remember something in our lives that we failed to accomplish. Which begs the question—What do you do when *At First You Don't Succeed? ... [Audience response] ... Try, try again!*

This leads Lance to point out that you can't try to raise your hand or lift a pencil. You just raise your hand or lift a pencil. You just do it. [This is similar to the advice Yoda gave Luke Skywalker in *Star Wars — Try not. Do. Or do not—There is no try.*] Lance's message was that when you try to do something, your heart is not fully in it—so don't try. Just do it!

Zig Ziglar's mind paralleled Lance's. In one speech I heard him deliver, he opened with an old truism handed down over time: *Anything worth doing is worth doing well*. He goes on to explain that novices and newbies can't do important things well initially, and then leads us, through various examples, to the realization that the truism needs replacing by: *Anything is worth doing poorly until you can do it well*. Zig and his twist certainly engaged my mind —that speech was delivered over 30 years ago!

4. Invite Audience to Join You Mentally on a Journey

- Come back with me to 1948—Harry Truman's campaign cupboard is bare... [BW]
- Come with me to Ancient Greece. One sculptor, Pygmalion, loved his statue so much it turned into life [AB^]
- Fast forward with me 10 years...
- I invite you come with me on an imaginary journey—into Inner Space...
- Let's go back to ...
- Let's do something together. [JO^]
- Let's walk down memory lane together...
- May I invite you to visit my Swimming Club? [Arm out, moving to Stage Left]
- Please turn your calendars [or wind your clocks] all the way back to 2001 ...
- Think about it like this ...
- Think of a moment...
- Think of a time when ...
- Think of a time when you suddenly found ...

5. Invite Audience to Be a Partner in the Whole Speech

Title: How to Use A Paper Towel

In his 5-minute TEDx Talk in 2012, Joe Smith created something remarkable that can be fully appreciated only by viewing it at TED.com. Joe introduces, and then orchestrates, full audience participation throughout. He opens by explaining that over half a billion pounds of paper can be saved each year in the United States by using a two-part process with paper towels. One part is shaking your hands after washing them; the other is folding one sheet of a paper towel. Joe then goes through a series of paper-towel scenarios (with dialogue) of washing his hands in a bowl, nods to the right half of the audience to shout out "Shake" which he does with his hands, and then nods to the left half of the audience to shout out "Fold" which he then does with the paper towel. It's an extremely effective demonstration speech with full participation … and acceptance of his point. A participating, engaging, unique speech.

6. Invite Audience to Respond to an Unexpected Statement

Attendees at Toastmasters 1991 Golden Gavel Award heard its recipient, Bill Gove, the first President of the National Speakers Association, give an amusing example of this when he interrupted himself during his own speech. It went like this:

I used to play golf each Tuesday with a group of oldies—
[Stops. Looks at audience]
You are supposed to shout out there—
"How old were they?"
[Starts over]
I used to play golf each Tuesday with a group of oldies …
[Audience shouts out]
How old were they?
[Stops. Looks at audience]
Well, I'm glad you asked that question —
Their average age was deceased; they … *[Laughter]*

Recent examples demonstrating this fun way of connecting come from two popular platform speakers, Jeanne Robertson and Kelly Swanson:

I am 73 years old—
Now you're supposed to gasp there—
So let's do that again—
I am 73 years old
[Audience: average gasp]
That's not good enough— so let's do it again—
I am 73 years old
[Audience: loud gasp] … [JR>] *[Laughter]*

I speak at physical fitness events—
I'll pause while you gasp in shock [~KS]

7. Invite Audience to Imagine Something

Imagine if you were born into a home with no books... [5 second pause] [RW^]
... This was the grabber opening to a memorable speech on tackling illiteracy.

Imagine a world with...

Imagine a world without computers, the Internet, or your cell phone—which would you miss most? Why? ...

Imagine what it would be like if ...

Imagine my parents' reaction (when I said)—*I want to be a comedian!* [DLC]

8. Invite Audience to Do or Say Something

... Show of Hands

A show of hands—
Have you ever wanted to
Go back to school, start a business, write a book,
But fear, procrastination, or the good opinion of others
Talked you out of it? [KRM]

... Invite Everyone to Put Their Hands Up (creating laughter)

Hands up those who have heard me before—or today are hearing me for the first time! [ZZ]

... Invite Everyone to Do Something with Their Clothing

Title: Finding the Right Shoes

So all of you take off your shoes right now! [Speaker became shoeless early in the speech.] I don't want to be alone. Come on—take them off. I'm serious! Take your shoes off and look at them—tell yourself—no one can fit into these shoes better than me. [PS^]

... Create a Cacophony (and also laughter)

I suspect every one of you remembers a teacher who made a difference in your life. On the count of three, shout his or her name out loud... [~RJH]

... Stand Up

Title: What We Knew Then

Come on, get up!
Stand with me!
I mean it—out of your chairs—hands in the air!
To live now as you lived then ...
It's time to wake yourselves up!
Jump on the bed of your life and shout with me
Good Morning!!!! [RH^]

... Earlier in the speech, Rich Hopkins had the audience participating in a limited way. Here, he steps up the level, so that the speech ends with the audience standing and shouting with their hands in the air—and enjoying it! This speech earned Rich third place in the 2006 WCPS.

... Reach Out in Your Mind

Sitting next to you ...
May be the friend of your heart, or of your times, or of your blood —
Reach out now in your mind—and heart—and touch them. [JE^]

... Ask a Question that Requires a "Yes" Answer

Title: Brain Lifting

Why not use the two most important words in the English language?
Without these two tiny words our world would not exist.
Do you want to hear what they are? —
Say yes. [Audience]—*Yes!*
What if? —Every great question that has advanced civilization
Has started with— "What if?" [SP^]

Phrases that Invite Audience Participation

- A quick hands-up if you think that...
- By a show of hands ...
- Clap if you have been a member more that 10 years...
- Come on, clap it up!!!
- Drum roll please ...
- Now, please do it with me. Turn to your neighbor and say... [~CV^]
- Raise your right hand. Put on your left shoulder. Pat yourself on the back. You deserve it!
- Say with me ...
- Hands up if you have ever felt this way...
- Please sing (the *Barney Song)* with me...[JK^]
- Raise your hand if ...
- That's great. Give yourself a round of applause!
- Hands up those who have or have had teenagers — [pauses, looks around] — Ah, the Fellowship of Suffering! [JK^]

What to Do When Your Participation Invitation Fails

When it happens—and it will—acknowledge, don't ignore, weak audience response. You can comment on it (e.g., *Well, I know one audience that was up too late last night*); suggest you do again (e.g., *That's not good enough—let's try that one again...* which usually achieves a good-hearted repeat); or, in a warm friendly style, mention that both you and the audience will need to do better next time.

Acknowledging such blips demonstrates your comfort level on the stage and with the audience; it also reminds your audience you are human, too, and things don't always work out as one wishes, making you more relatable.

Examples of Managing Weak Audience Participation

They did, in other words, what we all agreed is—
[Waits for audience response]— *Crazy*
<u>I can't hear you — it's —</u>
[Audience] *Crazy.* JM^

Keep going and draw strength from those three little words.
Say them with me –
[Audience] *You still should.*
<u>Aw!!! — That wouldn't burst a grape!</u>
<u>Say it like you mean it! —</u>
[Audience responds loudly] *You still should!!!* KRM

My mom's voice goes two octaves higher.
She smiles, she squints, and she squeals out an—
Oh, thank you! —
Regardless of the gift!
If it's a pair of diamond earrings — *Oh, thank you!*
If it's a book which she already has a copy of—
And has no intentions of reading—
She says— [Awaits audience response]
[Audience]— *Oh, thank you.* *[Delivered weakly]*
<u>We'll work on it.</u>
Mister Contest Chair... KH^

... Two lessons here: it shows how a great speaker humorously responds to a weak audience response; and it's a reminder that inviting your audience to "fill in the blanks" unexpectedly at the beginning of a speech (as this was) may not work as well as later in the speech when the audience is more in tune with you. It seems that what works best at the beginning of a speech is a simple question or inviting your audience to complete a well-known jingle, slogan or expression.

3.2 Wars over Words

Introduction

Words are a speech's building blocks—or its stumbling blocks. Words determine your speech's clarity and degree of connection between you and your audience. Two primary ways of assessing words when preparing or evaluating speeches are:

- Concrete vs Abstract Words
- Vivid vs Vapid Words

Understanding the warring sides in these two wars will allow you to choose words that paint clearer pictures enabling you to build a closer rapport between you and your audience.

There is some overlap between the two wars (e.g., a concrete word may also be a vivid word) so after learning their details you may decide to use the rules of just one of the wars or the wisdom of both.

To remove the suspense, here's a brief introduction to these two wars of words:

Concrete vs Abstract Words

Concrete words describe things we can see, hear, smell, taste, or touch (i.e., we are able to relate to them via our five senses). Their definitions are fairly clear and stable ("concrete") and commonly understood by speaker and listener alike. Examples include my wife's iPhone, your purple sweater, my daily walk.

Abstract words describe things with intangible qualities, such as ideas and concepts, which are difficult to attribute specific, stable meanings. Examples include: freedom, love, democracy, morality, compassion, and friendship. You can (and should) speak about them but when you do, understand that what's in your mind is unlikely to be the same in every listener's mind. For example, what you mean by freedom of speech will unlikely have exactly the same boundaries (or lack of them) in the minds of each listener.

When S. I. Hayakawa introduced this new way of looking at words, he linked the concrete and abstract concepts together with what he termed The Ladder of Abstraction. He imagined a tall ladder leaning against a wall, with the most concrete items at the bottom, the most abstract at the top, with gradations (rungs) in between. We'll explore these and show how to use them in our speeches.

Vivid vs Vapid Words

Vivid words are those that help paint vignettes, images, and pictures in listeners' minds. Typically, such words are fresh (vs stale), active (vs passive), bright (vs dull), colorful (vs bland), causal (vs pedestrian), simple (vs complicated), or strong (vs weak). The words in brackets are, most often, vapid words. As later examples will demonstrate, the good guys in this war are definitely the vivid words.

3.2A Concrete vs Abstract Words

Introduction

Words sit on a continuum—described variously from tangible to intangible, clear to cerebral, visual to conceptual, distinct to conjectural. Or, to use linguist S. I. Hayakawa's most famous continuum – concrete to abstract.

In his 1939 book, *Language in Action,* Hayakawa invites us to visualize his continuum as a ladder leaning against a wall, where the bottom rung (rung 1) is reserved for the most concrete term in the set of words under consideration and the top rung (say, rung 10) is reserved for the most abstract.

Other concrete words are then placed on the lower rungs, sorted in order of concreteness (the more concrete the word, the lower the rung) and the reverse occurs at the top of the ladder, where the more abstract the word the higher the rung. Words in the middle of the ladder are sorted similarly. The result is a continuum of words, from the most concrete to the most abstract, on ascending rungs of an upright ladder. Unsurprisingly, Hayakawa termed his creation the *Ladder of Abstraction.*

Concrete words describe distinct items. Abstract words describe ideas and concepts. Below is a simple 8-rung Ladder of Abstraction that you will readily relate to. It's about ice cream. Reading from the bottom rung upwards, the very concrete double-scoop waffle cone (well, unless it melts) is a unique, clearly tangible item, while food, on rung 8, is intangible because it's a concept, a generalization. Food to you will mean something different to the next dozen people who read this. It's meaning is fuzzy, not focused.

Food
^ Junk food
^ Dessert
^ Ice cream
^ Premium ice cream
^ Ben and Jerry's ice cream
^ Ben and Jerry's Chunky Monkey ice cream
^ A waffle cone of Ben and Jerry's Chunky Monkey ice cream [ISU]

Now let's review Hayakawa's favored 6-rung Ladder of Abstraction which ties together a farm and Bessie, one of its cows.

Wealth
^ Assets
^ Farm assets
^ Livestock
^ Cows
^ Bessie

As you climb each rung, you see how it moves from being very concrete (specific) to very abstract (conceptual). Part way up, note the words cows and livestock are part concrete and part abstract as the continuum morphs from concrete into abstract.

Concrete Words

Here's the key: the clearer its distinctiveness, the more concrete the word. The less clear the distinction, the less concrete the word. For example, my old silver 2002 ES300 Lexus sunroof sedan would classify as a clearly concrete term compared to, say, just a silver Lexus sedan, or even less concrete, a Lexus car, or even less concrete (higher-rung still), a Lexus. On the ladder's top rung about my specific car may sit an abstract concept relating to the genre of cars, such as the Lexus global fleet, an idea understood in a general but not specific way (because the global fleet changes in composition and number minute by minute).

The definition of concrete words is that they are connectable to by at least one of our five senses: Sight, Sound (hearing), Smell, Taste, and Touch (feel).

Thus, a coconut is a very concrete term. In fact, we can perceive it through all five senses as I heard in a recent speech. [MPW] We can see it as a unique item (*sight*); we can feel (*touch*) its coarse, stringy, outside covering; if we shake it we'll hear (*sound*) its milk inside; and, if we cut its top off with a machete, we can *taste* its milk and *smell* the coconut's fresh flesh.

Abstract Words

Abstract words are the exact opposite. They are ideas and concepts defined by our minds, not our senses. They have no physical attributes. Abstract words include love, hate, democracy, communism, freedom, socialism, patriotism, courage, honor, justice, truth, integrity, feminism, wealth, compassion, kindness, giving, understanding, racism, prejudice, and the Middle East, Middle Ages, and middle age. They are, in a way, just short-hand terms for concepts and ideas with fuzzy, imprecise definitional borders. Reaching agreement on each word's exact definition is often like trying to catch fog.

For example, ask different people what democracy means. It's unlikely they will answer these questions the same: Who is eligible to vote? Is it a presidential or parliamentary system? Is gerrymandering allowed? How easy is it for new parties to offer election candidates? Are there limits on monies raised for candidates? Is most legislation passed based upon the quality of ideas or the quantity of influence money? Does their definition apply to all countries?

Likewise, what is freedom of speech? Can you have freedom of speech if there are limitations on what you can say (e.g., words suggesting "hate speech?") If there are limitations to freedom of speech, who decides? Why? How?

Well, So What? You Ask

Why is the difference between concrete and abstract words important and how does it affect how we connect with our audience? Well, it's because our minds think in pictures rather than concepts; in concrete rather than abstract terms. We are motivated to act more by one specific injustice than the grand concept of justice for all; more by a person's living example than his lofty generalized utterances; more by a clearly explained path than a conceptual one. In other words, we are motivated more by concrete images than by abstract thoughts.

Consider the following statements:

> I have a dream [ABSTRACT] that [*for example*] my four little children will one day live in a nation where they will not be judged by the color of their skin but by the content of their character [MORE CONCRETE].
>
> I believe that each of you can be a success [ABSTRACT], to [*for example*] wear a Piaget watch, drive a Porsche, and live in a Penthouse at the Ritz [MORE CONCRETE]
>
> We need an honest democracy [ABSTRACT], we need [*for example*] fool-proof voting machines [MORE CONCRETE].
>
> To have a viable nation [ABSTRACT] we need border security [ABSTRACT], we need *[for example]* a big wall [MORE CONCRETE].
>
> Our Party wants to widen Obamacare these elections [ABSTRACT], we want to introduce free health care for all citizens up to their 21st birthday [MORE CONCRETE]
>
> You need some furniture [ABSTRACT], [*for example*] a La-Z Boy rocker would be ideal for you [CONCRETE].

In a speech, if any of the above statements ended after the abstract statement, the ideas would fizzle fast as they are easily forgettable. But when you add the concrete, specific examples, they become clearer, more memorable, and more actionable.

Concrete words connect. In contrast, abstract words are cloudy concepts.

The above statements illustrate how abstract and concrete words can work together in a speech. The abstract presents the concept, the concrete presents the specifics. But if you are forced to choose just one, the concrete is, most often, the more powerful.

It was about this stage when first reading about the Ladder of Abstraction that my mind drifted to that wonderful observation in George Orwell's *Animal Farm*—when Old Major, the grandfatherly pig, grunted to the others —*All animals are equal, but some animals are more equal than others.* So, too, with words: and those that are more equal are the concrete words.

Now, abstract words can and do play a key role in speeches, especially when you are calling upon the audience's higher principles and common values. But, when it comes to your call for action, the call is much, much easier to visualize, accept, and grasp when expressed in concrete terms.

Let me amplify, using examples from two speakers whom I greatly admire, whose speeches earned them runner-up trophies. Why not the winning trophy? Because, in my opinion, despite having a reasonable amount of concrete words in the speech's body, the ending invitation to action was couched in abstract terms so that the audience didn't have clear, specific steps to act upon the nobleness of each speech's message.

The two speech endings were:

The next time you're judged
I invite you to show compassion
Because that's when people get to see the real you
That's how we turn things — around.

Who in your life needs your understanding?
Who needs you to show a level of understanding
That brings courage where there may have been fear
To bring respect where there may have been prejudice
To bring passion where there may have been hate?
Because when we truly understand each other everyone gains.

The first speaker invites us to show *compassion*. The word is used five times earlier in the speech but, because compassion is an abstract term, in the few closing seconds of a speech it's difficult for an audience to clearly picture what it really is and in which occasions will they instantly know they are being judged.

The second speaker calls for our *understanding* when we find others (not ourselves) in situations of *fear*, *prejudice*, or *hate*, three more abstract terms that we are required to instantly filter. (What sort of fear, prejudice, or hate does the speaker mean?) That's a lot for we in the audience to process in a handful of seconds at a speech's closing.

Both speakers are polished, superb presenters: when they speak, they own the stage. Apart from their lack of closing clarity due to the absence of concrete terms, I wonder if the results would have been different if only...

What then, should a speaker do if speaking on an abstract theme such as, say, Freedom of Speech or Capital Punishment? One approach I have seen work effectively is to cover the abstract concept early and then work towards a concrete specific action that the audience can act upon. For example, a speech on Freedom of Speech might start with the general, uplifting principles of freedom but then narrows to a specific actionable case, e.g., why burning your country's flag should be upheld as a way of expressing this fundamental and constitutional right.

A similar structure would work for Capital Punishment (whether for or against). If advocating it, you could zero down to, say, the Boston Bomber and explain why he should be executed for his heinous act. If you are advocating against Capital Punishment, you could zero down to one or more known cases of people convicted and executed who were, posthumously, found to have been innocent.

Speeches comprising a mix of concrete and abstract ideas, as may occur in a three-part speech, should close by asking us to think or do something concrete.

The following is an example of an abstract concept, *appreciation*, that ends with a concrete suggestion. The speech starts with a mix of concrete and abstract words about those who have significantly helped us in life and ends by urging us to identify just one of those people to thank for his or her impact; it urges action of each audience member by acting now—now, before it's *Too Late* (the speech's title):

In each of our lives, right now
There is such a special person who cries out with the poet—
I'd rather have a rose, from the garden of a friend,
Than flowers strewn round my casket, when my days on earth must end.
I'd rather have a smile from a friend I know, like you,
Than tears shared o'er my grave, when I bid this world adieu.
Oh, bring me all the flowers today, be they pink, or white, or red.
I'd rather have just one blossom now, than a truckload when I'm dead.
Ladies and gentlemen, let each of us reach out
And touch that special gray-haired person now—
Now—before it's too late! BW

Simple Connectors Between Concrete and Abstract

If you think you have too much abstract language in your speech you can increase its concrete proportion by:

- Giving examples, e.g., *For example…*
- Asking clarifying questions, e.g., *How does this work for you?*
- Including sensory elements, e.g., something that smells or makes a sound
- Having your call to action expressed in concrete terms

If you think you have too much concrete language in your speech you can increase its abstract proportion by:

- Explaining why it is important
- Explaining what important values or principles lie behind your speech
- Appealing to shared values and ideals ~AD

Which Presidential Campaign Slogans are Concrete, Abstract, and In-Between?

Word choice influences not just speeches. Here is a selection of Presidential campaign slogans covering 150 years. The rankings are mine. Would you rank them differently? If so, your differences are more likely to be at the top rather than the bottom because abstract slogans are open to much more personal interpretation and definition. You will also note that the more concrete the slogan, the more memorable it is.

Slogans: Top (Abstract). Bottom (Concrete).

2016	Hillary Clinton	Stronger Together
1924	Calvin Coolidge	Keep Cool with Coolidge
2000	George W. Bush	Compassionate Conservatism
1988	George H W Bush	Kinder, Gentler Nation
1956	Dwight Eisenhower	Peace and Prosperity
1896	William McKinley	Patriotism, Protection, and Prosperity
2008	Barack Obama	Yes We Can! [aspirational]
2016	Donald Trump	Make America Great Again [aspirational]
1980	Ronald Reagan	Are you better off today than 4 years ago?
1928	Herbert Hoover	A Chicken in Every Pot and a Car in Every Garage
1864	Abraham Lincoln	Don't Swap Horses in the Middle of the Stream

The Benefits of Concrete Words

Concrete words tend to be more precise, such as your mailbox or the Eiffel Tower. They tend to be distinct things or objects rather than concepts or large groups of things or objects. They create clearer specific images in our minds.

Concrete words, understood via the senses, are also more readily remembered because they are often amplified by the senses involved, e.g., if you describe discovering week-old smelly socks under your kid's bed, the smell and the picture conjured by your words are vivid and memorable.

Next Steps

Throughout this book are some outstanding examples of persuasive speeches. As you read and reread them identify the strongly concrete and strongly abstract terms used. Assess their purpose and see where they appear in the speech. Look at the speech's call to action: is it concrete or abstract or somewhere in-between? Overall, ask yourself if the concrete-abstract balance seems appropriate for that particular speech?

Another exercise is offered by Roy Peter Clark in his excellent book, *Writing Tools*. He suggests that after you hear or read a speech, describe it using just one abstract term, e.g., is it about Friendship? Loss? Betrayal? etc. Then ask yourself if there are any ways to make that abstract concept clearer by being more specific, using more concrete words.

Finally, keep in mind that yes, you can wow audiences and win contests with a speech heavily flavored with abstract words and concepts —it's just usually a lot harder that way.

3.2B Vivid vs Vapid Words

Words are to a speaker what colors are to a painter TM+

Introduction

Words are not an indiscriminate rearrangement of the alphabet into random-sized groupings. No! They are the building blocks of audience connectivity. They are, in Rudyard Kipling's words, *the most powerful drug used by mankind.*

Words trigger thoughts, feelings, emotions. For example, during the 2016 Trump-Clinton Election, the children of illegal immigrants were described as Dreamers by some politicians who, at the same time, were describing many citizens as Deplorables. [And if that statement caused a reaction in you—positive or negative—it illustrates how words can trigger emotions, the engine of human action.] As Kipling, in 1923, told members of England's Royal College of Surgeons: *Words are drugs—they can blow your mind, make you feel euphoric or depressed, inspired, or overwhelmed.*

Words have power. Words change minds and outcomes. They move people—excite them, educate them, encourage them; and they demotivate people—put them to sleep. Vapid, tired words produce vapid, tired speeches. Our challenge as speakers is to include vivid, vivacious words that are perky, energetic, colorful. Should you find you have written a common, bland, vapid word like *asked*, check your thesaurus for alternatives. Candidates such as *begged, grilled, implored, inquired, insisted, pleaded, quizzed, requested, suggested, urged* will appear. Likewise, after completing this section, if you want more examples, google a phrase such as *vivid words* in your toolbar and explore the options triggered.

As a speaker, one of your first questions is what do you want your audience to do—something or nothing? The words you choose will influence that outcome. Choose and use to connect and convince. If you want to put life into your listeners, put life into your words.

Note there is a link between Vivid and Concrete words. Vivid words can also be concrete as they paint mental pictures while vivid adjectives can brighten and enhance concrete terms.

Our task is to paint pictures, or vignettes, in our audience's minds—of people, scenes, events—and the more vivid the vignette, the simpler and easier it is to visualize and recall. Vivid words create visual vignettes. Help your audience "see" and feel your speech weaving yet another connection between you and them.

Vivid Words include those that are…

active, bright, colorful, detailed, dramatic, eloquent, emotive, encouraging, energetic, fresh, graphic, imaginative, lively, lucid, original, picturesque, rich, striking, strong, vibrant, visual, warm.

Vapid Words include those that are…

bland, boring, commonplace, drab, dreary, dull, emotionless, feeble, flabby, flat, hackneyed, humdrum, insipid, limp, overused, passive, puny, routine, run-of-the-mill, tired, unclear, unnecessary, vague.

Vive la différence

To illustrate the difference, let's take the frequently-used, bland, vapid word *walk*. Now think of vivid words with a similar meaning that might replace it in a speech: possibly *sashayed, sauntered, scampered, shuffled, skedaddled, skipped, sprinted, staggered, strode, strolled, stumbled*. See the mental images they create. And that selection of words all start with just the same one letter of the alphabet. Many other vivid options await.

Examples of Vivid Words Injecting Vitality and Life into Speeches

We start our array of examples with the opening to Ted Mathew's speech which won third place in the 1979 WCPS. It was the first Contest speech that ever blew me away. Its title was *Knockout*—but its underlying message was about tolerance of others who hold different values. The six short opening lines clearly sets the scene; the following five has us there in the arena, amid the pandemonium, caught up in the surging crowd and then, almost as an aside, we catch a glance of the inert loser [Benny Paret.] Why is the opening such a grabber? — Its vivid, visual words: *Seven, Eight, Nine, Out! The vast arena erupts in pandemonium; surge forward; sweep; triumph; against the ropes; crumpled heap*. The words chosen are mostly short; verbs are active, not passive; not one word is wasted—all expressed in the current tense which heightens our sense of being there. We are instantly engaged.

Seven, Eight, Nine, Out!
The winner—
By a knockout in the 12th round—
And the new Welterweight Champion
Of the world—
Emile Griffith!
The vast arena erupts in pandemonium
Handlers, admirers, reporters
Surge forward to sweep the victor off his feet in triumph.
Against the ropes on the other side
The loser lies in a crumpled heap. [TM^]

I became desperate for an answer.
I turned to books, coaches, meditation—
You name it —I did it—
I even searched in the bottom of a bottle of whiskey.
I eventually found my answer—
Where many of our life's most important questions are answered.
My grandmother's kitchen was filled
With the aroma of freshly cooked bread.
And the quiet rhythmic chopping of vegetables
Was the only sound to be heard. [~MH^]

My mom cooked for dead-broke uncles, hung-over brothers, shade-tree mechanics, faith healers, dice shooters, hairdressers, pipefitters, crop dusters, and well diggers. [RB]

I can still see him sitting off to one side of the room
[Walks and sits in chair]
A tin of tobacco between his knees rolling another cigarette—
[Licks and seals cigarette]
Unreachable in his silence—
As if his shyness chained him to his chair. [JAG]

The whirlwinds of revolt
Will continue to shake the foundations of our nation
Until the bright day of justice emerges. [MLK]

Instead of strengthening my new marriage
I was already regretting it ...
Until one day I was watching TV
And some crazy guy came on and said
Everything in life is arranged...
And I jumped up and said—
You better believe it. [VJ^]

There's a tiny, tumbleweed town called Leadore, Idaho
That God has designated a winter misery test site.
There the bitter wind blows,
And it drives the cold to the marrow of your bones...
I shivered so
My teeth were ivory jackhammers
Just pounding in my head. [MM^]

Susan, I might have to eat my words
But you play like a double amputee ...
[Then, five years later...]
She took out a pen and wrote on a piece of paper
You play like a double amputee.
She tore it up in front of me and said—
And now, what would you like to eat these with? [HL^]

I was standing in a gas station pumping gas
And this beat-up old Datsun pick-up
Screeched to a halt behind me.
Out jumped this lanky young man
And walked straight toward me.
I looked him in the eye—
I knew I didn't owe him any money.
He walked right up to me.
With my quizzical look
He knew I didn't know who he was.
Raising his voice, he said
"Do you remember grabbing me

Standing me on a desk
And auctioning me off as a slave?"
He smiled.
Brent Larson. You were in my very first 5th grade class...
"I certainly was and I've been looking for you.
I want you to know I'm a teacher today
At this high school right over here because of you.
You made a difference in my life."
Well, there we were— two grown men
Crying and hugging each other in a gas station
As the local "lookie-loos" drove by and stared. [RJH]

The furniture was 50 shades of mauve—
The couch was shrink-wrapped in plastic. [~KS]

When Avanar passed on, he was 93 years old.
I will never forget that day.
When I entered his hospital room, he had just died.
[Gently tips a chair to lie flat on its back on the stage floor.]
I was alone with him.
He had become so thin that I could hardly recognize him.
For a moment —I thought I was with a stranger.
I wanted to touch him
But all I dared to do was to rest a finger on his big toe.
[Gently places a finger on the tip of a chair leg, representing Grandpapa's big toe.]
Thank you, Grandpapa.
Thank you for giving me your name.
I am so proud to be called Avanar—Bon Voyage. [JAG]

He was six-six, two-fifty — built like a brick outhouse
Hands like shovels — face like a catcher's mitt. [LC]

And now he's doing back flips down Hallelujah Avenue... [AN]

I shoehorned myself into one of America's shrinking airline seats [~GW]

There's something really special about coming home
To a furry ball of *happy*
Who's always over the moon to see you. [JR<]
... Speaker talking about his dog

My husband buys me a cord with a box on the end of it.
I shove it in my desk drawer
Where its only job for the next couple of months
Is to tangle itself around my office supplies. [~KH^]

One afternoon
Mom and I traveled to the old part of the city of Calcutta
Where the houses were so close that sunlight was a myth…
The aroma of spices drifted in the hot, humid air
And here in a small hut sat the holy man everyone called the Swami
His saffron robe drenched in sweat…
He tried solve the problems people put before him. [~VJ^]

I was tucking my young son into bed …
I was ready to flip the switch on another day of Mommy-hood
And relax for a while.
My best friend Chardonnay
Was waiting for me in the kitchen.
She's a good friend.
She was friends with my mother first.
She's the reason I had kids. [~KS]

A humungous horsefly shot through the window
In my mouth, and down my throat.
It came back up—
Lodged in my right nostril.
What would you do
With a horsefly buzzing in your nose—
Taking bites the size of Texas? [RJH]

Next Steps

The first step is becoming aware of the value of vivid words. This you have just done. The second is to understand where you currently stand. One way to do this is to review two of your recent speeches.

Assess their vitality level:

- What life lurks in your sentences and permeates your verbs?
- Do attention-getting adjectives pop out?
- Are there any vivid nouns?

Then consider setting up new file titled Language Log on your computer. Start populating it with vivid, ear-catching words and phrases for later audience enjoyment. Possible suggestions for your Language Log are the following vivid adjectives, verbs, and nouns.

A bell curve of opinions

A gaggle of ideas

A girl with nothing on her mind more interesting than nail polish

A jockey lot of ideas

A migraine-inducing problem

A monument of memories

A mosaic of magnificent minds
A mounting trash heap of misinformation
A small step for mankind, a giant step for me [WW+]
Age gifts us a generous dose of scar tissue research
America is a giant petri dish of extreme experiments
Are we just filling empty space with hollow time?
Catch those sneaky ideas that tiptoe through the corridors of your mind [BW]
Even Sherwin Williams couldn't match the color of his face
Exactly what hay wagon does he think we fell off? [DS<]
Grab a marker and color me excited [KS]
Have an eye-roll at this one
He added, with a significant eyebrow hoist — *You think you can do that?* [SL]
He sets rhetoric on fire like a crazy arsonist
He's a human pinball, caroming from temptation to temptation
Her silver hair, dyed by the passage of time
His stock of humility rose as his stock prices dropped
I could tell no amount of lipstick would make this pig look good
I was a workaholic — I was always busy being busy [KB^]
I was met with thunderous silence
It was a brilliantly mediocre idea
It was another bubble on its way to meeting a pin
It's a place where summer is an illusion
My life was a train wreck [JC>]
Our failures are our highways to success
Our kid's room was so bad we called it Mt Trashmore.
She gave me a look that would have raised the dead
She watched over her special vase like a prison warden [AD^]
Ten years of my life just vanished. Poof!
The ad triggered a rainbow of responses
The mountainside was a tattoo of scribbled ski tracks
There was a perfect thing to say at that point; alas, I couldn't think of it. [JC>]
Treasure your non-refundable fragments of eternity [CR]

3.3 Authenticity and Credibility

We buy from those we believe, know, trust, and like [KS]

Introduction

Authenticity and credibility are overlapping ideas that go to the heart of audience connection. Before buying your message, your audience first needs to "buy" you. From the outset, their subconscious minds are processing questions such as:

- What credentials do you have to give this speech?
- Are you speaking with knowledge and conviction?
- Do I believe you?
- Do I trust you?
- Do I like you?
- Are you "real?"

In other words, are you authentic and credible? Without many "yes" answers, strong connection is unlikely and the probability of "buying" your message is low.

Once aware of the importance of authenticity and credibility, there are different approaches you can take that will trigger "yes" answers in your speeches to the above questions. Helpful ideas follow.

Authenticity

Authenticity is what Aristotle called *Ethos*; it's your sincerity; it's you being straightforward and worthy of listening to; it's whatever you say or do that signals you are trustworthy and have integrity.

Authenticity is critical in a persuasive speech so start establishing your credentials early in your speech—even, if possible, before you speak. For example, if there is a pre-meeting brochure highlighting your speech, include why your experience and knowledge makes you the right person to be delivering this topic at this time to this audience.

More commonly, the meeting chairman will read a prepared introduction before you come to the speaking area. It's meant to answer some of the possible questions going through the audience's minds, such as: *Who is this speaker? What's special about him? How credible is he on this topic? Is the speech likely to interest me?*

Always accept the chairman's invitation to write your own introduction: it is your pre-speech, your opportunity to pre-shape the audience's minds about you and your topic. Well written, it increases your audience's anticipation to hear you and opens their acceptance level to both you and your message.

Remember, however, that it is an Introduction not a Biography, so keep it short. In that way, the audience will readily remember its key points.

Fortunately, there is a simple formula to speed you through the Introduction process. It has been a proven friend of mine for many years. Richard C. Borden shared it in his 1935 book,

Public Speaking as Listeners Like It. And it is still so relevant today. He tells us to build our written Introduction incorporating answers to four questions (mnemonic SATS):

1. Why this **Subject**? [Importance?]
2. Why this subject before this **Audience**? [WIIFM?]
3. Why this subject before this audience at this **Time**? [Relevance?]
4. Why this subject before this audience at this time by this **Speaker**? [Authenticity?]

Follow this formula and you will start connecting before you start speaking because it covers the key questions in the audience's minds, including your authenticity.

In those cases where an introduction is not read to the audience before you speak, such as in a speech contest, imbed your authenticity credentials early into your speech to answer some of their subconscious questions.

Other ways to allow your authenticity shine through include:

Be yourself. Trust your instincts. Be different. Speak in your own shoes, not someone else's. Don't worry about rehearsed gestures; let them flow naturally as you deliver your message. Even if you feel awkward doing something, e.g., singing badly, do it. The audience will love you being you.

Speak what you believe; really believe. For, as in a conversation, people see through lies and exaggerations. Let your passion flow. Sweat under the armpits. Show your emotions. As platform speaker Kelly Swanson advises, *If the audience doesn't believe it's the real you up there, they will disconnect.*

The speech has to be you—your beliefs, experiences, values, hope, ideals —not a regurgitation of someone else's. So be convincing. Let us hear your sincerity. You cannot have strong feelings on every subject, but you can speak sincerely on certain aspects of nearly every subject. As famous defence attorney, Gerry Spence, points out: *It's the sounds, not the words, that convince, for the sounds carry the conviction.*

Credibility

Credibility, or believability, builds trust. The last thing a speaker wants is to have his audience wondering *Did that really happen?* or *Does he practice what he is proposing?*

Speaking on something personal rather than impersonal is one way to have credibility — *The more personal your speech the more universal its reach* .[MM^] In other words, personal values, experiences, and observations that nearly every audience member can relate to have strong credibility because the audience can relate to them.

That's why personal stories are often chosen by speakers. Not only are they relatable and believable but, as you deliver them, listeners can readily recall and re-live similar events in their lives. Personal stories add to credibility because they communicate truth. On the other hand, if your speech is someone else's story, one way to establish credibility is to explain how the story affected you and how, now, you think or act differently because of it.

Of course, if you are already a well-known expert in a field, such as past House Speaker Newt Gingrich when speaking on politics or Tony Robbins on motivation, your credibility is already well established long before your first word is uttered.

In my experience, the most common credibility killer is when a speaker is preaching without proof of practicing. For example, you may have heard a speaker telling you of the benefits of starting each day at 4AM, yet doesn't demonstrate, or otherwise convince you, that he does so himself or demonstrate the great benefits he has gained by doing so in the past.

In recent years, I have heard two platform speakers talking of how they were bullied as children, urging us to take active measures against bullying—without demonstrating how their childhood experience influenced their later lives and what specific actions they have taken as adults to minimize childhood bullying. In my mind, they failed. They failed the Edgar Guest test (similar to the Gandhi Filter) which is captured in three couplets of his poem *Sermons We See*:

> *I'd rather see a sermon than hear one any day;*
> *I'd rather one should walk with me than merely tell the way.*
>
> *The best of all the preachers are the men who live their creeds,*
> *For to see a good put in action is what everybody needs.*
>
> *Though an able speaker charms me with his eloquence, I say,*
> *I'd rather see a sermon than hear one any day.*

It's the essence of credibility. Preach if you must—but only after you have demonstrated its practice.

Likeability, Vulnerability and Similarity

To the degree that barriers can be removed between you and your audience, the closer and more likeable you become. Identifying similarities or commonalities and exposing your failures and weaknesses are ways that achieve this. This process is descriptively labelled *Getting off your pedestal.*

Your goal is to have the "real you" come across rather than you appearing as flawless, a piece of perfection standing on the stage, separated from your audience by a chasm of awe. Michael Aun [MA^] stresses that you must let people see that you are human and like them—that you aren't up there on the platform above them all. His advice is reflected in a concept called *The Propinquity Principle* that states that we tend to like people who look like us or speak like us or have similar values. Choose words, ideas, and experiences that make you relatable.

Craig Valentine [CV^] says: *The quickest way to connect with your audience is to share one or more of your F's: your failures, flaws, and frustrations.* Why? Because most people have failed, most have flaws, and most have had frustrations — they can relate to such in others. Failure, in particular, intrigue audiences because they want to see how you handled it and what tools you used to turn your failure into a success. Don't be afraid of exposing your scars. Kelly Swanson reassures us that *It is your scars that make you beautiful.*

So how do speakers get down off their pedestals?

One obvious way is to avoid your speech appearing as an ego booster. This is usually done by making someone other than yourself the hero of your story. For example, Ryan Avery [RA^] achieved this in his WCPS Semifinal speech by having wisdom coming from his grandmother and, in his WCPS speech, wisdom came from his mother. In both speeches, he portrays himself as scared, as the one who thinks (and does) silly and immature things.

Putdowns of oneself is another effective technique. Several speakers in recent years included the question *Have you ever done something stupid?* in their opening, either before or after describing an incident. As everyone has, the audience warms to the speaker's open admission of not being on a pedestal but being "human" just like them.

Injecting Humorous Putdowns, like the following, usually receives smiles:

> *I don't practice what I preach—I just preach.*
>
> *I have stopped arguing with my teenage son about borrowing the car. Now, whenever I want it, I take it.*
>
> *I majored in extracurricular activities.*
>
> *I started my first job at 21 in a new suit bought with borrowed money — Now don't snicker, empires have been built on less!*
>
> *I'm donating my brain to medical science — I love creating laughter.*
>
> *I'm not ugly—just unhandsome.*
>
> *It was one week before Christmas. I still hadn't bought my wife a present. I'd been thinking and thinking what to buy—with my usual lack of success.*
>
> *Look, I'm far from perfect — Yes, I can see my wife nodding.*
>
> *You may have noticed I'm not 30 any more ...*
>
> *As far back as I can remember*
> *I was the butt of childhood jokes*
> *The goofy, scrawny kid—*
> *Who was aspiring to be one of those epic heroes*
> *You'd see in a movie—*
> *Maybe even get the girl.* [KJ^]

The bottom line is that audiences don't relate well to perfection. They don't mind you being excellent but they struggle when you position yourself as perfect.

3.4 Connection—Small Important Aids

It's the little things in life that count—you can sit on a mountain but not a tack

Introduction

This section covers three short but helpful connection techniques:

3.4A Connect with Contrast
3.4B Connect with Triples
3.4C Connect with Sequencing

3.4A Connect with Contrast

Contrasts connect because our minds are wired to catch opposites such as when:

We speak loudly, then softly
We speak quickly, then slowly
We speak, then pause to change the tempo or mood
We stand tall, then sometimes fall, crouch, stoop or kneel
We extend our arms wide, then drop them by our sides

And when …

We use opposite words and phrases.

Contrasts in speeches act as **mental speed bumps**—they shake minds out of their listening reverie; they grab our attention; they make things stand out; and they make audience members pay attention. They refocus wandering minds.

As you read the following contrast examples be aware of the thoughts and reactions each trigger in you. In this way, you'll begin to discover your preferred "contrast style." The first example is one you know and remember because it is such a catchy, compelling contrast:

To be, or not to be? [WS]

Americans are well-fed and poorly nourished. [NQ]

And you wonder why you have your ups and downs—and goods and bads—and backs and forths—and bottoms and tops—and ins and outs [CV^]

Don't cry because it's over, smile because it happened. [DS+]

Freedom for others to express wrong opinions secures freedom to express our right opinions.[BW]

Half the world is composed of people who have something to say and can't, and the other half have nothing to say and keep saying it [RF]

I'd rather be looked over than overlooked. [MW+]

In some decades, nothing happens; in some weeks, decades happen. [VL+]

It was a costly, yet priceless, experience...

It's better to live rich than die rich. [SJ]

Life can only be understood backwards; but it must be lived forwards. [SK]

Not to decide is to decide. [HC+]

One evening I hear this huge crash and then — something worse — silence! [KH^]

Real men love for a lifetime; not for a moment. [RJH]

Some call it a higher standard of living; others, a higher standard of waste.

That was Leviathan, the great blue whale, whose yesterdays are a hundred million years, yet of his tomorrows, there are none. [JE^]

The first step to getting what you want is to have the courage to get rid of what you don't. [ZZ]

United there is little we cannot do... Divided there is little we can do. [JFK]

War is a racket ... the only one where profits are reckoned in dollars and the losses in lives. [SB+]

We have enough religion to make us hate one another but not enough to love one another. [~JS+]

We listen too much to phones; too little to silence.

In a digital world run by Siri and Alexa, baseball seems as old fashioned as a record player [~MR+]

A society that has nothing to die for has nothing to live for; it's no longer a stream, it's a stagnant pool [MS>] [Double contrast]

You and I are told we must choose between a left or right, but I suggest there is no such thing as a left or right. There is only an up or down. Up to man's age-old dream—the maximum of individual freedom consistent with order — or down to the ant heap of totalitarianism. [RR]

Some lives are so vivid
It is difficult to imagine them ended.
Some voices so vibrant
It is hard to think of them stilled.
A man who seldom rested
Is laid to rest.
And his absence is tangible
Like the silence after a mighty roar.
... From George W. Bush's Eulogy of John McCain

3.4B Connect with Triples

Introduction

Triples, also called triads, are one of mankind's oldest ear-pleasers. The Greeks used them as did the Romans. They appear in Biblical stories. They have populated language and literature seemingly forever. And movies, too.

A Triple is an expression in three parts, such as the movie title, *The Good, The Bad, and the Ugly*; or Julius Caesar's *Veni, Vidi, Veci* (*I came, I saw, I conquered*); or the Biblical story of the Three Wise Men carrying gifts of gold, frankincense, and myrrh. A cereal commercial goes *Snap, Crackle, Pop!* And speakers use the concept when repeating a phrase thrice or expressing an idea three different ways.

Triples work well in speeches and elsewhere because they give an amazing sense of balance, are easy for the audience to remember, and they readily roll off speakers' tongues. They are in every speaker's toolbox and pop up in almost every speech.

The examples that follow illustrate how easy they are to create and use. Let them act as seed corn to help build your personal granary of Triples:

General Triples (Threes)

A kiss can be a comma, a question mark, or an exclamation point. [M]

Books are the windows of the world, the engines of change, the lighthouses in the sea of time.[BT+]

Emile Griffith—tall, slender, quietly spoken [TM^]

Every great cause begins as a movement, becomes a business, and eventually degenerates into a racket. [EH+]

I'm sorry to be so wishy-washy—but I am absolutely, unequivocally, and decidedly unsure.

Sixty years—sixty months —sixty minutes. What is time?

Some books should be tasted, some devoured, but only a few should be chewed and digested thoroughly [FB]

The graveyard contains books that will never be written, songs that will never be sung, ideas that will never be shared. [OW^]

Alliteration in Threes

Government is big, bloated, and broken.

Harry Truman was known for his courage, character, and common sense.

He was cool, calm, and collected.

The All Blacks showed the world how rugby should be played—with pride, passion, and panache. [LN]

Whatever you aspire to be—chemist, carpenter, or clown.[SD^]

Rhyming in Threes

A dentist drills, fills, and bills.

A leader knows the way, shows the way, goes the way. [RW]

Homeless, useless, worthless. [MB^]

I dream of a home that is spacious, gracious, and palacious. [MVH]

Make them high. Make them cry. Make them try. [DN^]

They were a sorry bunch—pale, male, and stale.

Martin Luther King's dream of a world without racism, militarism, and materialism remains a distant dream [JW+]

Three Integrated Ideas

Better Listening. Better Thinking. Better Speaking. ®

One People, One Country, One Leader *[German Motto]*

Liberty, Equality, Fraternity *[French Revolutionary cry]*

Duty, Honor, Country *[West Point Motto]*

Humor Three-Step (with Twist)

It was Bed, Bath, and—way Beyond! *[Describing the gift's cost.]*

It's as American as Hot Dogs, Apple Pie, and Political Scandals. [LM^]

Nervous about my upcoming trip I grabbed my blankets, my flashlight, and my mother-in-law. [DLC]

The day our boy left home, my soulmate stood at the end of the driveway watching his car, 18 years, and half our grocery bill disappear. [CM+]

The ring was beyond sparkling, beyond beauty, beyond my budget [TC^]

He was as good looking as George Clooney, as wealthy as Warren Buffett, and as sexy as Orville Redenbacher. [AN]

3.4C Connect with Sequencing

Introduction

To achieve impact, put your impact phrase last. Why? The impact phrase contains the life of the sentence. When delivered early, the words that follow tail off and attention droops; when delivered last, interest grows until the impact phrase hits, followed by the natural end-of-sentence pause which further helps highlight the impact phrase.

An example you'll likely recall was Johnny Cochran's iconic phrase in his defence of O. J. Simpson. Cochran could have said: *You must acquit if it doesn't fit*. Instead his carefully chosen words were: *If it doesn't fit, you must acquit* [followed by a pause.] Acquittal was the goal of the defence team. They achieved their goal.

Now compare some sentences to make the point from a speaker's perspective. The original (O) is first; the second sentence is sequenced (S) giving the original more impact:

O: May you do better than ever before when you mount that stage on Saturday.
S: When you mount that stage on Saturday may you do better than ever before.

O: Aristotle, Plato's prized pupil.
S: Plato's prized pupil, Aristotle.

O: A family drive is the easiest way to be happy.
S: The easiest way to be happy is a family drive.[CV^]

O: His giant intellectual vacuum cleaner mind is continually absorbing ideas.
S: His mind is continually absorbing ideas like a giant intellectual vacuum cleaner.

O: My wife Marie is perfect—she sits with me when I'm sick and she puts up with me when I'm well.
S: My wife Marie is perfect—when I'm sick she sits with me and when I'm well she puts up with me.

O: Review your draft to see where you plan to have impact in your speech.
S: Review your draft to see where you plan to make your speech impactful.

O: The weather told me I should start looking for a pair of shorts in my closet.
S: The weather told me I should start looking in my closet for a pair of shorts.

O: Our son's bedroom was so bad it begged us for a bulldozer every month.
S: Our son's bedroom was so bad every month it begged us for a bulldozer.

O: Do you ever find your mind wandering when listening to sermons?
S: When listening to sermons do you ever find your mind wandering?

Sometimes you will find you have two potential impact phrases in a sentence. When this occurs, choose the more important one to you. At other times, there may not be an impact phrase, in which case don't worry. If that occurs too often, however, you may want to review your draft to see how you can add impact with your speech.

Let's discuss some such situations:

O: You have an important decision to make today.
S: Today you have to make an important decision.

If you believe the impact phrase is "you," then the above would be expressed as:

O: You have an important decision to make today.
S: Today an important decision must be made by you. [~PF]

Consider these two options. The speaker has invited his Gramma to a family dinner. Which option would you choose? [There's no correct answer. It depends on which point you are seeking to emphasize.]

Hey, good-looking, where do you want to sit?
Oh, honey, you just do like you always do—
Put me some place out of the way. [~RK^]

Hey, good-looking, where do you want to sit?
Oh, honey, put me some place out of the way—
Just do like you always do.

After several times of tweaking and rearranging words—as seen in these two final examples—you'll start finding sequencing becoming second nature to you.

O: Each day, at noon, he gets out of bed.
S1: He gets out of bed each day at noon.
S2: He seems so disciplined. I bet he springs out of bed every day at—the crack of noon!

The following statement was made by Marion Barry, a past Mayor of Washington DC:

Outside of the killings, Washington has one of the lowest crime rates in the country.

Now if you wanted to rearrange that statement with the goal of creating impact (and bringing the house down with laughter) you'll likely attribute this to the Mayor:

Washington has one of the lowest crime rates in the country, outside of the killings.

Konnect Speech Examples

Introduction

Now that you know the basic tricks of how to connect with your audience, what follows are three seven-minute speeches that connected with their audiences extremely well. The first two won the WCPS title, the third won Toastmasters® highest-level Humorous Contest. Comments on their connection techniques accompany each speech.

The first two speeches won the WCPS title 25 years apart: in 1989 and 2014. They are completely different speeches but both, through their easy, inclusive, conversational styles connected strongly with their audiences. I chose them because their styles are particularly easy to identify and learn from.

Humorous speeches are successful only to the degree they connect. You will learn the techniques the speaker used that helped him connect so well. This humorous speech, delivered in 1982, included a then-current event (the royal marriage of Prince Charles and Lady Diana.) The speech still brings a smile to my face each time I think of it, even after many years, a reminder that great speeches and great lessons are timeless.

All three speeches exhibit excellence and demonstrate techniques that you will recognize and be able apply in your own speeches.

Later, when you reread the speeches in the other four Sections of this book, see if you can identify which connection techniques are used by the speakers.

Enjoy. Learn. Adapt.

I See Something

Dananjaya Hettiarachchi

Winner 2014 World Championship of Public Speaking®

www.iseesomethinginyou.com *View YouTube: Dananjaya Toastmasters*

001. [Takes red rose from his outside breast pocket, looks at it, smells it, pauses...]
002. You and I are not very different from this flower
003. Just like this flower is unique —— you are unique.
004. All of us have something special that makes us as beautiful.
005. Do you know what makes you special?

006. Now the answer to that can be a little difficult to find
007. Because sometimes life has a cruel way—
008. [Starts plucking petals from rose, dropping them & then the stem into a trash can]
009. Of taking out your petals and breaking you in two —
010. And throwing you into the trash.
011. And when you're broken—
012. It's very difficult to feel special.

013. Mr. Contest Chair, my fellow flowers
014. I can remember the first time I broke.
015. I was 17 years old.
016. I had already flunked high school—
017. And managed to get myself arrested.
018. Now, I wasn't afraid of the cops.
019. But there was one person I was very afraid of—
020. And that was my mama.
021. Raise your hand if you have an emotional mother —
022. Let me see. *[Raises his hand]*
023. Put them all out there together and you'll get my mama.
024. I could hear her scream outside the police station—even the cops were afraid!
025. She came up to me — held the iron bars — looked into my eyes. *[Simulating scene]*
026. And I saw a tear coming down her face.
027. Now I'd seen my mama cry before
028. But mothers cry three kinds of tears—
029. Tears of joy—tears of sorrow—and tears of shame.
030. And when a son sees a mother cry tears of shame—
031. That's a life-changing moment.
032. She looked at me and said
033. *Son — I want you to be a better man.*
034. That night when I drove home
035. My dad was waiting for me at home.
036. Now my dad is a cool dad.
037. Raise your hand if you have a cool dad. *[Raises his hand]*
038. Put them all together and you get my dad.
039. My dad came up to me and said—
040. "Son, it's okay.

041. You've flunked your exams.
042. You already got arrested.
043. That's fine — you get that from your mother's side.
044. I want you to start working immediately."
045. And I said, Okay.

046. So my dad took me to meet one of his friends called Sam.
047. Now Sam was an accountant who had an accounting firm
048. And had generously decided to make me his personal assistant.
049. And there he was.
050. He looked like a teddy bear — but this man was special ——
051. I looked at him and he looked at me
052. And then he said the most amazing thing.
053. He said—
054. "Son — **I see something in you — but I don't know what it is**.
055. If you decide to work with me, I can help you find that **something**."
056. And I was like . . . Whoa.
057. That's the first time in my whole life
058. Someone has said that **he sees something in me**.
059. And I started working for Sam
060. And every day after work he used to tell me stories—
061. About the world, about history, about culture, about philosophy.
062. And it was much more interesting than what I learned in school.
063. And I discovered I can dream.
064. And I started dreaming, ladies and gentlemen.
065. After one year
066. I went back into high school—completed my exams—and went into college.

067. After successfully completing college,
068. I found a great girl – but not a job.
069. I didn't know what I wanted to do with my life —
070. Have you ever had that problem?
071. And when you're lost, it's difficult to feel special.
072. So I went back to my cool dad and I said, "Dad I feel lost."
073. He said — "You *are* like your mother."
074. So my dad introduced me
075. To this strange club that had a strange name with strange people — talking.
076. On the first meeting
077. They told me to do something called a Table Topic
078. I aced it — but while I was speaking
079. I see a strange man seated in the back of the room
080. Humble, simple with the unfailing quality of kindness in his eyes.
081. As soon as I finished he walked up to me
082. Looked me dead straight in the eyes and said
083. "Son — **I see something in you — but I don't know what it is**.
084. If you come here twice a month maybe we can find that something."
085. And, ladies and gentlemen
086. I discovered I could speak — and I love speaking —
087. And that led me to become a teacher.

088. I know what it's like to not have enough money in your bank account.
089. I know what it's like to worry when the bills start coming in
090. And sometimes in the middle of the night
091. I wake up my beautiful wife and I ask her
092. "Honey, why did you marry me?"
093. She says, "**I saw something in you — but I still don't know what it is**."

094. Ladies and gentlemen — today—I'm a dreamer — I'm a speaker —
095. And I learned the unfailing quality of unconditional love from my wife.
096. I was broken —
097. And I've been broken — lost — and broke many times in my life.
098. But the people in my life
099. Were able to reach into the trash can and make me whole again.

100. [Reaches into trash can, pulls out a full red rose, holds it in one hand]
101. If it were up to me
102. I would never have been able to do that.
103. And this is why if you have great people in your life
104. No matter how broke—how lost—or how broken—you become
105. They can piece you back together.
106. Ladies and gentlemen–
107. When I look at you
108. I **see something in you — but I don't know what it is!**
109. [Smells rose — then — with a big smile — throws it into the audience]

I See Something — Dananjaya Hettiarachchi
Comment on Connecting

Before reading this commentary, I recommend you view the speech to allow you to visually and emotionally experience how effectively Dananjaya connected. [View YouTube.com: *Dananjaya Toastmasters*]

Note how the quirky title "I See Something" captures your curiosity (I wonder what he sees?) as does Dananjaya's appearance. We wonder who is this guy walking to center stage — solid, tall, bald, impeccably-dressed, self-possessed, brown-skinned, eyes sparking atop a broad smile and full black beard, a deep-red tie with a deep-red rose comfortable in his outer breast pocket. He gets our attention—he connects before his first word.

And the opening words surprise. Instead of a boldly spoken statement (as one might expect given his physical presence), we hear a slow, softly-spoken soliloquy on a beautiful red rose: how it is unique, as are we, followed by a question that draws us in, "Do you know what makes you special?" Ah, this speech must be about me—I'm hooked. But then he throws in an obstacle: "When you're broken, it's very difficult to feel special."

These opening words have my full attention and that connection is fully maintained throughout the whole speech. Here are some of the connection techniques he uses:

Connects with a Relatable Story

He tells us the story of his early life of being broken, lost, and broke, but is ultimately saved because others saw something in him, although they weren't sure what it was. We lean in to hear of his journey—for wouldn't we all love having someone see something special in us and help us discover it?

Connects with U's and Q's

"Yousifying" your speech and asking questions are simple but powerful audience connectors. This speech starts with both.

> <u>You</u> and I are not very different from this flower
> Just like this flower is unique—<u>you</u> are unique.
> All of <u>us</u> have something special that makes <u>us</u> as beautiful.
> Do <u>you</u> know what makes <u>you</u> special? [Lines 2-5]
>
> Taking out <u>your</u> petals and breaking <u>you</u> in two and throwing <u>you</u> into the trash. [9-10]
>
> Raise <u>your</u> hand if <u>you</u> have an emotional mother. [21]
>
> Raise <u>your</u> hand if <u>you</u> have a cool dad. [37]
>
> Have <u>you</u> ever had that problem? [70]
>
> And when <u>you're</u> lost, it's difficult to feel special. [71]
>
> When I look at <u>you</u> I see something in <u>you.</u> [107-8]

Connects with P's

Having the audience participate once or twice is a common trick of speakers to strengthen their connection. Dananjaya adds something special: he echoes his participation invitation. The second is unexpected, about a minute after the first. Yet it perfectly parallels and balances the first (mothers, then fathers.) It means that everyone in the audience and participated and connected with the speaker.

> Raise your hand if you have an emotional mother —
> Let me see. [Raises his hand] [21-22]
>
> Now my dad is a cool dad.
> Raise your hand if you have a cool dad. [Raises his hand] [36-37]

Connects Using Common Characters and Events

Morgan McArthur's [MM^] great insight, *The more personal your speech, the more universal its reach*, is clearly on display in this speech. What Morgan means is that when you speak about personal relationships, experiences, things, and events, it's easier for the audience to relate to you because they understand the context of who and what you are talking about and are able to translate them into their lives.

Dananjaya's speech is full of such relatable elements which hold our interest throughout. The speech's primary characters, besides himself, are his parents, a good friend of his father, a caring, helpful guy in his new Toastmasters club [the whole Contest audience related to that], and his wife. He talks of his failures and struggles in life which, if we didn't experience exactly the same things, we understand clearly what he is talking about: flunking high school, getting arrested, not having a job, being broken, lost, broke, and worrying about paying bills.

Events we relate to include his mother crying (and understanding what that means), having a "fix-it" dad, going to high school and college, finding the right job, seeking reassurance from his wife for his insecurity, and his first experience of Table Topics.

And he opens and closes his speech with the world's best-known flower, a rose. The audience clearly understands, and relates to, Dananjaya from beginning to end.

Connects by Being One of Us

This speech is a classic example of a speaker getting off his pedestal and openly sharing his fears and failings, his flunking school and of being arrested, and his having no job and having no money. He does not place himself above the audience. With his problems and failures, he actually places himself below the audience, speaking from a position of vulnerability, subconsciously making us wanting him to win in his challenges in life.

Dananjaya does not make himself the hero of his story. He gives that honor to the three who "saw something in him"—Sam; an unnamed Toastmaster; and his wife. This encourages the audience to think that others might help them in their lives, too. He offers us hope that we don't have to struggle all alone to make our lives better. Its format is a superbly-crafted "Failure to Success" speech, with most of the speech dealing with our non-hero's personal failing and struggles—something we can all relate to—before hope and success appear.

Connects with a Repetitive Humorous Phrase

The title ***I See Something*** acts as the springboard to the phrase that threads through the speech, ***I see something in you—but I don't know what it is.*** Imagine if the repeated phrase was just ***I see something in you.*** The speech would come across as flatter and more serious. Just the addition of the twist, ***but I don't know what it is,*** magically adds lightness. It allows the audience to laugh—and they do. It provides a moment to pause and digest. Not only that, when Dananjaya says the words ***I see something in you,*** the audience perks up awaiting the following tension-easing, smile-creating add-on. It is extremely effective. It is the memory hook that reminds us of the whole speech.

Actually, the speech is a mosaic of repetitive words that help make remembering its characters and vignettes easy. It is unique and is described on *page 173*.

Connects Emotionally with Words

Words that trigger emotions influence the audience's feelings towards the speaker and the speech (discussed in detail in the next section). Emotional connections are obviously more powerful than unfeeling, intellectual ones. This speech is full of words and phrases that trigger emotions. Here's a sampling:

Words:

Beautiful; flunked; arrested; afraid; cops; emotional mother; tears; scream; joy; sorrow; shame.

Phrases:

You are unique [3]

Life has a cruel way [7]

Breaking you in two and throwing you into the trash [9-10]

When you're broken, it's very difficult to feel special [11-12]

There was one person I was very afraid of ... my mama [19-20]

I saw a tear coming down [my mama's] face [26]

When a son sees a mother cry tears of shame—that's a life-changing moment. [30-31]

Connects with Charisma

Although charisma is not covered in this book, it is instructive to see how psychologists might view this speech through the filter of charisma's six common characteristics (as related to speaking): confidence, exuberance, optimism, a ready smile, expressive body language, and a friendly passionate voice [~JA] After viewing Dananjaya's presentation, I suspect you, like me, will rate his Charisma index highly.

Closing Comment

This speech on Dananjaya's is one of those special connecting speeches where reading the text alone doesn't do it justice. Viewing it, with text (and pen) alongside, is the best way to understand its full richness.

A Many-Splendored Thing
Don Johnson
Winner 1989 World Championship of Public Speaking®

001. Mister Toastmaster, fellow Toastmasters, Ladies and Gentlemen—
002. A family get-together can stir up a mixture of emotions.
003. Last Fourth of July for example
004. We had our traditional family gathering in the backyard.
005. What started out twenty years ago
006. To be a casual patio barbecue for the kids—
007. Now rivals Easter weekend at Palm Springs.
008. All eight of our kids showed up —along with their kids
009. And their husbands
010. And their wives
011. And their boyfriends
012. And their girlfriends
013. And their live-ins.
014. We call them our in-laws and outlaws.

015. As I was standing there
016. At my usual relegated place of that tradition –
017. In front of the charcoal grill–
018. My wife, Marie, came through the patio door
019. Carrying another load of potato salad and strawberry jello.
020. No sooner had she set it on the table
021. When she watched it disappear in one massive slurp.

022. And after patting the heads and tousling the hair
023. And squeezing the bodies of all the little sibs within her reach,
024. She meandered over to the grill to see how I was doing.
025. As she did, the backyard din caught her attention.
026. With a broad dramatic sweep of her arm, she indicated the yard full of bodies—
027. "See what you did," she said.
028. "Now" —she said—
029. "You could have had a boat and ski trips and even a Ferrari.
030. Why, in the smiles of those three alone over there,"
031. And she pointed out Theresa, Bernie and Celeste
032. "Are three round trips to Hawaii
033. Two to Europe
034. And six to Bakersfield."
035. I think she threw the last one in there just for the rhythm of it.
036. But I had never heard anyone describe our kid's orthodontic work
037. With such a poignant metaphor.
038. What she said though, started me thinking.
039. "Gee," I thought
040. "I hope I've given them more than pretty smiles—

041. I hope I've put more into their heads than braces."
042. And I asked myself—
043. As I often ask myself and as I know you who are parents ask yourselves—
044. "Have I given them good values?
045. Do they appreciate what they should?
046. Do they treasure the things that should be treasured?"

047. Suppose we were allowed to pass onto our kids
048. Just one thing—one item—one jewel of wisdom
049. What would that be? — Work hard? Achieve? Be a success?
050. Those thoughts danced through my mind that warm July day
051. Along with the images
052. Of braces and metallic smiles,
053. Countless trips to the dentist,
054. And Ferraris that will never call my garage home.

055. And at that moment, Celeste—our number three—came prancing by.
056. She pecked me on the cheek, said "I love you dad" and flitted off.
057. Well, the smoke from the grill got into my eyes and made them tear.
058. But her simple peck had answered my questions.
059. Squinting through the haze—
060. Drifting my way from the charcoal grill—
061. At that mass of bodies—yelling, laughing, talking, playing.
062. I could see it — I could feel it in the air—
063. Just as I could feel it every time that sea of humanity got together.
064. It was love.
065. It was a contentment in being together.
066. They truly cared for one another.

067. I can be sure that when growing up under one roof
068. I was certain they would end up slitting each other's throats.
069. But somewhere along the way this joy blossomed and there it was.
070. And as far as my teaching it to them
071. I think they taught more to me.
072. For when I was growing up
073. I could never tell my parents I loved them.
074. The words just wouldn't come out—and they never said it to me.
075. Oh, there was love—but no one ever said it.
076. To say it in words
077. Would show weakness and vulnerability.
078. And by golly, we were always strong and invulnerable.

079. But then I married an Italian.
080. What a beautiful cultural background
081. That allows you to say what should be said.
082. And it lets you have more fun.
083. Oh, you can bet that I tell my kids I love them now
084. And I say it to them often—
085. And they shower it back on me—

086. And it feels good.
087. They've taught me this one thing.
088. That if we have that single possession—
089. That ability to love—and be loved—and say it—
090. Then all else falls into place –
091. Achievement, happiness, success.
092. Whether it's a close and intimate love—
093. Such as that between husbands and wives
094. Or parents and children
095. Or the fellowship in a group like this.
096. It's the most precious possession of all.

097. Perhaps, that's why Toastmasters is so successful
098. Because you not only learn and grow
099. But you give part of yourselves to each other –
100. Your knowledge, your experience, your encouragement.
101. And I don't have to tell you that you get so much more in return.

102. So if I could leave my kids with just one piece of advice,
103. I would choose to return to them
104. That which they and their mother gave to me.
105. Love one another.
106. Show it. Share it. Say it.
107. Make that a part of building a better you.
108. For that feeling we share—
109. Call it camaraderie, call it conviviality, call it whatever you want,
110. Will last longer than boats or ski trips or Ferraris.
111. We cherish it more than we will trips to Hawaii or Europe or Bakersfield.

112. A man named Franklin Jones said it like this.
113. He said: *Love doesn't make the world go round.*
114. He said: *Love is what makes the ride worthwhile.*

A Many Splendored Thing—Don Johnson
Comment on Connecting

"Delightfully conversational" is my description of this speech about a family gathering which ends with Don Johnson sharing his realization of what it all means. It still resonates as real, fresh, and vibrant as when it was delivered 30 years ago— telling us that the theme of family and love is timeless.

After acknowledging the Chair and greeting the audience, Don's opening words — *A family get-together* — immediately connect because each audience member can think of, and relate to, one in his life. And the seven subsequent words — *can stir up a mixture of emotions*— activate our curiosity. Without wasting a word, he takes us to the scene of his story — *Last Fourth of July we had our traditional family gathering in the backyard.*

In just a handful of words, Don artfully captures our minds as we wonder what he means by a "mix of emotions" and what might come next. Our minds are ready for "the rest of the story" which unfolds in an easy-going, fun, expressive, conversational style. We are connected to Don throughout as he shares his thoughts and emotions while colorfully describing what he is seeing and thinking.

Not detected in the speech text, but obvious when viewing the video, Don is enjoying being on stage. He has an ever-present warm smile and a natural, seemingly non-stop flow of arm and hand gestures (perhaps thanks to Marie, his effusive Italian wife). Such expressive body language adds to his audience connection.

The following highlights some of the ways how Don connects well to his audience:

Connects with a Relatable Story

It's a story, a personal story, unique to the speaker, but about something we have all experienced. It's a solid base upon which a speaker can connect because each audience member is captured, not just by the speaker's experience (we are all voyeurs at heart), but also by each listener's own parallel story running in his mind. Don's story is easy to follow, picture, and remember. Our minds don't wander or get lost.

Connects with U's and Q's

Oh, you can bet that I tell my kids I love them now. [83]

And I don't have to tell you that you get so much more in return. [101]

As I know you who are parents ask yourselves—
"Have I given them good values?
Do they appreciate what they should?
Do they treasure the things that should be treasured?" [43-46]

Suppose we were allowed to pass onto our kids
Just one thing—one item—one jewel of wisdom
What would that be? [47-49]

Connects with Humorous One-Liners

Now rivals Easter weekend at Palm Springs. [7]

We call them our in-laws and outlaws. [14]

See what you did," she said. [27]

And Ferraris that will never call my garage home. [52-4]

Well, the smoke from the grill got into my eyes and made them tear. [57]

I was certain they would end up slitting each other's throats. [68]

But then I married an Italian. [79]

Connects with Conversational Asides and Inner Thoughts

I think she threw the last one in there just for the rhythm of it. [35]

But I had never heard anyone describe our kid's orthodontic work
With such a poignant metaphor. [36-7]

"Gee," I thought, "I hope I've given them more than pretty smiles." [39]

And I asked myself—as I often ask myself. [42]

Those thoughts danced through my mind. [50]

But her simple peck had answered my questions. [58]

Paints Pictures with Vivid Words

All eight of our kids showed up, along with their kids ... And ... And ... etc. [8-13]

She watched it disappear in one massive slurp. [21]

She meandered over to the grill. [24]

The backyard din caught her attention. [25]

With a broad dramatic sweep of her arm, she indicated the yard full of bodies. [26]

Uses Triples to Clarify Point and Increase Listening Pleasure

And after patting the heads and tousling the hair
And squeezing the bodies of all the little sibs within her reach. [22-23]

Just one thing—one item—one jewel of wisdom
What would that be? — Work hard? Achieve? Be a success? [48-9]

That ability to love—and be loved—and say it. [89]

Achievement, happiness, success. [91]

Your knowledge, your experience, your encouragement. [100]

Show it. Share it. Say it. [106]

[That feeling] will last longer than boats or ski trips or Ferraris.
We cherish it more than we will trips to Hawaii or Europe or Bakersfield. [110-111]

Love, Hillbilly Style

John Shepherd

Winner Toastmasters Region 8 Humorous Speech Contest

New Orleans, LA June, 1982

001. Mr. Toastmaster, Fellow Toastmasters and Friends
002. My Cousin Lester isn't what you'd call
003. An average citizen of Laurel Springs
004. My home town in the mountains of North Carolina.
005. Average would be way too sophisticated for Lester.
006. Some people would say he's stupid, slow, and ugly.
007. I'll admit to innocent, leisurely, and not too handsome.
008. You might sum it up by saying this—
009. *On the freeways of life*
010. *Lester would probably get a ticket for obstructing traffic.*

011. But on July 29, 1981
012. After 10 years of courtship—and 33 years of freewheeling—
013. Lester took his beloved Myrtle
014. And "jumped the broom"—so to speak—
015. At their favorite courting spot—
016. E.J. Mabe's Filling Station in Laurel Springs.
017. On that same day—4000 miles away—
018. Prince Charles hitched up with Lady Diana.
019. On that day— old Charlie got all the publicity—
020. The gold, the glitter—and the firecrackers.
021. But I'll bet you a dollar to a doughnut
022. He didn't have a dog for best man!

023. Last time they had that much commotion in Laurel Springs
024. Was when Uncle Jesse took his chainsaw
025. And cut the tires off the only school bus
026. Laurel Springs Elementary School ever had—
027. Claimed it made his cows so nervous
028. They wouldn't stand still to be milked.
029. After all, it was pathetic—
030. Watching ole Bess drag Jesse and his milk bucket
031. Through the meadow like that——
032. But that's another story.

033. Lester and Myrtle were star-crossed lovers from the very beginning.
034. They wanted to run off to Tennessee and get married
035. When they were in the third grade together.
036. Myrtle's momma wouldn't let 'em—
037. Claimed a 9-year old girl
038. Didn't have no business marrying a 23-year old man.

039. Of course, they were disappointed—
040. But true love makes a mighty strong bond.
041. Besides — Lester looked all over Alleghany County—
042. And couldn't find nobody else.

043. I guess you could say
044. It all boiled down to a question of class.
045. Lester just outright thought
046. Anybody who could read and write —was a communist.
047. Myrtle never outclassed Lester in that category—
048. Myrtle never outclassed anybody — in any category!

049. Now—no matrimonial contract is complete without a bachelor party.
050. *Something simple*, Lester said.
051. So we made it simple.
052. We just went down to the B&T Drug Store in Sparta
053. The night before the wedding
054. To look at the magazines—if you know what I mean—
055. And I don't mean *Better Homes and Gardens!*

056. Then—after about an hour—
057. We went over to the Western Auto store
058. And turned every one of their 17 television sets
059. To the same show – *The Newlywed Game.*
060. The only problem was—
061. We had to keep explaining to Lester—what they were talking about!
062. In the short space of 30 minutes
063. That boy must have said— *You don't mean it!*—25 times!

064. Then came the hour—
065. 12:00 o'clock high noon at E.J. Mabe's Filling Station.
066. Trucks–cars—tractors—bicycles—motorcycles—and mopeds
067. Littered the parking lot.
068. Throngs of the curious and interested
069. Jockeyed for the best view
070. On the hillside beside the store.
071. Hanging on the gas pump was a sign that said
072. Pump it yourself—or until two o'clock, do without.

073. Back in the stockroom
074. Lester was practicing his vows — "I do"— and "I will"
075. But he was having a little bit of trouble
076. Getting the best man to hold the ring in his teeth.
077. We tried to get him not to do it
078. But he insisted that *A dog is a man's best friend—*
079. And I'm not about to let old Herman down now.

080. Meanwhile, outside, here comes the bride and her family
081. Accompanied by the locally renowned marrying preacher—Bill Blevins.
082. Bill used to be mayor of Laurel Springs—
083. Until he was convicted on 39 counts of bribery.
084. While he was in prison — he took a correspondence course in evangelism.
085. Let me tell you something right now—
086. It's tough to top a corrupted evangelist!

087. As Lester and Herman took their places—
088. Under the eaves of the grease rack—
089. Size-16 Myrtle waddled up — in her Size-12 Sears Surplus wedding gown
090. To the strains of her favorite wedding march
091. The theme song to the old television show—*Bonanza.*
092. And as E.J.—the proprietor of the place—
093. Not so discreetly sidled up—
094. And slipped a $5 bill into the preacher's back pocket—
095. The reverend began.

096. Brothers and Sisters, hear me one and all!!
097. He shouted in the fiery tones
098. That a Sunday morning radio preacher would envy.
099. We are gathered here at the site of E.J. Mabe's Filling Station
100. To unite this man and this woman
101. Into the holy and irrevocable bonds of matrimony
102. Right here under the eaves of the grease rack—
103. Where E. J. has done many a tune-up —
104. Including points, plugs, and complimentary radiator adjustment—
105. For only $24.99—plus tax.
106. Can you say Amen?

107. As the hillside responded *Amen*
108. Another $5 bill found its way into the preacher's back pocket
109. And Brother Bill continued
110. Here begins a new life for Brother Lester and Sister Myrtle.
111. Here at E.J. Mabe's Filling Station—& Grocery Store
112. Where gasoline is going at last year's prices
113. And the loaf bread —I say the loaf bread — is fresh as the morning dew!
114. Can you say 'Hallelujah?'

115. As *Hallelujah's* echoed up the valley
116. A $20 bill changed hands and the preacher really got religion.
117. *BRETHREN!!!* he shouted —
118. The ground fairly vibrating
119. With his pulsating rhythm and pauses after each breath
120. My heart moves me (!)
121. To charge every one of you here (!)
122. To take these children into your arms (!)
123. Fill them with your love (!)
124. And see that they never lose (!)

125. That warm blanket of fellowship (!)
126. That we hold for them here this day (!)
127. *At E.J. Mabe's Filling Station, Grocery Store—& Dairy Bar*
128. North Carolina's lowest prices
129. For auto parts, dairy products, and fine, friendly service—
130. OH, IT'S MOVING ME NOW! —
131. To this young couple I say—
132. In front of these friends around you —
133. Who love and dearly care for you—
134. Do you—will you—'til death do you part?
135. Speak now or forever hold your peace.

136. Well, they did —and they would —
137. Except for one little hitch.
138. About half-way through the wedding ceremony
139. The Best Man got so wrought up
140. He swallowed the wedding ring—
141. Fortunately, they were able to get another one for a real good price
142. At *E.J. Mabe's*
143. Filling Station, Grocery Store, Dairy Bar—& Fine Jewelry Store.

144. And finally—this touching conclusion—
145. That would have even brought Prince Charles and Lady Di to tears.
146. I now pronounce you man and wife.
147. You may hug the bride—
148. If you want to kiss her, it'll be $10 extra —
149. Naturally, Lester took the economy package.

150. Now—like the royal couple
151. This star-crossed pair are well on their way to living happily ever after.
152. Myrtle got her a good part-time job
153. Helping uncle Jesse holding his cows still.
154. With Myrtle around—those cows wouldn't dare make a move.

155. And Lester—I'm telling you now—
156. That boy got himself a terrific job with the Highway Department—
157. When their mechanical flagman broke down.
158. His boss says you can't tell the difference
159. Between him and the real thing.
160. In fact—he may even be a little bit better.
161. He's been on the job for four months now
162. And they ain't had to grease him yet!

John Shepherd, DTM, won this, the highest level of humor contests in Toastmasters, representing Goldmine Toastmasters, Concord, NC.

Love—Hillbilly Style — John Shepherd
Comment on Connecting in a Humorous Speech

The Special Case of a Humorous Speech

This speech superbly demonstrates the special case of how humor cultivates connection—and vice versa. It is one of my two favorite "funny" speeches I have heard in all my years in Toastmasters. The other is Jay Nodine's *(see page 165.)* John and Jay were great friends and members of the Goldmine Toastmasters Club in Concord, NC. I have had the pleasure of calling them both warm, wonderful, and witty friends ever since I joined their club in 1981. John is still a member. Jay has passed. But mirthful memories of their humor remain as exemplified in both their speeches.

A humorous speech is designed to entertain a specific audience. This speech did that. It was not meant to convulse the whole world—in fact, some people outside of "the South" likely will not fully understand it and, today, some non-Southerners may feel it's not "politically correct." We can all agree, however, that we can learn how its humor was triggered and think how that insight can be transferred to our own individual situation. Humorous speeches don't require a message — just the yin of laughter and the yang of connection. Accordingly, this commentary will take a different tack from the previous two.

Context

Laurel Springs is a tiny town, a 2-hour (110 mile) drive from the Concord-Charlotte area of North Carolina. The elevation of Laurel Springs and its nearest "big" neighbor, Sparta (population 1,770 in 2010, 20 minutes from Laurel Springs), approaches 3,000 feet. The wider area includes many mill towns, reminders of an earlier era—a credible setting for a hillbilly wedding.

The speech is anchored in authenticity. John drew upon actual places, e.g., E.J.'s filling station, and based his characters on people he grew up with in Laurel Springs. A second real, but diametrically-opposite, anchor is the Royal Wedding of Prince Charles and Lady Diana, which took place a few months before the speech was written. It offers reality and an extreme contrast (and, therefore, numerous humorous opportunities.)

Conversational Style

In persuasive speeches, speakers usually rely on U's, Q's and P's (*You's, Questions*, and *Participation* invitations) to build their audience connection. In this speech, only U's are drawn from that trilogy. But the *You's* are augmented by several other tools, including an easy conversational style established at the beginning:

> My Cousin Lester isn't what you'd call an average citizen of Laurel Springs
> My home town in the mountains of North Carolina.
> Average would be way too sophisticated for Lester.
> <u>Some</u> people would say he's stupid, slow and ugly.
> <u>I'll admit to</u> innocent, leisurely and not too handsome.
> <u>You</u> might sum it up by saying this—
> On the freeways of life Lester would probably get a ticket for obstructing traffic. [2-10]

From John's conversational opening, we learn that Laurel Springs is the speaker's actual home town (giving credibility to later observations), it's in the mountains, and it's about Cousin Lester who is "not average" (indicating he is the Hillbilly in the speech's title.) To widen our smiles, we are exposed to an interesting technique of expressing why "average" would be "too sophisticated" a term for Lester: what some would say, what the speaker would admit to, and how you, the audience (directly including us in the conversation), might sum it up. In the opening 70 words, we meet the main character, Cousin Lester, connect with the speaker, and we are ready for the rest of the story.

One feature of John's engaging, and easy connecting conversational style is his use of **explanatory asides,** such as:

> They "jumped the broom"—so to speak [14]
>
> But I'll bet you a dollar to a doughnut he didn't have a dog for best man! [21-2]
>
> Last time they had that much commotion in Laurel Springs was when... [23]
>
> But that's another story. [32]
>
> Let me tell you something right now—
>
> It's tough to top a corrupted evangelist! [85-6]
>
> *He swallowed the wedding ring—*
> Fortunately, they were able to get another one for a real good price—at E.J. Mabe's [140-2]
>
> *If you want to kiss her, it'll be $10 extra —*
> Naturally, Lester took the economy package. [148-9]

Twists

Twists, a humorist's most favored tool, pop up throughout the speech. A Twist occurs when your mind is being taken in one direction and the speaker then turns it in a completely unexpected, new direction. Here are some of them:

> The gold, the glitter—and the firecrackers. [20]
>
> They wanted to run off to Tennessee and get married—
> When they were in the third grade together. [34-5]
>
> The only problem was—
> We had to keep explaining to Lester—what they were talking about! [60-1]
>
> As Lester and Herman took their places—
> Under the eaves of the grease rack [87-8]
>
> Size-16 Myrtle waddled up — in her Size-12 Sears Surplus wedding gown [89]
>
> To the strains of her favorite wedding march
> The theme song to the old television show—*Bonanza.* [90-1]

Amplifying Statements

In many humorous speeches the speaker plays a key role. Not this. It's an easy-to-follow-and-visualize story where humor is created as John highlights, in vivid living color, the various steps in the hillbilly version of courtship and marriage.

One technique he uses effectively is taking a statement and amplifying it with exaggeration, with each amplification triggering added laughter. For example:

> Lester and Myrtle were star-crossed lovers from the very beginning.
> They wanted to run off to Tennessee and get married
> When they were in the third grade together.
> Myrtle's momma wouldn't let 'em—
> Claimed a 9-year old girl didn't have no business marrying a 23-year old man.
> Of course, they were disappointed—but true love makes a mighty strong bond.
> Besides —Lester looked all over Alleghany County—
> And couldn't find nobody else. [33-42]

Humorous amplifications also follow these statements:

> Lester just outright thought [45]
> No matrimonial contract is complete without a bachelor's party [49]
> Then… we went over to the Western Auto store [57]
> Lester was practicing his vows [74]
> Here comes the bride and her family [80]
> As Lester and Herman took their places [87]

Two speech segments use amplification, too; not in sequential lines but threaded through the speech. One is about E.J. Mabe:

> *E.J. Mabe's Filling Station* [16]
> *E.J. Mabe's Filling Station* [65]
> *E.J. Mabe's Filling Station* [99]
> *E.J. Mabe's Filling Station—& Grocery Store* [111]
> *E.J. Mabe's Filling Station, Grocery Store—& Dairy Bar* [127]
> *E.J. Mabe's Filling Station, Grocery Store, Dairy Bar—& Fine Jewelry Store* [143]

The repetition of a key phrase throughout the speech adds a smile, an element of rhyme, and helps thread the speech together embellished in three ending references: Grocery store? — likely. Dairy Bar? — maybe. Fine Jewelry Store? — definitely not.

The second repetitive segment unfolds Bill Blevins character, a preacher who loves Mammon more than God. This was a play on US society at that time when some televangelists were found "straying from the right path," monetarily and otherwise. His character becomes increasingly vivid in these image-rich lines and sales pitches:

> And as E.J.—the proprietor of the place—
> Not so discreetly sidled up—
> And slipped a $5 bill into the preacher's back pocket [92-4]

> As the hillside responded Amen
> Another $5 bill found its way into the preacher's back pocket [107-8]

> As Hallelujah's echoed up the valley
> A $20 bill changed hands and the preacher really got religion. [115-6]

> You may hug the bride—If you want to kiss her—it'll be $10 extra [147-8]

We are gathered here at the site of E.J. Mabe's Filling Station
To unite this man and this woman into the holy and irrevocable bonds of matrimony
Right here under the eaves of the grease rack—where E. J. has done many a tune-up —
Including points, plugs and complimentary radiator adjustment—
For only $24.99—plus tax. Can you say Amen? [99-106]

Here at E.J. Mabe's Filling Station—& Grocery Store
Where gasoline is going at last year's prices —
And the loaf bread —I say the loaf bread — is fresh as the morning dew!
Can you say 'Hallelujah?' [111-114]

At E.J. Mabe's Filling Station, Grocery Store—& Dairy Bar
North Carolina's lowest prices—
For auto parts, dairy products, and fine, friendly service—
OH, IT'S MOVING ME NOW! [127-130]

Not seen in the text, but well-remembered by those present, was John's easy switching from normal speaking to the rhythmic pulsating pace, pitch, and pauses of a real, fired-up, revivalist preacher to the accent of a hillbilly as he rolled off such phrases as:

33 years of freewheeling [12]
Jumped the broom [14]
Prince Charles hitched up with Lady Diana [18]
Old Charlie [19]
Watching ole Bess [30]
Myrtle's momma wouldn't let 'em [36]
Didn't have no business marrying a 23-year old man [38]
Couldn't find nobody else [42]
Lester just outright thought [45]
Pump it yourself—or until two o'clock, do without [72]
That boy got himself a terrific job [156]
And they ain't had to grease him yet [162]

Closing Comment

Many factors made this speech a success. Covering two unique weddings occurring on the same day allowed for contrast and exaggeration. Exaggerating a hillbilly wedding (or was he?) measured against our "normal" weddings and against a Royal Wedding allowed us to laugh out loud. Developing Lester and Myrtle into lovable, well-developed, colorful characters, and folding in the prototype of a scurrilous preacher added to the reality, and hilarity, of this entertaining speech, a speech tied together by twists, asides, and exaggeration, three common humor tools. It was, and still is, an unforgettable speech!

SECTION 4

EMOTION

As a general rule, we make decisions emotionally and justify them later with the aid of logic [~SA]

Centuries ago, when the word "emotion" was coined in France, it meant "to stir up." It still does. In most cases, emotions are stirred up by others, i.e., emotions are triggered from the outside, such as when a speaker is stirring the hearts of his audience, exciting their feelings, and otherwise is encouraging and lifting them. [~TM+]

Ever been to a rock concert? Remember how you quickly felt good about the lead singer, about the band, their rhythmic lyrics, your favorite songs being sung, and your decision to attend? It wasn't by chance. They were influencing your emotions—they wanted to make you feel good, to like them and their music, and have a good time.

A speaker's challenge is similar. Speeches become great when they are not only heard, but felt, by the audience. We must awaken the heart to move the mind to action. [RJH]

Each of us has experienced emotion's power: occasions when emotion influenced our feelings, decisions, and actions. We need to harness and apply such power when we are seeking to persuade others. In this section you will learn the key techniques, supported by examples. And where, you might ask, does one start? The easiest place is choosing and using emotive words as Jerry Starke did to win his World Championship:

> *The bride came over to us and said, "Mom, Dad, we're leaving now. Thank you for everything and we love you very much." And as the two of them left, I could see her mother's lips quivering, her eyes welling up. It wasn't just our only daughter that was married but the last of three children to leave the nest. And that evening the two of us went home to an empty house. And we were placed on the parent's inactive list. And my role as Ivan the Terrible came to an end.* [JS^]

In ninety-three simple words we feel touches of nostalgia, love, hope, joy, and then sadness, as we hear of this major life change. We feel warmth for, and connection with, both the speaker and his wife.

As Maya Angelou observed:

> *I've learned that people will forget what you said, people will forget what you did, but people will never forget how you made them feel.*

Make them feel.

4.1 Emotions—A List

The more senses and emotions you touch, the more of the speech the audience remembers. [AP]

Over 2300 years ago, **Aristotle** offered his students a list of nine emotions to help improve their persuasiveness. Other lists over time have appeared as thinkers, writers, and speakers have studied the subject and labelled their observations.

Half a century ago, **Paul Ekman** gave us six core emotions: happiness, surprise, sadness, fear, anger, and disgust. Within each lie many gradations. Fear, for example, covers the gamut from mild concern to terror. Ekman was a pioneer in the study of emotions, each manifested in a different combination of our 43 facial muscles.

The shortest scientific list was released in 2014 by **Dr Rachael Jack** at the University of Glasgow. Using the latest photographic and software technology, her research team recorded every facial expression imaginable and discovered there are four core emotions—Happy. Sad. Afraid/Surprised. Angry/Disgusted. All other emotion descriptors are subsets or variations of these four.

In 2017, **Alan S. Cowen and Dacher Keltner**, of Berkeley University, approached emotions from a classification perspective and found 27 distinct categories of emotions.

The Emotion Thesaurus by Angela Ackerman & Becca Puglisi, an excellent, practical book, lists 75 emotions. Not only is each emotion defined but helpful descriptors for speakers and writers are given: physical signs (e.g., flushed look, frequently moistening the lips); internal sensations (e.g., breathlessness, tingling nerve endings); and mental responses (e.g., a desire to move closer.)

Other lists come from the mystic Thomas Merton (4 emotions); James C. Humes (4 emotions to close a speech); Cavett Robert (5 motivational emotions); Christopher Kokoski (7 primary emotions); Robert Plutchik (8); Charles Darwin (8); and two encyclopedia lists titled Universal Emotions (7) and Basic Emotions (10).

In total, I found 13 helpful lists with a total of 173 emotions. Removing cross-list duplicates, **108 uniquely-described emotions** emerged, shown in the following table. Of these 108 emotions, 24 (22% of the total) populate two or more of the 13 lists. The most frequent duplications (on five or more lists) are: Anger. Disgust. Fear. Joy. Love. Sadness. Surprise. [Numbers in the table indicate how many lists they populate (when more than one).]

The table introduces you to the wide variety of ways you can stir the hearts of your audience. Choose one or two and experiment with them. Using your thesaurus, find similar-meaning words. Take heart. A recent Google search of the term *emotive words* produced, within a second, a list of 23 million results!

Emotions —A List

Emotion	Count
Admiration	
Adoration	2
Afraid/surprised	
Agitation	
Amazement	
Amusement	2
Anger	8
Angry/disgusted	
Anguish	
Annoyance	
Anticipation	2
Anxiety	2
Appreciation	
Awe	
Awkwardness	
Boredom	
Calmness	
Confidence	
Conflicted	
Confusion	2
Contempt	3
Craving	
Curiosity	
Defeat	
Defensiveness	
Dejection	
Denial	
Depression	
Desire	2
Desperation	
Determination	
Disappointment	
Disbelief	
Disgust	6
Distrust	
Doubt	
Dread	
Eagerness	
Elation	
Embarrassment	
Empathy	
Entrancement	
Envy	2
Excitement	3
Faith	
Fear	10
Friendship	
Frustration	
Gratitude	
Grief	
Guilt	2
Happiness	2
Happy	
Hatred	
Hope	4
Horror	
Humiliation	
Humor	
Hurt	
Impatience	
Indifference	
Indignation	
Insecurity	
Interest	
Irritation	
Jealously	
Joy	5
Kindness	
Loneliness	
Love	5
Need	
Nervousness	
Nostalgia	3
Overwhelmed	
Pain	
Paranoia	
Peacefulness	
Pity	
Pride	3
Profit	
Rage	
Regret	
Relief	2
Reluctance	
Remorse	
Resentment	
Resignation	
Romance	
Sadness/sad	7
Satisfaction	2
Scorn	
Sexual-desire	
Shame	4
Skepticism	
Smugness	
Somberness	
Suffering	
Sulkiness	
Surprise	6
Surprise/shock	
Suspicion	
Sympathy	
Terror	
Trust	
Uncertainty	
Unease	
Wariness	
Worry	

4.2 Emotive Words in Action

The best and most beautiful things in the world cannot be seen or even touched. They must be felt with the heart. [HK]

Words affect emotions. Be they happy, hurtful or hateful. Cuss words, bitter words, or loving words. Patriotic words, rebellious words, or conciliatory words. Inspirational, motivational, or despairing. Grateful, regretful, or sad. Active, passive or dull. Funny, witty, or serious. Fast, slow, or rhyming. Challenging, thoughtful, or persuasive. Loud, soft, or silent.

They may be single words, or phrases, sentences, or paragraphs. What words you choose and combine influence how your audience feels. Even the most common of words influence, such as house vs home—*house* is a cold term, and *home* emotes warmth and love. What feelings do you want to convey? What words convey them best?

It sounds overwhelming but there is, fortunately, a framework that points speakers towards more vivid pictures, towards more emotive words and phrases. Randy Harvey terms it SCREAM, based on Churchill's CREAM method. CREAM is clearly described in *Speak Like Churchill Stand Like Lincoln,* a superb book for speakers by James C. Humes.

SCREAM

Simile … saying one thing is like another
Contrast … saying an opposite word or phrase
Rhyme … using rhyme is always fine
Echo … repeating a word or phrase
Alliteration … repeating the first letter sound
Metaphor … saying one thing is another

Examples of each are:

Simile (S)
I woke in a hospital with machines lurking over me like vultures [RM+]

Contrast (C)
He didn't answer me. Or did he? [CV^]

Rhyme (R)
The more personal your speech, the more universal its reach. [MM^]

Echo (E)
The President took a fancy to someone who was not his to fancy. [JE^]

Alliteration (A)
He brings hope to the helpless, calm to the chaos. [MA+]

Metaphor (M)
Are there empty chairs in your life … those who need to be called back to the banquet of life? [CR^]

Lines and paragraphs that have touched me in some way, ranging from happiness to sadness, from humor to anxiety, and the many points in between, follow. See how emotive words are used to influence audiences and also note the role that SCREAM elements play. Letters after the quote indicate SCREAM elements, e.g., S = Simile.

His eyes were as blank as marbles. S

It's like driving around the country roads of Ireland—no idea where you're going but great fun getting there. [AN] S

It's like a painting by Hieronymus Bosch where there is so much going on you can't quite tell what it all means. [BB] S, M

Sometimes in life, when we don't have love, it feels like a year without summer. It's been many years without summer. [KN^] S, C, E, M

I've seen things you couldn't pay your therapist enough to help you un-see [JA>] C

Your mouth can spit venom—or mend a broken soul
Ladies and gentlemen—let that be our goal. [MQ^] C, R

I was a radiant light in a 40-watt world. [AN] C, M

I'd rather be disliked for what I am, than liked for what I am not. [MJ] C, R, E, M

It's not what you've lost but what you have left that counts. [Describing the feelings of a man who had lost both hands in an accident.] [PKP] C, E, M

Losing people is part of loving people, but if you do it right, they'll never leave your side even after they're gone. [DH+] C, E, A, M

Our nation is in an Indiana Jones crisis moment. The cave has collapsed. Snakes are slithering. Vehicles are vaporized. And the crushing ball is rushing down the mountain at us. Will we, like Indy, escape? Or will we have our lights knocked out? It depends on how quickly we can cut through this thicket of fear and greed. [AN] C, M

There we were — two grown men crying and hugging each other in a gas station as the local "lookie-loos" drove by and stared. [RJH] R, A

The life of the Negro is still sadly crippled by the manacles of segregation and the chains of discrimination [MLK] R, M

Be thankful for what you have. Your life, no matter how bad you think it is, is someone else's fairy tale. [WA+] M

I tore that letter up until my hands were filled with a thousand paper tears. [PH^] M

There is no prosthesis for a wounded heart. [HL^] M

Too many women are caught up in lives of secrets and lies. [JB*] C, A, M

[1]The shadows are lengthening for me. [2]The twilight is here. [3]My days of old have vanished—tone and tint. [4]They have gone glimmering through the dreams of things that were. [5]Their memory is one of wondrous beauty, watered by tears and coaxed and caressed by the smiles of yesterday. [DMC]

... 82-year-old General Douglas MacArthur starting the close of his Duty, Honor, Country farewell speech to the cadets at West Point.

> *SCREAM ANALYSIS by Randy Harvey— [1]Metaphor. [2]Metaphor. [3]Metaphor, consonantal alliteration "t." [4]Metaphor, consonantal Alliteration "g," Lincoln's "th" Alliteration "They, through, the, things, that," Metaphor "things that were." [5]Transitioning Alliterative "th," Metaphor "memory/wondrous beauty, compounding Metaphor memory (implied) watered by tears, Metaphor emoting sorrow, Metaphoric Alliteration "c" "coaxed and caressed." Metaphor "smiles of yesterday." This are particularly delightful display of compounding and contrasting "meta-metaphors." Very masterfully written speech that connects to the subliminal reaches of the mind.*

Tonight, I represent an AIDS community whose members have been [1]reluctantly drafted from every segment of American society. [2]Though I am white and a mother, I am one with a black infant struggling with tubes in a Philadelphia hospital. [3]Though I am female and contracted this disease in marriage and enjoy the warm support of my family, I am one with the lonely gay man sheltering a flickering candle from the cold wind of his family's rejection. [MF+]

... Speech at 1992 Republican Conference encouraging open minds and help in addressing AIDS.

> *SCREAM ANALYSIS by Randy Harvey— (1) Metaphor, Alliteration (2) Metaphor, Echo "I am", "I am," compound Contrast "white/black"/ "mother/infant," Metaphor " struggling with tubes in Philadelphia" (internal Alliteration of the hard "t" in white, struggling, tubes and hospital—consonance); (3) compounding Echo "I am" , Contrast female/male, support/lonely straight/gay (implied contrast), acceptance/rejection (implied contrast), warmth/cold (implied contrast), Metaphor "cold wind of family rejection." This paragraph is reminiscent of John F. Kennedy's 1961 Inaugural Address's use of Meta Scream which is the use of three or more SCREAM constructs in a single line or group of connected lines. It drives the listening mind into hyperdrive with myriads of cognitive connections mnemonic, cognitive, psycho-social and emotional.*

4.3 Senses

The mind is not a debating chamber, it is a picture gallery. [JE]

Incorporating any of the five senses—sight, sound, smell, taste and touch— enhances and sharpens the pictures you are painting in the mind of each audience member, making them more vivid and alive. The five senses are constant friends of advanced speakers.

To introduce you, here are five examples. The first line (B) is a basic sentence; the second (S) is enhanced by one of the senses, making the scene easier to "see" and remember.

B. His well-polished shoes.
S. His shoes were drill-sergeant, spit-polish shiny. [Sight]

B. The school bus is almost here. I shout to my kids to put on their shoes.
S. The school bus is almost here. I shout to my kids to put on their shoes. I shout SO LOUD that even my neighbors put on their shoes. [WN^] [Sound]

B. Much of the President's route through Havana was on newly-repaired roads.
S. Much of the President's route through Havana was traced by the scent of fresh tar. [Smell]

B. Have you ever been in a life-threatening situation?
S. Have you ever been in a life-threatening situation? Do you still remember the acrid taste of fear? [Taste]

B. Her phone rang again.
S. Her phone shivered with another incoming message. [DS=] [Touch]

A strong champion of peppering speeches with senses is World Champion Ryan Avery [View YouTube: *Ryan Avery Toastmasters*] At presentations following his win, Ryan would hold up his speech showing certain words highlighted in five colors: each representing one of the senses. He explained how, when writing and reviewing his draft, he would look for, and alter, sense gaps and imbalances. But, like pepper, don't over-flavor your speeches with senses; add just enough to make them distinctive.

Another speaker I admire says: *When describing your scenes, ask yourself—What do you smell? What do you hear? What do you taste? What do you touch? How does this moment make you feel?* [KS]

Following are examples of how speakers in diverse situations have employed the senses. Use them as inspiration.

The Senses in Action — Examples

sight. smell.

One afternoon, mom and I travelled to the old part of the city of Calcutta, India. Here, the houses were so close that sunlight was a myth. The aroma of spices drifted in the hot humid air. And in a small hut sat the holy man everyone called the Swami. His saffron robe drenched in sweat, he tried to solve the problems put before him. [VJ^]

sight. sound.

When the last ding-dong of doom has clanged and faded from the last worthless rock hanging tideless in the last red and dying evening, even then there will still be one more sound; that of his puny inexhaustible voice, still talking. [Faulkner: Nobel Prize Acceptance 1950]

sight. touch.

The building I knew as a child was now sad and stained with the tears of 54 monsoons and an exuberant coat of black mold. [PL]

sight. smell.

The devil came here yesterday. Right here. And it smells of sulfur still today, this table that I am now standing in front of. [Hugo Chavez at UN Sep 2006, referring to previous day's speaker]

sight. touch.

There's a tiny, tumbleweed town called Leadore, Idaho, that God has designated a winter misery test site. There the bitter wind blows, and it drives the cold to the marrow of your bones. Bob called at midnight. He had a cow trying to have a calf. He needed a vet in Leadore. At 20° below zero in January exposed flesh freezes in minutes. [MM^]

sight. sound.

I was standing in a gas station pumping gas
This beat-up old Datsun pick-up
Screeched to a halt behind me.
Out jumped this lanky young man.
Walked straight toward me. [RJH]

... *The screech not only added sound but painted an image of an urgent sudden stop.*

sight. smell. touch. sound.

I realized for the first time that I had lived my whole life like a—postcard — flat and incomplete. I had always been so busy building the future I had never lived in the moment — the moment that had the smell, the touch, the sound and the emotion. [VJ^]

sight. smell.

He was tall and trim; his suit and overcoat were perfect; his cologne smelled of money. [DS=]

sound.

Ding! Ding! Ding! Ice cream truck! [RH^]

sound—a scene created completely by sounds.

[It was Christmas Eve.] And in the pause between hymns, if one listened with care, above the pant of the horses, above the whistle of the wind, one could hear the bells of St Michael's ten miles away—and then the bells of St Sofia's even further afield—calling one to another like flocks of geese across a pond at dusk.

... From the absorbing book, A Gentleman in Moscow by Amos Towles

sight. sound.

If I joined Twitter or Facebook I could have hundreds of brand-new friends— just like that! [Snaps fingers.]

... The snapping of Jock's fingers at eye height effectively activated two senses—sight and sound.

touch. taste. sight. sound.

The speedboat hit me and I submerged into a touchless, tasteless, sightless, soundless abyss. [~RM^]

sound. sight.

When that final bell rings—
Ding, ding, ding.
The fighters and the coaches
Will raise their hands in victory singing—
"I'm still standing, yeah, yeah, yeah."
"We're still standing ... [Audience sings "yeah, yeah, yeah."] [RJS]

sound.

He answered with the quiet sound of snoring.

sight. smell. touch. sound.

The keys clattered. The door thuds behind me. An eerie blue light spills out from the kitchen. The digital numbers 11:58 stare me down as I sink into my only chair. A musty glow appears at the other end of the room. Month-old laundry looms in the back corner; the scent tries to escape its mesh prison. I dig through my bag, drag out a soggy cardboard box. The lid flips open, a crusty pizza slice greets me. The fridge rumbles louder than my stomach. Overhead, the lightbulb buzzes like an insect. I look around, then quietly eat. [~B+]

taste.

Mom, in her nightgown and bunny slippers, smiled sweetly. [RA^]

touch.

Goose bumps appeared — right after she did.

sight. smell.

On the pool deck there was music playing, people dancing, and children splashing in the pool. Oh, the smell of popcorn. [KS>]

touch. sight.

We climb over a rise, and a smile creeps onto my face. We had been hiking through dense alpine forest all day, when ... [KM]

sight.

His fair hair had gone white years ago. He carried a spare tire around his middle. His red-rimmed eyes were milky with the onset of cataracts, likely sped up by a two-pack-a-day smoking habit. The end of his large nose was a sea of broken capillaries, brought on by his alcoholism. [BT]

sight. sound.

They fell silent as she entered the room, their faces turned to her like sunflowers to the dawn [DS=]

Linking Emotions to Senses
Eckman's Six Core Emotions Linked to the Sense of Sound

Happiness	Baby giggling
Surprise	*You've won a holiday vacation!*
Sadness	*Adieu, my friend*
Fear	Ugly shouting from a nearby riotous mob
Anger	Your child shouts abuse at you
Disgust	Someone spitting on the street [~DK]

Linking Emotions to Senses
The Emotion Calming/Calmness Linked to the Five Senses

Sight	Watching fish in an aquarium...
Sound	Listening to a relaxation tape...
Smell	A soothing scented candle...
Taste	A cup of mint tea...
Touch	Having a massage... [AN]

4.4 Humor

The emotions of man are stirred more quickly than man's intelligence. [OW]

Amusement and humor are listed among the 108 emotions. Laughter (soft or loud) is involuntary assent and is an effective tool for persuasion.[SL] Smiles and laughter relax your audience, make them more inclined to like you, be more open to your message, and they act as tension-releasers.

And if you are not a naturally funny person (like 97% of the world, it seems!) there is a simple technique that will help you begin your journey of smiles and laughter—today! It's called the Twist. A Twist has your mind moving in one direction when—*Wham!*—you are redirected in a surprising, completely different direction. It's the surprise change that triggers the smiles and laughter. A favorite example is:

> I showed my mother my report card.
> It was my worst ever.
> She smiled.
> *I'm proud of you son—*
> *I can tell from your grades you don't cheat.* [JB^]
> ... The speaker has us laughing in just four simple steps followed by his Twist.

Many Twists comprise only two steps: a statement, then the Twist. For example:

> *Thrift is an admirable virtue—in your parents.*
>
> *Hospitality is the art of making guests feel like they're at home—and you wish they were.*

There is no magic number of steps for a Twist. Twos and threes are the most common but Twists comprising double-digit steps appear regularly. Once aware, you'll find Twists everywhere. Although less common, Twists are also effective in making serious points.

For many years I avoided humor in my speeches as my efforts at making people smile or laugh were usually stilted, and usually failed. When laughing during others' speeches, I found myself thinking, *I wish I could do that.* Having an analytical mind, I finally decided to see if there was a "special way," so I read humor books, watched many videos, and attended speaker seminars. I discovered that humorists extensively used Twists. Twists are, without question, the simplest and easiest way to build your humor skills. Three other simple, smile-creating techniques also discovered were Asides, Putdowns (of oneself), and Exaggeration. They are explained, with myriad examples, in a book I later wrote: *The Non-Humorist's Handbook.*

Enjoy the Twist examples that follow. Personalize and add them to your speeches.

4.5 Twists—Examples

My plane left at 5:25—and I didn't. [AN]

This organization doesn't need McKinsey to sort things out—it needs Freud! [AN]

I know my golf game is improving—I'm hitting fewer spectators [~GF]

I cook with wine—sometimes I even add it to the food. [WCF]

Friends, you have no idea the amount of human electricity generated by a love letter—until your spouse intercepts it! [~JAG]

She laughed so hard her water broke—and she wasn't even pregnant. [JR>]

Without promotion, something terrible happens—nothing. [PTB]

I was really nervous about my long trip so I took my sleeping bag, my flashlight — and my mother-in-law. [~DLC]

Say what you like about Facebook, it has totally revolutionized how we waste our lives. [AN]

I love all children—except the boys. [LC>]

Happiness is having a large, loving, caring, close-knit family—in another city. [GB]

Last year there were 15,000 accidents on golf courses—and that doesn't include holes-in-one. [DB+]

I like my coffee strong, black—and made this year.

The tragedy is that the most knowledgeable people who should be in Congress don't have the time—they're too busy cutting hair and driving taxis. [GB]

My people skills are well above average. My tolerance for idiots needs some work.

Never underestimate your abilities. That's your boss's job.

I promise to tell the truth, the whole truth, and nothing but the truth—unless I think it adds to my story! [BH^]

I've learned that being a parent is the easiest job to get—and the hardest to have.

We both grew up in small towns. Jay's hometown was larger. It actually had a traffic light. My hometown didn't need one. We didn't have an intersection. [BM^]

The US is living on momentum, memories, and borrowed Chinese money. [DC+]

I found my husband on Match.com. At first no one liked him. Now, 10 years later — I understand why. [SK^]

If the phone doesn't ring — you know it's me. [JB>]

When I was 22, I got a job as a hydration specialist — a bartender [JL^]

By working faithfully eight hours a day, you may eventually get to be boss — and then work twelve hours a day. [RF]

Today a man knocked on my door and asked for a small donation towards the local swimming pool — I donated a glass of water.

God created the 10 Commandments — man created a billion laws to say the same thing.

There's only one thing money can't buy — poverty. You need a credit card to do that.[PW]

He's not against freedom in principle — only in practice. [JG+]

Hallmark just announced the launch of an economy card — it's for those who don't deserve the very best. [~DB+]

We Southerners aren't fatter — we're just more honest.

I can remember two emotional scars in my life.
The first was my divorce.
I was a mother left with—
Two children—
Two dogs—
Two cats—
And too much debt. [AFT]

I was so excited to get into the real world and get a real job.
I applied everywhere,
But this was right after the economic crisis
And everyone was looking for work.
I waited and waited . . . and waited.
Not a single phone call.
I started to panic.
Maybe they lost the resumes I sent out–
Yeah, all 100 of them...
That night I asked my roommates for advice—
Mom, Dad... [lots of laughter] [JL^]

Examples of Serious Twists

Civilizations die from suicide—not murder. [AT]

Europe's cathedrals are so inspired, so magnificent—so empty. [MR>]

Fifteen minutes early is on time; on time is late; late is unacceptable. [VL]

Growing up, I had the privilege of being underprivileged. [RWK]

Life is a banquet, and most poor suckers are starving to death! [MAM]

I want to tell you some good news—but I have to tell you the truth. [DP+]

Is there life before death?

Reading gives us a place to go when we have to stay where we are. [EMS]

Ready, aim, blame! [MH>]

The most unsafe place in America today for a black child is in the womb. [CO]

War does not determine who is right — only who is left. [BR+]

4.6 Threading Emotion Through a Whole Speech

Emotion in a persuasive appeal is only effective inasmuch as it is a shared emotion. [SL]

Now let's review two speeches with completely different subjects and styles. Each employ emotion, from happiness to sadness, woven throughout adding to its memorable message.

David Henderson's World Champion Semifinal Speech is about Hope. [Two days later he won the World Championship with a completely different speech.] Randy Harvey's World Championship speech is about Love. Both are uplifting messages, both employ lots of contrasting emotions.

To gain a full appreciation, I suggest that after reading each speech, and before you read the comments, you view it on YouTube. This will allow you to "see" and feel it, and sense its flow and emotions. [Note: due to a contest audio glitch, David's video is not his actual winning speech but a later club recording.]

Both speeches display many aspects of excellence, not just emotion. Return visits to explore them more deeply will be helpful as you continue your climb up Speech Mountain.

One simple way to understand emotion in a speech is to compare it to music in a movie where the sound helps create the mood — fast or slow, up or down, relaxed or sad, suspenseful or joyous.

When writing an important speech consider asking yourself: *How do I want the audience to feel at the end of the speech—and at different milestones along the way?* One WCPS [VJ^] does this and chooses his words and scenes accordingly. Composers of music for movies work with the same mindset. Have you ever wondered where would memorable movies be without their mood-creating music—from *Rocky, Star Wars,* and *The Lion King,* through to *Bonanza, High Noon*, and *The Good, the Bad, and the Ugly*?

Likewise, where would memorable speeches be without their emotion?

The following two 7-minute speeches demonstrate how emotive words, the senses, and humor, the three basic tools of influencing feelings, are used. You will also readily recognize the SCREAM elements that flow freely through both speeches.

Comments on the first speech focus on its emotional structure; on the second, its techniques.

Following these two speeches are two shorter emotive examples: an award acceptance speech and the key section of a speech to a business audience. They are included to remind us that emotion is critical across the spectrum of communication.

The Best Medicine

David Henderson

Winner 2010 Semifinal World Championship of Public Speaking®

View YouTube: David Henderson Toastmasters
Text below is a blend of the original and re-given speeches.

... Enters wearing a long white doctor's coat, with items from child's medical kit: stethoscope, pager, etc.

001. The best doctor in the whole wide world
002. Does more than stitch up cuts, push pills, or take out tonsils.
003. He gives people hope.
004. Fellow Toastmasters
005. Hope is the best medicine
006. Because you can't always cure people—
007. But you can give them strength to push on—
008. And that's what hope does.
009. It gives you strength even when you're dying.

010. Miss Mamo was obviously dying.
011. She had lots of tubes
012. Tubes to her wrist
013. Tubes to her nose—
014. Tubes to this BIG machine
015. That went BEEP, BEEP.
016. She had thick, beautiful hair—once
017. But it was all gone
018. And so were all the relationships she took for granted.
019. Now she accepted dying from cancer
020. Because she had to.
021. But no one can accept dying alone
022. Without hope
023. And they don't have to—
024. They just need help from the best doctor in the whole wide world.

025. Now this doctor I'm talking about became a doctor in 1981—
026. At the age of six—
027. When he got a Fisher Price medical kit for his birthday.
028. And his mom told him—
029. "Since you want to be a doctor so bad
030. You can bring your little butt to work with me
031. And take care of a real patient."
032. Now the doctor had already had a few mishaps with the neighbor's pet
033. So this time his mom picked the patient—Miss Mamo.
034. You see—the boy's mother was a nurse in the ICU
035. Which, by the way—never made much sense to him.
036. Every time somebody asked about it, he said
037. "I see you too."
038. But, I'm digressing—

039. What the boy remembered most
040. About his first visit to the ICU
041. Was the smell.
042. It smelled like somebody threw up
043. Or somebody's puppy had an accident
044. And whoever cleaned it
045. Used buckets and buckets of Pine Sol
046. To try to hide the smell.
047. But—fellow Toastmasters—
048. No matter how hard grown-ups try
049. They can't hide the stench
050. Of despair or suffering or hopelessness from children.

051. By the time that boy got to Miss Mamo's room
052. He didn't want to be a doctor any more—
053. Especially not when his mom told him to go inside all by himself.
054. "I don't want to," he told her.
055. "Why not?"
056. "Because she's scary looking. That lady's bald-headed!"
057. "Boy—you'd better hold your voice down."
058. "I'm serious, mom. I'm just a kid. You're a nurse— you go."
059. "I tried to—but can't."
060. And she cried.
061. And the boy said —
062. "I'm sorry mommy. I'll go."

063. Now Miss Mamo must have known that boy was coming
064. Because as soon as she saw him
065. Her eyes got really big like it was Christmas
066. And she said—Ooooooh!
067. That's how old Black women talk—
068. "Oooh, sweet Baby Jesus." —
069. But the boy said—"No, I'm your doctor."
070. "Well, of course, you are, Baby.
071. What kind of medicine do you practice?"
072. "My mom says I'm a good doctor
073. So I don't think I have to practice.

074. *...Puts on plastic stethoscope*
075. Let's have a look—shall we?
076. Can you take a deep breath
077. And blow out all the candles on a birthday cake
078. Just like this— *[Breathes in and out]*
079. Again— *[Breathes in and out]*
080. Good.
081. Now I want you to stick out your tongue and go *Haaaaah.*
082. Again. *Haaaaah.* *[With tongue stuck out.]*
083. Excellent!
084. Well, your heart is beating 55 miles per hour –

085. That's normal.
086. Your breath is a little stinky—
087. But it's nothing I think you need worry about.
088. May I see your arm please?
089. *[Pretends to give an injection with plastic syringe]*
090. Now if that wears off during the night
091. I want you to take two Hershey's Kisses
092. And call me in the morning.
093. *[The toy pager rings (activated by the speaker)]*
094. "They're paging me. I have to go."

095. And, fellow Toastmasters, he did go
096. Every day—that entire summer.
097. The boy went inside—
098. His mom stayed outside.
099. And for the first time in a long time
100. Miss Mamo was hopeful.
101. She went from waiting to die to dying to live—
102. Each day—for one more visit
103. From the best doctor in the whole wide world.

104. Until one day during a routine visit Miss Mamo went "Ugh." *[Puts hand on his chest]*
105. And that machine that goes BEEP, BEEP
106. Starts going BEEP, BEEP, BEEP, BEEP
107. And a nurse rushed in
108. And the machine beeped even faster
109. And a doctor rushed in
110. And when it seemed like that machine couldn't beep any faster
111. Or Miss Mamo's face couldn't get any tighter
112. Something happened—
113. That even the best doctor in the whole wide world
114. Is not prepared for at six years of age.
115. His mom walked into the room.
116. She knelt down by Miss Mamo
117. And took her hand.
118. Miss Mamo tried to talk
119. But the boy's mother just said
120. "Shhh! —I know you love me — and I love you too."

121. Fellow Toastmasters,
122. Sometimes a single act of forgiveness changes everything.
123. Miss Mamo relaxed.
124. She looked peaceful.
125. And that machine went *BEEEEEEEEEEEEP* *[Draws straight line with hand]*

126. Confused, sad, and scared,
127. Our young doctor had melted into a corner.
128. A nurse took him by the hand and said
129. "You know, she left something for you — a letter."

And, fellow Toastmasters,
Would you believe thirty years later
That young doctor still has it *[Takes letter from his pocket]*
It reads—
Dear Doctor David,
I never properly introduced myself.
My name is Joyce Janik Cunio
And I'm your grandmother.
As you get older
Keep in mind there's only one thing you cannot find again
Once you have lost it –
That's lost time.
I lost six years of your life
Because I abandoned your mother when she was a child—
A mistake I thought was as incurable as cancer
Until a young doctor taught me
I didn't need a cure—
I needed hope.
I was able to endure my suffering because my grandson—
The best doctor in the whole wide world—
Brought me kisses every day.
I love you, David.
Always,
Miss Mamo.

I don't know if I could find the strength to do what my mom did—
But I sure am glad she did it.
Fellow Toastmasters —Hope IS the best medicine.
So if you've lost touch with someone who needs it
Write them a prescription—before it is too late.

The Best Medicine — David Henderson
Comment on Emotion

Overview

At their most basic level, stories involve sympathetic characters encountering complications that change their lives (providing) potential for provoking emotion, says Jack Hart in his valuable book, *A Writer's Coach.* David's story of Miss Mamo meets that definition. Facing death, seemingly alone, she dies peacefully three months later after finding love she never expected.

David Henderson, in his warm conversational style, takes us on a winding emotional journey of curiosity and surprise, sadness and hope, anxiety and happiness, amusement and humor, love and admiration.

We are teased, and pleased, as we learn about the characters, and delighted by the details of each unfolding scene. We are there with David as he describes the sights, smells, and sounds. We enjoy the story's language, especially that of a child expressing a child's thoughts. We experience the speaker's emotions. And we are kept absorbed and engaged right through to the closing invitational call to action.

The Speech's Emotional Structure

The title is a teaser. It piques our curiosity. We muse what might be the best medicine. We assume it must be medical, given the title and the long doctor's coat. Will it be exercise? Sleep? Yoga? Of course, *Readers Digest* subscribers think laughter is the best medicine! We're surprised to learn that its hope. Arousing curiosity at the outset is good, especially when the title is part of a fuller title and the message—*Hope is the best medicine.*

Our curiosity continues with David's opening words as he walks us through a short logic-flow statement that underpins his message. He explains:

> The <u>best</u> doctor (in the whole, wide world) … gives people <u>hope</u>.
> <u>Hope</u> is the <u>best</u> medicine because
> You can't always cure people but you can give them <u>strength</u> to push on.
> That's what <u>hope</u> does —it gives you <u>strength</u> even when you're dying.

At the outset we hear his reasonable, up-lifting premise which makes us more open to what might follow and, with increasing curiosity, wonder where this white-coated speaker is planning to take us. We haven't a clue—but are interested and ready.

We immediately find out [L-10] as we meet Miss Mamo, whom Jack Hart would describe as the story's *sympathetic character*. Miss Mamo is an "older" woman with three months to live. She is "not in a good place." Besides having lost her once-beautiful hair, she has lost her friends and family. Alone in an ICU room, Miss Mamo is dying of cancer, dying without hope. We instinctively feel sad for her.

A paradox appears. Hope is the best medicine but what hope can there be for a woman whose only companion is a sterile, emotionless, big machine whose tubes are attached to her body? Where is this best doctor in the world we just heard about?

Well, a young "doctor," age six, with his plastic Fisher-Price medical kit, appears [L-25] in the next scene. How can he be the "best doctor in the world" able to give hope? David answers our mental question, telling us "this is the doctor I am talking about." We just don't understand how. Our curiosity grows as we learn of the boy's medical kit and his mother telling him "you can bring your little butt to work with me and take care of a real patient." We warm to the boy, enjoy his mom's "real" language, appreciate that "the doctor has already had a few mishaps with the neighbor's pet," love the boy's ICU humor, and David's transition, "But, I'm digressing."

At this point, we have met Miss Mamo, the boy, and his mother, and have learned that he is going to take care of a real patient, Miss Mamo, although he doesn't yet know her name or condition. Willingly, we are being drawn into a fascinating story.

Suddenly, the tempo changes. "What the boy remembers most about his first visit to the ICU was the smell." [L-39] Our senses receive a shock—a triple assault:

> *It smelled like somebody threw up*
> *Or somebody's puppy had an accident*
> *And whoever cleaned it used buckets and buckets of Pine Sol*

Not one, but three unpleasant smell images that most of us readily recognize and react to. And David follows with an observation, emotively using the smell as a metaphor:

> *No matter how hard grown-ups try, they can't hide the stench*
> *Of despair or suffering or hopelessness from children.*

A conflict scene —"I don't want to [do it]"— follows. The 6-year old is upset by the smell; he's upset being told he has to go into the room alone; and he's upset to find that Miss Mamo is bald. We feel his anguish, aggravated by the emotional parent-child conversation which ends in mother's tears, the boy saying sorry and then "I'll go."

Now, at last, the meeting.[L-63] Is this how you thought the first meeting between Miss Mamo and the boy would go? Surprised me too, but after the previous two scenes covering "the stench of despair" and a mother crying, a big dose of light-heartedness was due and we smile and laugh enjoying the "Ooh, sweet Baby Jesus" moment and the boy's humorous Twist response to the "What kind of medicine do you practice?"

The doctor's first examination of Miss Mamo also amuses our visual, hearing, and smell senses. After the repeated in and out breathing, a tongue sticking out (with big *Haaaahs*) we learn that the patient's heart is beating 55 miles per hour and she has stinky breath. To top it off, the best doctor in the whole wide world gives an injection (from a child's syringe) and offers pain-killers of two Hershey's Chocolate Kisses, just as we are surprised by the loud ringing of his Fisher-Price pager [unobtrusively activated by David.]

The above two scenes have lifted our sprits as does the next where we learn the boy is visiting every day [L-94] that summer. We understand how this encounter would raise Miss Mamo's spirits and give her hope "dying to live" for just one more day. We feel good, despite knowing the inevitability of what lies ahead for Miss Mamo.

This sad moment occurs during one of the boy's regular visits. We witness a scene [L-104] of sight and sound, full of movement and BEEPs. And, in those final few minutes of life, Miss Mamo's daughter walks in, kneels, holds her hand, and with words of love closes years of pain, allowing Miss Mamo to die peacefully—being loved by her daughter and grandson. All the pieces fall into place: grandmother, mother, son. Surprised, as an audience member, I feel tears welling. But the boy—he is bewildered.

We find him "melted into a corner." With yet another surprise to follow. Miss Mamo has left the boy a letter which David produces and reads. The letter fills in the final gaps, triggering more feelings.

Imagine a boy learning that his patient of three months, someone he had never seen before, was his grandmother. Imagine a boy learning that his mother had just forgiven her mother, his grandmother, on her deathbed, after being abandoned by her as a child. Imagine a boy vaguely understanding his daily presence gave hope and love to his grandmother. Of course, a six-year old wouldn't fully grasp all the implications. But we, the audience, do and are affected by it.

The speech closes. We are emotionally "sold." We agree with David's message that "Hope is the best medicine," and anticipate and welcome his invitational next step — *Who, in our lives, needs a prescription of hope?*

Insight from The Speaker

In an interview [SS+] two years later, David elaborates:

> ✦ In this speech, I shared the story of watching my mother forgive her mother on my grandmother's deathbed for abandoning her as a child. It was about hope which I called "The Best Medicine." When you lose someone it feels fundamentally unfair, so I focused on finding a way for people to move forward from loss in a positive way.
>
> ✦ Take something that is unique to you and make it something that other people can relate to. Done the right way, people forget that you are telling a story about yourself and they think about things that have happened to them [i.e., they are absorbing your story into their lives.]
>
> ✦ When you tell a personal story drawn from your experiences, the mechanics such as humor, hand gestures, and vocal variety get automatically corrected [i.e., with a personal story you are more naturally emotive—and more authentic.]
>
> ✦ Come up with a way to make the audience feel the emotions with you.
>
> ✦ The one thing you must do is make people laugh. Laughter is not just about entertaining people, it is about generating an emotional response.

Closing Comments

As with music in a great movie, David composed a speech that changes our feelings and mood as the story unfolds. This is clear in the structural analysis where the sadness of meeting Miss Mamo is followed by the joyful innocence of the boy, followed by the highs and lows, sadness and smiles of the contrasting interlocking scenes. The alternating mix of emotions triggered is, in part, driven by the story's unfolding surprises which keeps us fully involved throughout.

In addition to the speech's curiosity and surprise, some other emotion-building techniques used are worthy of comment:

Blandness is banished

Throughout the speech emotive words and phrases conjure up images, memories, and the feelings we personally attach to them. They include:

> abandoned, accident, bald-headed, best doctor, best medicine, cannot find again, Christmas, cried, cure, doctor, dying alone, eyes got really big, grandmother, grandson, hope, hopelessness, I know you love me, I love you too, ICU, kisses, lost touch with someone, mistake, mom, obviously dying, our young doctor had melted into a corner, peaceful, relaxed, scary-looking, she knelt down, single act of forgiveness, sorry, stench, stinky, suffering, took for granted, took her hand.

Repetition is used to magnify emotion

Repetition is used in different ways including:

To magnify sadness

> Miss Mamo was obviously dying. She had lots of tubes—tubes to her wrist—tubes to her nose—tubes to this BIG machine that went BEEP, BEEP.

To magnify worry

> And that machine that goes BEEP, BEEP starts going BEEP, BEEP, BEEP, BEEP and a nurse rushed in and the machine beeped even fast and a doctor rushed in and when it seemed like that machine couldn't beep any faster...

The repetition of the idea of emotional loss was cleverly linked by a Twist

> She had thick, beautiful hair—once
> But it was all gone—
> And so were all the relationships she took for granted.

In Closing

Speeches like this are a pleasure to read, view, enjoy, and learn from as they allow us to appreciate how a carefully chosen mix of words, senses, and laughter trigger emotions that are blended together to create something very special.

Lessons from Fatdad

Randy J Harvey

Winner 2004 World Championship of Public Speaking®

001. When I was seven
002. We drove to my cousin's for dinner—
003. And to show off Fatdad's new car —a 1960 Ford Fairlane.
004. I fell asleep in the back seat.
005. And my folks left me sleeping as they went up to the house.
006. When I woke up
007. I stumbled out of the car and headed for the porch.
008. Woof! —— OWWWOOO!!!
009. I WAS surrounded by a pack of black and tan hunting hounds —
010. OWWWOOO!!!
011. My heart jumped — and then so did I—
012. First to the trunk—and then the roof—of his new car. c1up
013. Mr. Contest Chair, Fellow Toastmasters, and guests
014. I was frozen like a treed raccoon
015. I was bawling and screaming —
016. The hounds were circling and howling.
017. An ugly one-eyed dog
018. Clawed and scratched its way onto the trunk.
019. His yellow teeth snapping and foaming—
020. Uhh!—I was standing in water—— *[looks down briefly]*
021. It was mine!!!
022. Its claws screeched and slipped on the glass when I heard—
023. *Son*!!!
024. And I dove at the voice — c1down
025. To be caught in Fatdad's arms.
026. Safety was a flannel shirt *[inhales]*
027. That smelled of cherry tobacco
028. And a thunderous bellow
029. That scattered hounds like cottonseed on the wind.

030. The next morning—
031. Fatdad was buffing the scratches out of his new car c2+
032. I said — *Fatdad, I'm sorry you had to rescue me.*
033. He scooped me up in his big arms—
034. Said: *Son, in life —*
035. Sometimes you're the catcher — sometimes you're the caught.
036. When you love somebody — their trouble is your trouble.
037. Fatdad was my Daddy—
038. And that loving nickname Fatdad
039. Has been handed down through four generations of men in my family.

040. When I was sixteen
041. Fatdad bought me a 63 Volkswagen Beetle
042. Wide tires, chrome wheels.
043. I was driving it one sunny afternoon— c3sit
044. Listening to Simon and Garfunkel on the eight-track—
045. *Cecelia you're breaking my heart!* *[leaning back singing loudly]*
046. A humungous horsefly shot through the window—
047. In my mouth — and down my throat——
048. It came back up —
049. Lodged in my right nostril!!!— *[points to right nostril]*
050. What would you do *[asks audience question]*
051. With a horsefly buzzing in your nose
052. Taking bites the size of Texas???

053. I steered with my knees— *[on chair, with knees up]*
054. And tried to fire that bug out my nose. c3up
055. The car shot to the left —
056. Then it catapulted back to the right— *[runs to left, then right]*
057. Cut down Morrison's fence—
058. Sailing across their yard
059. Right at Mossburger's fountain —
060. Where Mary Poppins stood—
061. Holding her umbrella *[on one foot, one arm up]*
062. Pouring water from a can.
063. I hit that fountain so hard I launched it like Sputnik
064. Mary Poppins hovered briefly
065. Then went down faster than a spoonful of sugar!

066. Well, the Morrisons and the Mossburgers—they were a bit excited.
067. Not Fatdad!
068. He rode in like the Cavalry — made peace with the Neighbors.
069. I—sat on a rock—in shock— as Fatdad put his arm around me. c4rock
070. I burst into tears.
071. *Shssssh—we can fix the fence——I'll buy another fountain——*
072. *We can even replace that ol' car — those are just things.*
073. *But — I could never replace you* —— c4up
074. *Besides — the town will talk about this for weeks——*
075. The lesson—Love!

076. Now teenage boys—they don't always think about cars——
077. Sometimes they think about—GIRLS!
078. Fatdad overheard me and my buddies
079. Bragging about our adventures with women!
080. Not being the shy type—he joined right in-—listened for a while—
081. And then —like ice water thrown on you in a hot shower— said
082. *Boys—real men love for a lifetime —*
083. *Not for a moment!*
084. Ruined the whole conversation!!!

085. But Fatdad loved my Mama.
086. When they walked in the garden
087. Or when they sat on the sofa c5+
088. Their hands seemed to find each other.
089. And when Mama was sitting watching TV
090. Fatdad would come up behind her
091. Wrap his strong arms around her c6wrap
092. Rest his chin on her shoulder
093. Kiss her on the cheek. *[gives soft smooch]*
094. Ooh, as a teenager c6up
095. I couldn't believe old people carried on that way!!!
096. But Fatdad's love was more than romance.
097. When my Mama battled the cancer that eventually took her life
098. Fatdad—
099. Like a good shepherd caring for a wounded lamb—
100. Fed and bathed—
101. Read and sang to her—
102. And when my mama's sunset fell—
103. And turned to starlight
104. Fatdad held her close—
105. Whispered words of love — and faith —
106. To calm her fear.

107. Fatdad's love for my Mama was a gift to my wife and children.
108. Because watching him —
109. I learned to love them—
110. For a lifetime.

111. This year I had my first Father's Day without Fatdad.
112. And I miss him. *[holding back tears]*
113. But the lessons he taught me will last a lifetime.
114. When you love—
115. Sometimes you're the catcher —
116. Sometimes you're the caught.
117. When there's trouble—
118. Love rushes in—
119. Wraps its strong arms around you.
120. Real men— well —
121. They love for a lifetime—
122. Not for a moment.

123. Fellow Toastmasters
124. **THE LESSON IS LOVE**
125. And I'm proud to tell you
126. My children call me—**Fatdad.**

Lessons from Fatdad — Randy Harvey
Comment on Emotion

Overview

This is an emotive speech, both in words and presentation. It is an emotive topic. "Fatdad" —Randy Harvey's dad— had died in a farm accident only six months earlier. Randy misses him and relates some of many memories and lessons Fatdad left behind.

The advantage of reading a speech is the uncovering of subtleties missed when viewing it, such as word selection and usage. On the other hand, viewing a speech shows many elements that are not transmitted clearly when reading it, such as movement and facial expressions indicating emotion. This speech is rich both in its viewing and reading.

The speech covers a span of over 40 years. From four decades, how does one choose a few points illustrating your father's influence to share with 2,000 strangers and hold their uninterrupted attention for 7 minutes? Randy does it with vividly painted personal stories, connecting emotionally, and a superb use of speaking techniques.

The Opening Scene

The first scene provides a wonderful array of emotive skills that are repeated throughout the speech so it shall be our focus.

The title, *Lessons from Fatdad,* tweaks our curiosity. Is he Randy's father? Grandfather? A relation? A store owner? One's thoughts race. Okay, we're interested.

The opening scene is one to which the audience readily relates: a kid visiting relatives as his dad proudly shows off his new car. A child falling asleep in a car adds more memories. This low-key recounting of common memories starts the speaker's connection-building process with his audience.

It seems a comfortable, quiet and sleepy scene—a perfect set-up for the sudden surprise shock that jumps up at us in the form of fearful hounds. The tempo (and adrenalin level) instantly changes. Not just because of the dogs but because of the words describing them: *the hounds are circling and howling, one ugly one-eyed dog has clawed and scratched his way onto the trunk, his yellow teeth are snapping and foaming, and his claws screeched and slipped (on the car window.)* Certainly, enough fear to understand a 7-year old reacting by *bawling and screaming and feeling frozen like a treed raccoon* (i.e., a raccoon trapped in a tree surrounded by circling baying hounds.)

What major emotive techniques are being used here?

- First, the surprise shock—the sudden shift from tranquility to fear.
- Second, the choice of highly-emotive, easy-to-visualize (and feel) words.
- Third, the vivid mental picture of the character's reaction.

Question. Which has greater impact: "circling" or "circling and howling?" The latter, obviously, delivering more than twice the emotive power of just the single word "circling."

Why? Because when two active verbs are paired, their combined power trigger more than twice the emotion of one of them, particularly when the paired words also have a repetitive, rhyming, or alliterative element. As do all the picture-painting couplets that help create this visually-vibrant scene.

But the opening's scene's descriptive words go beyond paired verbs. They include amplifying adjectives attached to lonely nouns, such as *treed racoon, ugly one-eyed dog, yellow teeth (snapping and foaming), and a thunderous bellow*. Each adjective magnifies its noun, enriching our mental picture and touches our feelings.

Triggering the audience's emotions via a character's reaction is another emotive technique because people typically react to another's state of emotion. This is demonstrated by our reaction to this 7-year old boy bawling and screaming, and being frightened and fearful of those circling, snapping hounds.

Yet another excellent emotion-enhancing technique in the opening scene is Vocal Perambulation. Perambulation means walking around. Randy defines Vocal Perambulation as vocally walking around and uses it in speeches to build emotional suspense and then suddenly releasing it. It adds to a speech's roller coaster effect. In this opening scene he uses it twice to build and then ease tension.

The first time is when Randy tells us of climbing to the roof of Fatdad's car because of his fear of what those circling dogs may do to him—and we naturally feel his fear. This taut tension is suddenly snapped by a digression: *Uhh!—I was standing in water—[looks down]—It was mine!!!* That classic Twist triggered laughter and the tension melts.

But only temporarily. We must return to the boy's escalating fear as the ugly one-eyed dog's claws are now *screeching and slipping* on the car's rear window. The tension holds until Randy hears Fatdad shouting "son" and he dives into his arms. The opening scene ends with Randy's view of Fatdad as a haven of safety, security, and happiness, amidst the turmoil of life. And he shares his image of Fatdad in an unforgettable way—a flannel shirt smelling of cherry tobacco tied to a booming voice—a *thunderous bellow that scattered hounds like cottonseed on the wind.*

This carefully-crafted opening scene has taken us on a ride from quietness to fear (with humor intertwined) to the quiet, solid security of a rock-like father.

But that's not all. There are two more major emotive areas to discuss:

- **Senses**
- **Delivery**

Senses

Three senses are employed in the opening scene: **sight, sound, and smell**. All add impact.

Sight is obvious. We have a clear mental picture of the scene: the dogs—what they look like (*black and tan hunting hounds, one-eyed, yellow teeth snapping and foaming)*, and their threatening movements and actions—together with appropriate introductory images of the two primary characters.

The sounds we hear add a real-life dimension of emotive fear and anxiety to the scene. They include: *Woof! OWWWOOO!!! OWWWOOO!!! bawling; screaming; howling; clawed; scratched; screeched; thunderous bellow.*

And the sense of smell: *Safety was a flannel shirt* [Randy inhales to emphasize what follows] *that smelled of cherry tobacco.* A memorable metaphor for Fatdad.

Delivery

Randy's delivery is different. He makes the speech multidimensional. He does not give this speech—he lives this speech. The first scene of 90 seconds typifies his style, beginning the moment he confidently strides onto the stage with his warm smile.

His opening is conversational, warm and inclusive (including panning the audience.) After his opening words, *When I was seven we drove to my cousin's for dinner,* the two subsequent phrases, *and to show off Fatdad's new car—a 1960 Ford Fairlane*, were like asides in a conversation, even to the detail of looking over his glasses to explain that to us. Initial impression: Randy is easy to listen to, to relate to, to open up to.

He speaks, moves, and gestures naturally as he includes all of us in the audience. The surprise fear on his face and in his voice when he hears the hounds barking and snarling is in perfect contrast from his opening quiet audience conversation. Our emotions move in unison. As he relives his childhood reaction, he moves quickly to a chair (the car) and climbs onto it, carrying on his dialogue. We see his words in action as his gestures reflect them so naturally. For example, he shrivels his shoulders as he describes being *frozen like a treed raccoon*, sways his body as he describes his *bawling and screaming*, looks down (at the dogs) from the chair as he talks of the hounds circling, and his hands reflect the clawing and scratching of the ugly one-eyed dog. He is helping us see and hear what is happening. We are in the scene. We are absorbed. Our minds are not tempted to wander. We are on the roller coaster with him.

The closing lines of the scene, *Safety was a flannel shirt that smelled of cherry tobacco—and a thunderous bellow that scattered hounds like cottonseed on the wind*, is visual poetry. To watch him caringly rub the sleeve of that flannel shirt of safety and inhale that remembrance of Fatdad's cherry tobacco, then shock us with his own thunderous bellow as he echoes Fatdad's *thunderous bellow*. The ups and downs of the opening scene foretell the emotional roller coaster that follows through the rest of the speech. We expect a ride of surprises, of ups and downs.

Special Feature

As mentioned, the emotive techniques and delivery style of the opening scene appear throughout the speech. However, there is one special feature and we shall close this commentary on *Lessons from Fatdad* with it:

Visual Speaking Height (VSH)

A unique feature of this speech is a simple single chair. It is seamlessly integrated into the speech six times (*identified in the margin of his speech as c1 ... c6.*) The chair is used when:

1. It becomes the car Randy jumps onto to escape the dogs. He acknowledges the Toastmaster and audience from there, too, before jumping off it into Fatdad's arms.

2. Fatdad briefly has his hand on his car (chair) as he is buffing it.

3. Randy sits in his VW (chair) and leans back in it singing *Cecelia,* and then sits, with his knees up, when steering it (with his knees). He stands as the car shoots to the left.

4. Fatdad crouches next to Randy on the rock (turns chair 45 degrees to see both Randy and the audience) talking, with arm around Randy. He stands as he says: *Besides, the town will talk about this for weeks!*

5. Fatdad briefly rubs his hand across the top of the chair as Randy describes his parents sitting on the sofa.

6. Fatdad approaches the sofa (chair) from behind and wraps his arms around Mama (on the chair), resting his chin on her shoulder, and kissing her. Randy reacts by standing and expressing surprise about "old people's" behavior.

A chair is a great prop as it allows a speaker to easily change his or her visual speaking height (VSH), i.e., varying it from its normal, expected position. Randy's earlier doctoral studies had taught him that when this happens audience members subconsciously becomes more alert.

Using a chair six times in a 7-minute speech is a record — from the top of Fatdad's car, to leaning back singing *Cecilia*, steering his car with his knees, to wrapping his arms around it (and Mama.) Note that another example of changing his VSH occurred when he was describing the Mary Poppins statue with one arm up holding her umbrella, while standing on one leg. These unexpected images add to the multidimensional aspect of the speech and its memorability.

The Lesson: The clearer we "see" the scene, the stronger the feelings it creates.

The George P. Hoffmann, Jr. Distinguished Dentist Award
Pete Hoffmann

Receiving an award can also be an event that evokes emotion.

Every year since 1979, in memory of one of its great dentists, the South Carolina Dental Association has awarded the prestigious *George P. Hoffmann, Jr. Distinguished Dentist Award.*

In May 2019, the selected recipient was Dr George (Pete) Hoffmann, who has been following in his father's footsteps for 40 years and has, among other projects, been involved in promoting programs to lower South Carolina dental costs. Prior to practicing in SC, Pete served in the USAF in Vietnam where he received the Distinguished Flying Cross three times and the Helicopter Rescue Award four times.

Following is the brief, emotive speech Pete delivered to the Conference:

Pete (Intro)— I called Director Phil about two weeks ago and told him this was all new to me. I asked if I should give an acceptance speech and, if so, how long should it be.

Pete— So Phil, what do you think? Like fifteen minutes?

Phil — Oh my! No. No. No — We'll be on a very tight schedule that day.

Pete — So like five minutes?

Phil — Try one!

Pete (to Audience)— Friends, I know you would all LOVE to hear that 15-minute speech I had planned, but today please bear with me for just one more minute. [Pause]

Now, would you all please close your eyes. [Pause]

I'd like for you to think of <u>your</u> Dad.

See…him…here…with…you. [Pause]

Imagine that you are being given an Award — named in his honor over 40 years ago — shortly after his death.

Picture him looking at you — and see how very proud he is of you today.

Think how lucky you are to be his son — and how exceedingly happy you are – at this very moment.

Please open your eyes—

Now you know exactly how I feel.

Thank you all for this wonderful honor. This is a very special day for me and one that I will never forget.

Thank you. [PH+]

BPW Note: Attendees tell me there were many moist eyes in the audience … triggered by this simple, short, heartfelt acceptance.

Comment on the Speech

After receiving the details of Pete's speech, I shared it with a friend [GP] who appreciates speaking excellence. He wrote back:

Pete did an awesome job and provides a great example of eliciting emotions from an audience. His speech provides a number of lessons:

✦ He honored the request to present a one-minute speech, showing respect to the wishes of the host/association.

✦ He told his audience why his speech was one minute and not fifteen by telling a back story.

✦ He engaged the audience with twelve (12) "you's" and saving the few "I"s appropriately for the last sentences.

✦ He emotionally positioned his audience with three simple phrases (steps):

- *I'd like for you to think of your Dad;*
- *Imagine that you are being given an award; and*
- *Now you know exactly how I feel.*

Without *Think of your Dad* or *Imagine,* the audience would *not* have been prepared to know exactly how he felt.

Finally, the speech illustrates the powerful lessons in Konnect. Incorporating just a few of its concepts, he helped create a memorable speech despite the brevity of time.

As I think of this speech, I am reminded of the word *Eloquence* — whose dictionary definition reads: *marked by fluency, persuasiveness, and the power to stir emotions.*

The Woman with a Mop
Kelly Swanson

http://motivationalspeakerkellyswanson.com

You could hear her singing
All the way from the parking lot.
Some sweet morning
When this day is over
I'll fly away—
Loud, staccato, jubilant notes
Of a life well lived.

The glass automatic doors opened
And I could see her standing there
Holding her mop
As if it were a beloved dance partner
As if her faded cotton dress were made of the finest silk.

I sat in the corner of the lobby
Trying not to stare at this woman
Who was oblivious to everyone around her—
As if it were the most normal thing in the world
To be singing and twirling her way
Across the marbled floors of a hospital lobby
While the beeps of the monitors—
And the dings of the elevators
Sang to her in sweet harmony.
I could smell the perfume of my changed perspective
As I watched this woman
Turn her job into an art—
Turn her work into an act of worship.

She didn't know I was in the restroom
Close enough to hear her stop working
To go pray for a stranger's wounded child.
She didn't see me standing here
Watching her help that old man
Wrap the blanket tighter
Around his wife's shoulders.
She didn't know I saw her give away her lunch.

So many moments throughout that day
I watched
As her songs—her smile—her very aura
Affected everyone who crossed her path.
I watched—

039. As in those cold, unexpecting, antiseptic corners
040. Of that hospital
041. Pain found healing—
042. Sorrow found comfort—
043. Hopelessness found hope—
044. Wrapped in a faded cotton dress and comfortable shoes.

045. You could hear her singing
046. All the way to the parking lot
047. When she went to meet her bus at dusk.
048. I stood by the large glass window
049. And watched her go
050. Wishing she wouldn't
051. Wondering if I would ever see her again
052. Knowing I would never forget her.

053. Just outside that window
054. Hung a large, slick, commercialized sign
055. That had—no doubt— been created
056. By a group of marketing intellectuals—
057. "Excellence starts here."

058. I wondered
059. If the CEO knew
060. Just how true that really was.
061. That day—
062. A woman with a mop
063. Had changed my perspective.
064. A woman who smelled of bleach and blessings
065. Showed me—
066. How I want to serve my customers.
067. And—the funny thing was—
068. She had no idea.

069. If a woman with a mop can find a way to sing—
070. Why can't we?

The Woman with a Mop—Kelly Swanson Comment

This section on Emotion ends with Kelly Swanson, a speaking "emotion expert," a professional storyteller who creates stories as metaphors that businesses understand, adapt, and use in persuading others. Her practical, successful approach, which differs somewhat from traditional speaking, is something you should be aware of. Each visit to her website is a learning experience.

The Woman with A Mop is one of my favorite pieces of emotional persuasiveness. In just 404 words, Kelly's story captivates me completely. She tells me that individual employees can be more valuable to an organization than all the monies spent on large, slick billboards and neon signs. I relate to that. Some of her words lift my spirits, a few dampen them, and my emotions rise and fall in unison. Her picture-creating, emotive words make her speech touching, different, and memorable. She creates a vivid vignette with fresh, colorful words which linger long after I hear them. I aspire to be able to write and present something so emotive and touching.

And there is no reason why I—or you—can't achieve that goal. Like everything else in life, it's about understanding and mastering the game.

Consider Kelly's goal: to create a real or fictitious story that pulls her audience right into the center of it and holds them there. For she believes that when your audience is engrossed they are emotionally engaged and "will follow you anywhere."

Her belief is that that connection with your audience lies in four words: Like, Trust, Know, and Believe. Ask yourself: *Is that how you feel about others when you hear them speaking? Is that what others feel about you when you are speaking?*

She teaches newer speakers:

- Facts (and some speeches) push; emotion and visually-absorbing stories sell.
- Let your audience laugh. Don't focus on being funny, focus on being fun.
- Passion is contagious. Channel it. Show the audience that you really care—be yourself—be authentic—even if you feel awkward (e.g., singing badly). Let your audience bond with the "real" you.
- Emotions are the basis of trust and, in a crowded market, it's not about being heard above the noise, but being trusted.

Let your authentic you be heard.

SECTION 5

Remember

Speak to be remembered and repeated [PF]

Audiences don't have perfect memories. If we want our message to matter, we must help them remember what it is. Myriad techniques are available. This section covers three of the most effective:

5.1 Repetition

5.2 Differentiate

5.3 Closing

Repetition is the most recognized rhetorical tool. It is the basis of oral tradition in most civilizations. To remember long stories or poems such as the *Iliad* and the *Odyssey*, Homer's two epic poems, repetition played a key role, just as it does with the songs we sing today. Likewise, in speeches—audiences remember what is emphasized through repetition. The Ancient Greeks and Romans, with their strong speaking traditions, developed repetitive techniques appropriate to the desired emphasis and impact when seeking to persuade. In this section, you will find their techniques still in play.

Differentiate means doing something that will make you and your speech noticed. A purple cow stands out, is remembered, and is talked about; a brown cow isn't. Adding purple cows to your speeches will make you and/or your speech different. Nancy Duarte, author of *Resonate*, coined the term, **STAR**. She urges that, in each important speech, we offer a STAR—**S**omething **T**hey'll **A**lways **R**emember. In this section, a selection of STARs is shared demonstrating how you can make your speeches different and memorable.

Closing your speech is your last opportunity to leave your imprint. It's an important opportunity because last words linger in listeners minds. Your final paragraphs, where you summarize your speech and tie it all together, are obviously pivotal in your final effort to persuade. In this section, you will learn some of the closing techniques of successful speakers. The type of closing you choose will depend upon the speech's purpose and audience, although they both share one common denominator: for best results, end positively and end on a high.

The above three elements will help you assist your audience to remember, recall, and repeat your key message. Domino's founder, Tom Monahan, expresses it well:

It's not what you say—it's what they take away

5.1 Repetition

Introduction

What is repetition? The traditional definition is using a word, phrase, or clause more than once, typically in a short span of a words. However, in the world of speaking, repeating a word or phrase throughout a whole speech is an effective connection technique and is included.

Why repetition? Because a repeated word or phrase emphasizes a speaker's point, helps an audience remember the point, and sometimes produces a rhyming effect which also helps an audience remember what was said.

Some examples of repetition:

As he turned to walk, I noticed a familiar grimace and a familiar limp ——"Knee or hip (replacement)?" [AT^] *[Example of one-word repetition]*

What lies behind us and *what lies before us are tiny matters compared to what lies within us.* [RWE] *[Example of two-word phrase repetition]*

If you think you can win, you can win. [WH] *[Example of three-word phrase repetition]*

In Florida, to buy a gun you do not need a permit, you do not need a gun license, and once you buy it you do not need to register it. You do not need a permit to carry a concealed rifle or shotgun. You can buy as many guns as you want at one time. [EG]
[Example of four-word phrase repetition]

Repetition has many applications. For example, it may be a single word, phrase, or sentence that is being repeated; it may occur at the beginning, middle, or end of sentences; it may be a phrase repeated in normal or reverse order; or it may be a phrase, thread-like, repeated throughout a speech.

Repetition is not just of words. Ideas and sounds are also arrows found in a speaker's repetition quiver. There's rarely a speech where some form of repetition cannot be used. In essence, if you're not into repetition you're not into speaking.

Aristotle defined rhetoric as the art of persuasion. Repetition, to many, is the king of rhetoric. Becoming familiar with the Repetition family is essential. On the next page your introduction to twenty family members, each with a unique characteristic, begins.

The first three forms of Repetition discussed—Repetition at the Beginning, the End, and as Threading—are the family's major members; powerful and effective in almost any speech. The others, more specialized in use, should also be studied carefully for they, too, will enhance your speeches' power, flavor, richness, and memorability.

1. Repetition at the Beginning

[Rhetorical term: anaphora, pronounced an-AFF-or-a*]*

One of the best-known forms of repetition is when a word or a phrase begins a series of consecutive (or almost consecutive) clauses, sentences or paragraphs—thus the term Beginning Repetition. Its rhetorical term is *anaphora*. A simple example is:

Bad defense. Bad coaching. Bad planning. Bad football.
... Coach Bill Belichick explaining the Patriots surprise defeat in their 2017 opening game.

Beginning Repetition is considered the king of repetition because it's easy to create, easy to recall (for both the speaker and the audience), and it's an easy way to add impact. It may be as short as two consecutive clauses or as long as having 15 consecutive sentences open with the same phrase, as you'll see shortly. Frequency of repetition depends upon the speech's occasion and goal. To introduce you to the power and opportunity of Beginning Repetition we shall look at two memorable speeches:

I Have a Dream

On August 28 1963, from the steps of the Lincoln Monument in Washington DC, Martin Luther King Jr delivered his seismic speech on racial injustice to a crowd of almost one-quarter-million people. The speech has subsequently become known as the *I Have A Dream* speech.

What is often overlooked is that King used eight different repetitive phrases to emphasize different points during his moving message. The 17-minute speech is an archipelago of paragraphs in a sea of emotive images, with half of the speech's 16 paragraphs injected with different anaphoric repetition.

You can easily access an Internet copy of this iconic speech. Open it and see how King employs repetition. Below are his eight anaphoric phrases, their frequency of use, and the paragraphs in which they first appear.

One hundred years later ... (the Negro is still not free)	[4x, Para 3]
Now is the time ... (to make real the promises of democracy)	[4x, Para 6]
We must... (not be guilty of wrongful deeds)	[4x, Para 8]
We can never be satisfied ... (as long as the Negro is the victim of the unspeakable horrors of police brutality)	[7x, Para 10]
Go back ... (to Mississippi)	[6x, Para 12]
I have a dream ... (that one day this nation will rise up and live out the true meaning of its creed)	[8x, Para 13]
With this faith ... (we will be able to hew out of the mountain of despair a stone of hope)	[3x, Para 14]
Let freedom ring ... (from the prodigious hilltops of New Hampshire)	[8x, Para 15]

You can see that as the speech moves towards its finale, repetition develops a pile-driver aspect, with repetitive phrases not only becoming more frequently stated, but also appearing in every paragraph. Now, when sentences begin with the same words the speaker gains two benefits—the audience develops rhythmic expectations that carries them along which tends to make them more open to the message; and using the same phrase to begin consecutive sentences helps the speaker remember the words that follow, allowing him to pour his energy into persuasion rather than trying to recall his script.

Dr King delivered his 1,655-word (98 words per minute) address with eight significant repetitive phrases. Obviously, in longer speeches repetitive phrases can easily be inserted. So, you might be thinking, what if you are giving a shorter speech? Say, as short as the 272-word Gettysburg Address which Lincoln delivered in just over two minutes? Can anaphora be effective there, too? The answer is an emphatic *Yes*!

Such a speech follows. It was prepared from notes scribbled in a car as the speaker was being driven to the event, his final speech of the campaign, two days before the 1983 British General Election. The Labour Party's poll numbers trailed Prime Minister Margaret Thatcher's Conservative Party by a huge margin. This anaphoric speech by senior Labour member, Neil Kinnock, is considered by William Safire to be one of the finest ever delivered in British politics.

I Warn You

This speech is reproduced with the permission of the speaker, Lord Kinnock.

If Margaret Thatcher is re-elected as Prime Minister on Thursday—

I warn you.

I warn you that you will have pain—when healing and relief depend upon payment.

I warn you that you will have ignorance—when talents are untended and wits are wasted, when learning is a privilege and not a right.

I warn you that you will have poverty—when pensions slip and benefits are whittled away by a government that won't pay in an economy that can't pay.

I warn you that you will be cold—when fuel charges are used as a tax system that the rich don't notice and the poor can't afford.

I warn you that you must not expect work—when many cannot spend, more will not be able to earn. When they don't earn, they don't spend. When they don't spend, work dies.

I warn you not to go into the streets alone after dark or into the streets in large crowds of protest in the light.

I warn you that you will be quiet—when the curfew of fear and the gibbet of unemployment make you obedient.

I warn you that you will have defence of a sort—with a risk and at a price that passes all understanding.

I warn you that you will be home-bound—when fares and transport bills kill leisure and lock you up.

I warn you that you will borrow less—when credit, loans, mortgages and easy payments are refused to people on your melting income.

If Margaret Thatcher wins on Thursday—
I warn you not to be ordinary
I warn you not to be young
I warn you not to fall ill
I warn you not to get old. [NK+]

... And no, this unique, anaphoric, passionate political speech of 284 words did not push Margaret Thatcher out of office although, four months later, it did help push Neil Kinnock into office as leader of Britain's Labour Party. Great speeches usually have consequences—just not always immediately.

The lesson? Anaphora—the repeating of words or phrases at the beginning of clauses or sentences—is a powerful communication tool in speeches of all lengths.

Repetition at the Beginning is Widespread

To start your speech synapses snapping, following is a wide selection of examples, starting with a snippet from Steve Jobs' June 12, 2005 *Stanford Commencement Address.*

> My doctor advised me to go home and get my affairs in order—which is doctor's code for prepare to die.
>
> It means to try to tell your kids everything you thought you'd have the next 10 years to tell them in just a few months.
>
> It means to make sure everything is buttoned up so that it will be as easy as possible for your family.
>
> It means to say your goodbyes. [SJ+]

When we cease to be challenged—and we don't do something about it
We are frozen—
Frozen because we are afraid to change.
Frozen in a hell of our own choosing;
Frozen alive...
... We get stuck to tired excuses.
I'd do it, but I'm too old.
I'd do it, but I'm not smart enough.
I'd do it, but I never have time.
But . . . But . . . But.
If we don't get off those butts—
We'll be forever frozen to a bucket. [MM^]

Sometimes I wake up grumpy; sometimes I let him sleep. [AN]

We're gonna learn. We're gonna grow. And we're gonna get better. [DS*]

That's not who we are;
That's not what we do. [BO]

There is no proof that [college football] players need waterfalls in the training room.
There is no divine directive that demands a $5 million salary for head coaches.
There is no evidence that the difference between a 9-4 record and 6-6 is an indoor practice facility. [MR+]

I immediately thought of the things that she would never do:
She would never know the feeling of love's first kiss
She would never hold the hand of a boy who would take her on a date
She would never know the thrill of graduation and looking forward to college
She would never hope for the day of a wedding and a honeymoon
She would never know a home other than that she shares with her sister
She would never discover the news of a new life growing within her
She would never hold her own child in her arms. [KT]
... A father recalling the loss of his 9-year old daughter.

And you can be like the first doctor and based on what has already happened, conclude that there's no hope. You can be like the second doctor, make your thorough examination and based on what you think should happen, conclude that there's no hope. Or you can be like the third doctor and take a look within and always find hope where there's life. [DLM]

Is there someone out there
Someone in your workplace
Someone in your neighborhood
Someone in your home
Who has heard your beast roar? [MB]

It means you're not just here to inform.
It means you're not just here to entertain.
It means you're not just here to persuade.
Those little pixels on the computer screen— can change somebody's life. [JM]

My mom's voice goes two octaves higher—
She smiles
She squints, and
She squeals out an "Oh, thank you!" —
Regardless of the gift! [KH^]

Here I learned the importance of self-love.
Self-love helps you accept your flaws but focus on the beauty.
Self-love is the cure to self-hatred.
Self-love is the foundation for happiness.
Self-love is the cure to self-hatred.
So go ahead and fall in love with yourself. [DB>]

I remember when there were no black students at Clemson.
I remember segregated bathrooms and water fountains in department stores.
I remember what they used to call white people who praised Martin Luther King. [RB+]

You don't understand!
I coulda had class.
I coulda been a contender.
I coulda been somebody—
Instead of a bum—
Which is what I am. *... Marlon Brando (as Terry Malloy) in movie On the Waterfront*

Ron Paul Before Congress, Feb 12, 2009 [YT+] [Paul's *What if?* speech, abridged]

Madam Speaker, I have a few questions for my colleagues.

What if our foreign policy of the past century is deeply flawed and has not served our national security interest?

What if we wake up one day and realize that the terrorist threat is the predictable consequence of our meddling in the affairs of others, and has nothing to do with us being free and prosperous

What if occupying countries like Iraq and Afghanistan and bombing Pakistan is directly related to the hatred directed toward us?

What if it is finally realized that war and military spending is always destructive to the economy?

What if all war-time spending is paid for through the deceitful and evil process of inflating and borrowing?

What if we finally see that war-time conditions always undermine personal liberty?

What if we as a nation came to realize that the quest for empire eventually destroys all great nations?

What if Christianity actually teaches peace and not preventive wars of aggression?

What if diplomacy is found to be superior to bombs and bribes in protecting America?

What happens if my concerns are completely unfounded? — Nothing.

But what happens if my concerns are justified and ignored? — Nothing good. [RP]

2. Repetition at the End

[Rhetorical term: Epistrophe, pronounced e-pis-tro-fee]

Repetition at the end of consecutive (or mostly consecutive) paragraphs, sentences, clauses or phrases is considered more powerful than repetition at the beginning because a natural pause —a comma or period—follows. This allows more time for reflection on the repeated phrase. The power of ending repetition is often seen in songs. Mark Forsyth, author of *Eloquence*, points out that Leonard Cohen ends every verse of his iconic song with *Hallelujah* and Don McLean ends each verse of his well-known song with *Bye, bye, Miss American Pie.* Audiences will remember you when you do likewise.

My two favorite examples of *epistrophe* were delivered 2000 years apart.

Around 200 BC, Cato the Elder, the great Roman soldier and statesman who felt so strongly about Rome's major enemy, ended almost every speech with these words: *Carthage must be destroyed.* Everyone in the Roman Senate, and in Rome, knew Cato's cry. His epistrophe is so memorable it is still repeated both in and out of classrooms today. As a side note, in 2008, Presidential candidate Barack Obama borrowed Cato's use of epistrophe in the political arena by completing many a paragraph and speech with what became his well-known phrase of hope: *Yes we can!*

My other favorite is the cry-from-the-heart of Harriet Tubman — the illiterate, escaped slave who, prior to the US Civil War, helped other black slaves escape to freedom via the Underground Railway. Her emotional set-up clauses, followed by her short, repetitive, inspirational phrase is a perfect illustration of *epistrophe.*

> *If you hear the dogs—keep going.*
> *If you see the torches in the woods—keep going.*
> *If they're shouting after you—keep going.*
> *If you want a taste of freedom—keep going.*
> *Don't ever stop—keep going.* [~HT]

Now let's discover how others have built repetitive endings into clauses or sentences to strengthen their point. We start with a whimsical favorite:

I've had good days, and bad days, and going half-mad days. [JB>]

Words have power. Words are power. Words could be your power. [MQ^]
... Note two repetitions, words and power, in each sentence, with the heavier emphasis on the ending word.

If you get out of Toastmasters
All you can get out of Toastmasters
You'll never get out of Toastmasters. [HB]

To avoid criticism—do nothing; say nothing; be nothing. [EH]

What do most people say? — *No problem.*
There is no problem for which their answer isn't *No problem.*
Medicare will go bust — *No problem.*
Social Security will go bust — *No problem.*
The unemployment rate keeps rising — *No problem.* [GN+]

It has been the mark of manhood and civility
And longstanding American tradition
To leave politics out of the way we honor our veterans.
They fought the battles—we did not.
They shed the blood—we did not.
They reconciled with their enemies—we did not. [SWD]

The information age is actually a media age—
We have war by media.
Censorship by media.
Demonology by media.
Retribution by media.
Diversion by media—
A surreal assembly line of obedient clichés and false assumptions [JP+]

I was born an American; I live an American; I shall die an American. [DW*]

My older son knows—not to go near the chess set.
My younger son knows—not to go near the chess set.
My husband knows—*not to go near the chess set [silently mouths the final phrase]* [KH^]
... Note that by using the set-up word "knows," the repetitive ending phrase flows easily. This snippet is made more memorable by silently mouthing the last repetition.

Hardly anyone noticed her.
Those who did, hurried by.
Some looked right at her
And yet right past her.
Others looked right through her
As they thought—Homeless. Useless. Worthless. [MB^]
... Note that repetition is not only at the end, but the scene is made more memorable with the associated repetition of "right," as well as the rhyming repetition of "less" in the last line.

Take whatever idiot they have at the top of whatever agency and give me a better idiot.
Give me a caring idiot.
Give me a sensitive idiot.
Just don't give me the same idiot. [AB+]
... Frustrated Hurricane Katrina official in an emotional interview with CBS News.

3. Repetition by Threading

A key word, phrase, or sound that threads its way through part of or all of a speech explains Repetition by Threading. Its usual purpose is to remind the audience, consciously or subconsciously, of the speech's theme or message. It has two great strengths: it forces the speaker, before choosing the threaded phrase, to clarify and really sharpen the point he or she wishes to make, and it helps listeners more readily understand and follow the speaker's thought process.

There is no fixed path when threading repeated words or phrases. Nor does the word or phrase need to be identical each time—it can be repeated fully, partially, or with word variations, so long as the thread is clear. For example, in one speech I admire, intertwined throughout are the words *perfect*, *perfectly*, *perfectionist*, *imperfections*, leading us to the speech's climatic final words, *perfectly imperfect.* [AD^]

This section covers seven types of Threading:

3.1 Classic Threading
3.2 Dual Threading
3.3 Humor Threading
3.4 Phrase That Stays—General
3.5 Phrase That Stays—Motivational
3.6 Constant Object
3.7 Speech with A Threaded Phrase and High Level of Repetition

3.1 Classic Threading: Harold Patterson — *The Pain Passes*

Harold Patterson in his World Champion Speech, *The Pain Passes*, uses the title to foreshadow his inspirational message, *the pain passes—but the beauty remains.* To illustrate the message's universality, Harold shares five disparate stories — Renoir, Toastmasters, Wilma Rudolph, Will Rogers, and the worrying birth of his first child—threading them all together with his repetitive phrase.

Before the first word is spoken, the title *The Pain Passes*, arouses curiosity (without giving away the speech's point) and begins the thread that weaves throughout the speech and ends in its closing words, a callback to the opening paragraph's poignant statement: *The pain passes—but the beauty remains.*

Harold's technique is the classic form of threading: the point is alluded to in the title, explained in the opening, summarizes each story, and is included in the speech's closing words. In addition, the speaker reinforces his message with related supporting words (*pain, beauty, joy*) peppered throughout the speech. This popular format is effective because despite different stories it shows their common thread of the speaker's point.

The Pain Passes
Harold G. Patterson
Winner 1987 World Championship of Public Speaking ®

View YouTube: Harold Patterson Toastmasters

At the beginning of this century
In a home in Southern France
The great French impressionist Henri Matisse
Watched as an easel was propped in front of a crippled old man.
And he watched as a nurse placed a paintbrush
Between the fingers of the old man's twisted rheumatic hand.
Then Matisse turned to his friend—the aging artist, Pierre Auguste Renoir—
And asked him why he continued to paint—when the **pain** was so intense.
Renoir's answer was this—
My dear friend
The pain passes—But the beauty remains.

What a magnificent thought.
The pain passes—But the beauty remains.
Renoir's **pain** eventually took his life
But the **beauty** of his works—
The creation of his art—
Remains with us even today.

The very nature of our human existence
Ensures us that we too will experience **pain**.
And whether it be physical, emotional, or both—
Long term, short term, or lasting a lifetime—
We must remember to be true to ourselves—
And to **do those things which bring us the greatest joy**—
And then, too, like Renoir—**Our pain will pass.**

Sometimes our pain may be emotional.
Someone once said that the human mind
Is the most remarkable of all creations.
Think about that!
It starts working even before we are born
And works continuously 24 hours a day
Collecting and storing information
And never stops until we—
Stand up to give a speech.

At Toastmasters
The greatest **pain** we will experience
Will be in those anxious moments
Just before we give our first speech—
Our first icebreaker — remember!?
That knot—
Right in the pit of your stomach
Those trembling legs—
The blood racing through your veins—
Those sweaty palms———
Yet, **no matter how great that pain is**
There is no greater beauty
Than the feeling of accomplishment
As we take our seat when it's over.
And that's a feeling
A beauty that remains
With us always.

On June 23, 1940,
A girl was born to a couple in Clarksville, Tennessee.
The **joy** of this birth was overshadowed—
By the complications of its prematureness.
The child developed double pneumonia—
Scarlet fever—
And by the time she was 6 years old
It was determined that she had polio.
That meant braces—confinement—and excruciating pain.
Yet with each visit to the doctor
Her questions were always the same—
When can I take the braces off?
When can I walk?
When will I be able to run with my friends?
And each time the doctor's answer was this—
I don't know—maybe never.
The little girl's **pain was great**—
Yet not strong enough to overcome her spirit.
Because one day she did take the braces off—
And she did walk—
And she did run—
And did she ever run.
In Rome, in 1960, she ran for the whole world!
To the French she was known as *La Gazelle*—

To the Italians, *The Black Pearl*—
And to the rest of the world—
Her friends—
And especially her 18 brothers and sisters—
She was known as Wilma Rudolph—
Fastest Woman in the World—
Winner of 3 Olympic gold medals.
In Rome in 1960, Wilma Rudolph was living proof that
The pain passes—But the beauty remains.

The **pain** of losing a loved one
Is something that never quite goes away.
Yet, in time, even the **pain** of a loss is eased
By the remembrance of that person's life.
In 1935—a man died tragically
In a plane crash in Alaska.
The entire world felt the **pain** of this loss—
His gift was laughter
And at this time
He was helping a troubled world laugh its way
Through a great depression.
The loss of Will Rogers was a **painful** one indeed
Yet the beauty of his life—
His wit and wisdom—
Remains with us to this very day.
Will Rogers said this—
In Oklahoma
We have an average annual rainfall of 31.2 inches—
And, boy, you ought to be there the day we get it——
Again, **the beauty remains**.

Sometimes our **pain** may be both physical and emotional.
In 1983—
A man and woman were married at the age of 34
And two years later they decided to have a child.
Not an unusual decision
But because of their age
They knew that certain precautions must be taken.
After several thorough examinations—
The doctor said— *Go for it.*
Their dream of having a child of their own
Would soon become true.
And for the first seven months

The pregnancy progressed flawlessly
But then the doctor noticed that something was wrong—
A condition called preeclampsia—
Would send the mother to bed—
Under 24-hour hospital observation—
Threatening the lives of both mother and child.
The only cure was to deliver the child now—
But it was too soon—too early—to do that.
Valuable time was needed.
So they waited—
And they prayed.
Three agonizing weeks went by—
And finally, the doctor said
We must deliver this child now.
And at 5:21 pm on July 24, 1985
The doctor handed me—
My newborn daughter.
And he looked at me and said
She's six weeks premature—
And only 4 pound, 4 ounces—
But she's a fighter and she'll be just fine.
And as the tears flowed freely
My wife and I now knew that
The pain had passed—And the beauty was here.

The **pain of life** is inevitable for each of us—
And whether it be physical, emotional, or both—
Long term, short term, or lasting a lifetime—
We must remember to be true to ourselves—
And to do those things which bring us the greatest joy.
And then, finally—
To remember—listen to—and embrace—
The words of Renoir
As they are brushed across the canvas of our soul—
When he said —*My dear friend—*
The pain passes—
But the beauty
Oh, the beauty remains——*Forever!*

3.2 Dual Threading: Lance Miller — *The Ultimate Question*

Lance Miller's World Champion Speech, *The Ultimate Question* has a unique construction: it intertwines two related threads—a word and a sound—and ends with a speaker-audience sound duet.

To address the curiosity triggered by his bold title, Lance begins his first thread in the opening paragraph by asking "The Ultimate Question" — *Do you validate* (the goodness in others)? But we wait over a minute longer (150 words) before the word is heard again. That's when the *validate/validated/validation* thread really leaves the spool. And, then, after another 45 seconds (100 words) we hear *Chi-Chink* (the onomatopoeic sound emitted when a parking-ticket validation machine is activated.) Then on, both threads, *validate* and *Chi-Chink*, are used frequently until they come together in the finale.

Despite the apparent slow start of the threads, both unroll briskly once started. In this 7:18 minute speech, we hear the word *validate* (or a variant) 13 times and the sound *Cha-Chink* 13 times, a healthy 2 per minute for each. The two threads of word and sound stitched into Lance's audience dialogue leaves us clearly understanding his point and actionable message.

What's important to note is that neither thread appears either in the title or early in the speech (with one exception) illustrating threading's great flexibility of application.

The Ultimate Question
Lance Miller
Winner 2005 Toastmasters World Championship of Public Speaking ®

Website: http://www.lancemillerspeaks.com
View YouTube: Lance Miller Toastmasters
Laughter Levels (see superscripts): Light [L1] Healthy [L3] Loud & Long [L5]

The Ultimate Question!
That question that has plagued man since the dawn of time.
And that question that each and every one of us must ask
At some point in our life.
[Pulls a parking ticket from jacket front top pocket, holds it up.]
Do you validate? [L2]
[Returns parking ticket to pocket.]

Mr. Chairman, Fellow Toastmasters, and Friends—
I was 26 years old.
I was living in a small town in Indiana.
I had a job I didn't like.
I hadn't a date in three years.
And I had a couple of roommates named Mom and Dad! [L3]

I felt like my life was going nowhere
So I took control—
I left my home and my family
And I headed to Los Angeles to start over.
6 months later —
I had a job I didn't like.
I was dating a girl
Who was trying to make me "better"—
By pointing out all my faults. [L1]
And I had a couple of roommates that made Dumb and Dumber
Look like Einstein and Oppenhiemer. [L2]

I had changed everything in my life—
But nothing had changed.
I still felt like I was going nowhere.
And then, one day after a business meeting
All I wanted to do was get my parking validated.
[Pulls parking ticket from jacket pocket, holds in hand.]
And I walked over the receptionist and said
"Excuse me—do you validate?"
And she looked up and said
"Well, yes I do—you have a lovely smile." [L4]
Showing her the ticket, I said
"No, I was just in a meeting with your boss—
Do you validate?"
And she said
"Well, let me compliment you
On what a fine choice of business associates you have." [L1]
Catching on, I said—
You have such a keen sense of humor
I'm going to go tell your boss how lucky he is to have you out here.
And she goes — "Give me that ticket!" [L1]
She took her little machine and she went **Chi-chink.** *[Stamping the ticket.]*
And then as she handed it back
She looked at me and said—
"There's something special about you."
I took the ticket and headed for the elevator.
But I stopped and I turned around and just said—
"Thank You." *[Returns parking ticket to pocket.]*

I don't how long it had been since I felt validated.
Her words stayed with me all the way home.
And as I was looking at my life
I started to wonder how long it had been
Since I'd validated somebody else.
I wanted to do that!
I wanted to make people feel good!
But I felt that I needed to be important —
I needed to be successful—

So that when I said something to somebody
It would mean something to them.
But that receptionist had just made my day.
Heck—she made my month!
With one little **Chi-chink** she stamped my ticket.
And I thought — I can do that!

So I went home to see Dumb and Dumber. [L3]
These guys were constantly bringing people back to the apartment.
It was driving me nuts!
But I went in and I said
"You make friends faster than anybody I have ever seen—
And that is a gift."
To see their faces—
I swear they got smarter right before my eyes! [L3]
Chi-chink.
I went to see my girlfriend —
And I thanked her for caring enough about me
To want to see me be as good as I could be.
You know what? — She got nicer! [L1]
Chi-chink. [L1]
I went to work, and I thanked my boss for hiring me.
He'd done me a favor—
And I started enjoying my work a lot more.
Chi-chink.
I used to think that I had to be important
Before I could validate other people.
I used to look at people as obstacles to my success.
But what I discovered was—
I became important when I validated other people.
I became important to that person — and that person.
People were the pathway to my success.
I started trying to find something I could stamp on everybody I met—
That little piece of goodness — That little piece of rightness —
Just a little **Chi-chink.**

I started to feel like a SUPER HERO.
Underneath this mild-mannered exterior
Was a blue and red spandex suit with a giant V on the chest—
YES! — I was the VALIDATOR! [L2]
When things would get tense
They'd tighten up.
I'd come in and—
Chi-chink — **Chi-chink** — **Chi-chink** —
I had plenty of ink!
I'd hear people say, "Who was that man?"
"I don't know—
But I heard this **Chi-chink** —
And suddenly I feel so much better now!"

And then I figured it out—
Do you know what's wrong with world?
Do you know what's wrong with me?
Do you know what's wrong with you? ——
WHO CARES!!!! L4
The question is—
What is right with the world?
What is right with me?
What is right with you?
The common denominator of all humanity
Is the fact that we are human.
We are—by nature—imperfect.
It takes no special talent to find an imperfection in another person. L3
But every person goes through life—
Wanting to be RIGHT
Wanting to be VALUABLE.
Find that —
Bring it out in them.
I started to discover in my life that I got what I validated.
I found out that I brought out
The goodness— the value in others—
By validating that.

We have a lot of problems in this world.
But I've learned
That there is not a problem that exists—
Between a parent and child
Between a husband and wife
Between a worker and his employer
Or between races, cultures, or nations—
That does not stem directly
From an inability or an unwillingness
To validate—
The rightness
The value
And the goodness
In another.
This is the Ultimate Question –
Do Your Validate?
But this is not what's important.
What's important is
Can you – **Chi** – [Audience response: **Chink**]?
Can you – **Chi** – [Audience response: **Chink**]?
Can you – **Chi** – [Audience response: **Chink**]?
You've been a great audience!!!! L3

3.3 Humor Threading: Jay Nodine — *The Golden Years –Yeah! Right!*

One technique that humorous speakers often use is a repeatable clause or vignette to start each section of the speech. This was vividly demonstrated by Jay Nodine in the 2007 Toastmasters District 37 (NC) Humorous Contest.

Jay chose an easy-to-visualize vignette to thread through the speech:

I live for the Senior Citizen Early Bird Special
Of HA-BA-NERO pepper-crusted trout
At McCabe's Restaurant—
Every Friday afternoon.

And then he repeats it, or variations of it, or recognizable parts of it, six times, tying each to a different part of his story. Each repetition brings a smile, partly because of the scene created, partly because of the sing-song rhyme Jay uses when expressing his words, and partly because of the amusing expectation of what might follow.

Opening each scene is his amusing repetitive phrase (with variations):

Now—It seems like only yesterday—
But it MUST have been a Friday

Repetition plays a key role in creating smiles and laughter throughout. In addition to his core vignette (and its variations) we find repeated phrases such as:

Golden Years
Senior Citizen Discounts
Fixed income
Shortness of breath /Loss of stamina / Numbness in my arms.

Understanding Jay's speech construction will add to your appreciation of a repetitive thread and provide ideas you might experiment with in your next humorous speech.

The Golden Years—Yeah! Right!

Jay Nodine

Winner 2007 Toastmasters D37 Humorous Speech Contest®

With age comes wisdom
With wisdom comes the Golden Years.
With the Golden Years
Comes Hardees 99-cent biscuits—
And—Senior— Discount—Coffee.

Mr. Contest Master, fellow Toastmasters and Guests
I'm not knocking Senior Citizen Discounts mind you—
For when you reach the Golden Years
Every penny counts!

Plus—I live for the Senior Citizen Early Bird Special
Of HA-BA-NERO pepper-crusted trout
At McCabe's Restaurant—
Every Friday afternoon.

However—each time I find a place
That offers a Senior Citizen Discount
I find a bunch of people in their Golden Years
Telling the person next to them—
Oh— I'm on a fixed income!
I'm on a fixed income!
Well—I want you to know
That is not true in my case——
I am on a declining income!!!!——
And the only thing golden about the Golden Years
Is the gold I transfer from my bank account
To the medical profession.

Now—It seems like only yesterday—
But it MUST have been a Friday
Because I picked up my Senior Citizen—Early Bird Special
Of Habanero pepper-crusted trout
At McCabe's on my way home.
Before that—I was sitting in my doctor's office
Complaining about—

- Shortness of breath
- Loss of stamina
- And numbness in my arms.

He was saying —
All the tests looked normal
But I'm thinking it could be the heart.
We need to run a few tests.
In the meantime—
I am prescribing these pills that are expensive
And may have some side effects—
Side effects!!! —I wasn't worried about my sides—
It was

- the shortness of breath
- Loss of stamina
- And numbness in my arms

That I worried about.

Now—It seems like only yesterday—
But it MUST have been a Friday
Since I barely made the Senior Citizen—Early Bird Special
Of Habanero pepper-crusted trout—at McCabe's.
There I was at the Heart Center
Taking stress tests—CAT Scans — EKGs — MRIs.

After the tests the doctor said
Everything looks normal
And that I had a strong, healthy heart.
However—I am sending you to a specialist in Charlotte
In the meantime—take the pills I am prescribing.
They are very expensive—
And may have some very serious side effects! <Wiggles waist>

Now—It seems like only yesterday
But there I was—on a Friday
At the Presbyterian Hospital
On the examination table
Worried about missing
My Senior Citizen—Early Bird Special
Of Habanero pepper-crusted trout.
I was heavily sedated
When I heard this far away voice—
Mr. Nodine—Mr. Nodine—can you hear me?—
Yes!
Again—the voice—
Sir—we are going to take this sharp probe
Put it into your groin
Push it up to your heart
So we can run a test —
I said—*OK!*
As it turned out –
Diagnosis—the same!!!
The heart appears strong and healthy.
The doctor was telling me again—
I'm going to prescribe these pills that are very expensive—
I know, I know—they may have side effects—
No—but they will enhance the symptoms you have now.

Now, it seems like only yesterday,
But it must have been—
No, I'm sure it was—yesterday. *[Play on repeated phrase]*
I got a call from the Heart Center
at North-east Medical Center.
They told me to come by their office
They wanted to discuss my case further.
As I was pulling into the North-east Medical Parking deck,
There was a sign that read—SPEED LIMIT—5 mph.
You can't drive 5 mph.!!!
When you start your car—
What are you doing—7 ????!!!!
Well—you guessed it.
I was stopped for speeding
Pulled over by the Security Police.
He wasn't in a car—

He was just walking along beside me.
A big burly fellow with those mirrored sunglasses.
Leaning over and looking into my car—
Buddy—do you have any idea
How fast you were going? he asked—
I don't know—maybe 6?
Without changing expression—he said
We have you on radar—you were going 9!!!!—
Nine!!!! — No way! I said
My front-end shimmies at 8!

As I was lamenting over the $90 ticket
The doctor was saying
Mr. Nodine your heart seems to be in good shape—
But you are taking far too many pills.
He also said—
We have had over a hundred people this month
With the same symptoms as you—
We have traced it to McCabe's Restaurant.
We have discovered—
That habanero pepper and fish oil will cause—

- Shortness of breath
- Loss of stamina
- And numbness in the arms

SO, DOC, YOU ARE SAYING
NOTHING IS WRONG WITH MY HEART???
Mr. Nodine, I can safely say
Your heart will last—as long as you do!!!

Well then, I asked—
DO YOU THINK I WILL LIVE TO BE 80?
He asked—do you smoke or drink in excess?
Oh no, I said.
He asked—do you eat red meat?
I shook my head—Noooo.
He asked—do you drive fast cars—and chase loose women?
No, I said —I DON'T DO ANY OF THOSE THINGS.
He said——
THEN—WHY DO YOU CARE?
Mr Toastmaster…

Jay Nodine, DTM, was a member of the Goldmine Club in NC (District 37) for decades. He also served as a member of Toastmasters International Board of Directors. Jay, always warm and funny, won D37's Humorous Speech Contest in four consecutive years—a record. This was one of those speeches.

3.4 Phrase that Stays — General

Sometimes, a speaker repeats a certain meaningful phrase not just to connect with the audience but also to build a memory link and, ideally, an emotional link with his or her audience so that it lingers for weeks, months and, sometimes, years. When that happens, the speaker and his message has really connected. The phrase can be threaded into the speech anywhere, not necessarily as a tidy summary of each speech story. The term, *Phrase That Stays*, describes it well but other names are also used: Randy Harvey calls it a *Legacy Line*; Pres Vasilev, a *Message Phrase*; Craig Valentine, a *Foundational Phrase*; and Doug Stevenson dubs it a *Phrase That Pays*®

It is a potent, frequently-used repetition tool. Some examples follow:

Manoj Vasudevan [MV^] — *Pull Less, Bend More* (see speech, *page 216)*

The cryptic title is the speech's message and the start of its primary thread, even though it does not appear again until two-thirds through the speech, when Manoj's mother explains that *Pull Less, Bend More* is the answer to his relationship problems with his wife.

Despite its late appearance in the speech it's this Phrase That Stays that we remember most afterwards. Why? Several reasons. Besides being mentioned in the title, it is repeated six times (including the last two lines on the speech, the last of which was with audience participation.) In addition, variations of the phrase along with supporting related words are threaded throughout the speech, such as:

Argue (and variants) ... 4 times
Bow bends ... 2 times
Cupid (and variants) ... 5 times
Differences (and variants) ... 3 times
Fix it ... 4 times
Holding hands ... 3 times
I joined her ... 2 times
Perfect/perfect partner ... 6 times

Simply stated, A Phrase That Stays and its associated threads stitch a tapestry making the message clear, repeatable, and memorable.

Dananjaya Hettiarachchi [DH^] — *I See Something* (see speech, *page 91)*

Dananjaya superbly threads a Phrase That Stays through this, his World Champion winning speech. Its title, *I See Something*, arouses curiosity without giving the message away, a common technique. As the speech unfolds, however, the title morphs into *I see something in you—but I don't know what it is,* his Phrase that Stays skillfully placed in four places throughout the speech.

The first three are related to the key influencers in his life. They all said the same thing about him but were prepared to help him anyway. Dananjaya then brilliantly concludes by turning and talking directly to the audience: *I See Something in You—But I Don't Know What It Is.* That really resonated, for attendees repeated it in a fun way during the rest of the Convention in Kuala Lumpur—and even after they returned to their homes in different parts of the world. I know—I heard it from attendees. His phrase is truly one that has truly stayed.

Ed Tate [ET^] — *One of Those Days*

After almost 20 years, Ed Tate's WCPS winning speech *One of Those Days*, is still remembered because of its title-based Phrase That Stays. It's a story of the ups and downs in one day of Ed's life, starting with a speeding ticket on his way to the airport and ending with him receiving a First-Class flight upgrade—with a series of easy-to-visualize ups and downs in between, each ending with Ed saying, "It's going to be one of those days." The audience loved the threaded roller-coaster story, not knowing when or what twist or turn was next. And, as often is the case when using a repetitive phrase, the speaker was able to close with strong audience participation...

> And it was like I always said—
> I knew it was going to be ... *[Opens arms to audience]*
> *One of those days*! *[Audience response]*

And then, at the 2018 World Championship of Public Speaking ...

Two records were broken. The top three place-winners were women and all had a title-based, readily repeatable Phrase That Stays threading through their speeches (all three speeches may be viewed on YouTube.)

1. Ramona J. Smith *Still Standing*
2. Zifang "Sherrie" Su *Turn Around*
3. Anita Fain Taylor *It Is What It Is; And It Ain't What It Ain't*

The winning speech was unique with its high-energy boxing theme. Ramona loses in three rounds to different life challenges ... but she fights back and states proudly, at the end of each round, she's *still standing*, the goal of all boxers.

Her phrase and theme also brought into play Elton John's 35-year old song, *I'm Still Standing*. Ramona moves into her close with ... *the fighters and the coaches will raise their hands in victory singing* (and she sings) *I'm still standing — yeah, yeah, yeah*. She then puts her hand out towards the audience and sings: *We're still standing*—and the audience automatically responds— *Yeah, yeah, yeah*.

Ramona connected. Her speech resonated. Many attendees were repeating it after the contest. Some attendees still repeat it.[PM^] Her speech was an example of exceptional, multi-dimensional connecting of a Phrase That Stays.

3.5 Phrase that Stays — Motivational

Speeches with a motivational or inspirational message often use a Phrase That Stays threaded throughout to make and reinforce the speaker's point. When you are listening to motivational speakers it doesn't take long to identify their repeatable phrase. Typically, memorable motivational phrases are short, positive, action-oriented, and rhyme. You'll understand why when you choose your favorites from the following list:

Accept the pain, reap the gain.
Act your wage. [DR]
Be a will-be, not a has-been.
Be the rage of the stage.
Begin the journey.
Begin your day the right way. [JS>]
Build your own habit hutch.
Choose to choose or choose to lose.
Devote daily a dime of time.
Do 3 Daily Do-Its.
Don't compete—create! [JW+]
Don't die until you're dead. [SS]
Don't motivate—Inspirate! [RM]
Fake it till you make it. [TR]
Fall forward. [DLC]
Freedom to choose means freedom to lose.
Lift your Gratitude Attitude.
Live the dream.
Problems are guidelines, not stop signs. [~RS]
Sell the sizzle, not the sausage.
Speak from your heart and the world will listen. [RJH]
Stop selling. Start helping. [ZZ]
Stop stewing, start doing.
Success comes in cans, not cannots. [JW+]
Take a check-up from the neck up. [ZZ]
Turn setbacks into comebacks. [BK]
Turn your scars into stars.[RS]
Wag more, bark less.
What got you here won't get you there. [CV^]
Your day's power is in your first hour.
Your dream is not for sale. [CV^]

3.6 Constant Object

Ryan Avery advocates a Constant Object as one way to thread your speech together. He means planting something tangible and recognizable in just a few different places of your speech. It is a subtle way of linking your speech together. For example, in his World Champion speech, *Trust is a Must* YT+ Ryan's Constant Object was "bunny slippers" and they appear in three different contexts early, middle, and late in the speech:

> When asking permission to go to a party:
> *Mom in her nightgown and bunny slippers smiled sweetly— All right, son. I trust you.*
>
> When Ryan is caught by the police for under-age drinking:
> *There is some angry southern woman—yelling in a nightgown and bunny slippers.*
>
> When dreaming of his wife-to-be:
> *I dreamed of still holding [my wife's] hand at ninety—decided no bunny slippers.* RA^

Ryan says the bunny slippers were a good constant object because they were appropriate to the speech and everyone could picture them in their own minds, based on their own experiences, because he gave no details of them (color or shape). Another benefit of a constant object is that it can indicate a person (without mentioning his or her name).

A Constant Object is effective and worthy of experimentation.

3.7 Threaded Phrase and High Level of Repetition

Everyone I know who is familiar with Dananjaya Hettiarachchi's World Championship speech, discussed earlier, rates it highly. All mention his threaded phrase, *I see something in you—but I don't know what it is.* Most mention the rose, his command of the stage, and his audience connection. But few notice his subtle, repetitive use of words which also contributes to the speech's success. Let me explain...

Following are key lines showing Dananjaya's amazing pattern of word repetition. [The line numbering is from the full speech, *page 91*.] As you will see, his repetition of words builds and strengthens our mental image of each vignette so that, afterwards, we can easily recall the speech's different scenes and characters.

In my first hearing of the speech, I didn't appreciate the extensiveness of its repetition. Only later, when studying the text to see what made the speech special, did the repetitive word patterning become apparent. The following selection of lines with their thoughtfully planned, repetitive words comprise an extremely high 40% of the speech.

It is the first time I've seen this technique in action. I'm sure it won't be the last. Study and experiment with this technique to make your speeches more memorable.

Dananjaya Hettiarachchi's Technique of Threading and Repeating

[Title] **I See Something**

L2. You and I are not very different from this flower.
Just like this flower is unique—you are unique.
All of us have something special that makes us as beautiful.
Do you know what makes you special?

L7. Sometimes life has a cruel way
Of taking out your petals—
And breaking you in two
And throwing you into the trash.
And when you're broken—
It's very difficult to feel special.
Mr. Contest Chair, my fellow flowers,
I can remember the first time I broke.

L18. Now, I wasn't afraid of the cops
But there was one person I was very afraid of—
And that was my mama.
Raise your hand if you have an emotional mother.
Put them all out there together and you'll get my "Mama."

L26. And I saw a tear coming down her face.
Now I'd seen my mama cry before
But mothers cry three kinds of tears;
Tears of joy, tears of sorrow, and tears of shame.
And when a son sees a mother cry tears of shame
That's a life-changing moment.

L35. My dad was waiting for me at home.
Now my dad is a cool dad.
Raise your hand if you have a cool dad.
Put them all together and you get my dad.

46. So my dad took me to meet one of his friends called Sam.
Now Sam was an accountant who had an accounting firm

53. He said:
"Son, **I see something in you—but I don't know what it is.**

74. So my dad introduced me to this strange club
That had a strange name with strange people — talking.

81. He walked up to me
Looked me dead-straight in the eyes and said:
"Son, **I see something in you —but I don't know what it is.**

L88. I know what it's like—
To not have enough money in your bank account.
I know what it's like—
To worry when the bills start coming in.

L92. "Honey, why did you marry me?" —She says:
I saw something in you—but I still don't know what it is.

L96. I was broken —
And I've been broken,
Lost and broke many times in my life

L106. [Closing] Ladies and gentlemen
When I look at you
I see something in you—but I don't know what it is!

Note also his recurring audience connection phrase:
L64. And I started dreaming, ladies and gentlemen
L85. And, ladies and gentlemen, I discovered I could speak
L94. Ladies and gentlemen, today I'm a dreamer, I'm a speaker
L106. Ladies and gentlemen, when I look at you…

4. Repetition in Parallel

[Parallel repetition at beginning and end of clauses or sentences is Symploce, pron. sim-plo-see]

Repetitive parallel patterns in sentences create a sense of balance and often an ear-pleasing rhythm as well. Perhaps it's our structured minds that make us comfortable with words and phrases that run in parallel. See for yourself how you respond as you read the following examples:

Examples that meet the strict definition of *symploce*

Much of what I say might sound bitter, but it's the truth.
Much of what I say might sound like it's stirring up trouble, but it's the truth.
Much of what I say might sound like it's hate, but it's the truth. [MX]

My brother [Robert F. Kennedy] need not be idealized
Or enlarged in death beyond what he was in life—
To be remembered simply as a good and decent man who
Saw wrong and tried to right it,
Saw suffering and tried to heal it,
Saw war and tried to stop it. [EK]

When there is talk of hatred —— Let us stand up and talk against it.
When there is talk of violence —— Let us stand up and talk against it. [BC]

Age is the newest four-letter word.
Oh, we know what ours is—But
We don't want to say it;
We don't want to write it;
We don't want to remember it. [SJ^]

There would be so many times in my life—
Where I've looked at my own reflection—
And I've said, "I'm —
Not good enough
Not smart enough
Not tall enough
Not rich enough
Not talented enough—
I'm just *not enough.* [KYY]

The madman is not the man who has lost his reason.
The madman is the man who has lost everything except his reason. [GKC]

Examples with a less-restrictive definition of parallel repetition

At Toastmasters—
We don't criticize, we praise.
We don't comment, we compliment.
We don't degrade, we encourage.
We don't pinpoint faults, we look for positive traits.
We don't put down people, we bring them up. [TN]

I was told there would be
No Mt. Everest too high,
No Grand Canyon too deep,
No Sahara Desert too wide
If I could live in one thousand, four hundred forty minutes. [AT^]

By "retirement" I mean the sudden stoppage of work—
Going from the dynamic career to the doldrums—
From vigor to vegetation. [RF^]

First they came for the Communists
And I did not speak out—because I was not a Communist.
Then they came for the Socialists
And I did not speak out—because I was not a Socialist.
Then they came for the Trade Unionists
And I did not speak out—because I was not a Trade Unionist.
Then they came for the Jews
And I did not speak out—because I was not a Jew.
Then they came for me
And there was no one left—to speak out for me.

... Martin Niemoller, a German anti-Nazi Lutheran pastor was imprisoned for his views in Dachau and another concentration camp 1938-45. His statement comprises five parallel statements, each comprising three parts. Each part is repeated apart from a couple of words. The parallel statements build in power until the last, when it unleashes a twist with a powerful sting.

And after that blue house
Every time they said—"Not interested"—
I heard —"Keep going. Someone down the street is interested."
Every time they said—"Get out of here"—
I heard — "Hurry up. Someone is waiting to tell you, 'Get in here.'"
Every time they said—"Go back to your country."—
I heard — "Go back to your country." [PV^]

... This shows the height one can take repetition. It's constructed with three sets of beginning repetition on alternate lines, plus three sets of ending repetition, concluding with a twist in the final line. That's the mark of a master craftsman.

5. Repetition of a Word

Repeating a single word (or short phrase) surprises, catches one's ear, and occasionally causes smiles. The effect is even stronger when the repeated word increases or decreases in intensity or if long deliberate pauses are inserted. This technique adds a subtle memorable difference to your speech. What is surprising, as you will discover in the coming pages, is the number of different ways a single word can be repeated. Below is an introductory sampler before we view diverse techniques with this oft ignored, yet often powerful, tool.

To jaw, jaw is always better than war, war. [WC] *Meeting at White House, June 26, 1954*

Never give in, never give in, never, never, never–
In nothing, great or small, large or petty–
Never give in—except to convictions of honour and good sense.
Never yield to force;
Never yield to the apparently overwhelming might of the enemy. [WC]
Speech at Harrow School, Oct 29, 1941

Never in the field of human conflict was so much owed by so many to so few. [WC]
Praising the Royal Airforce's Defence of Britain, Aug 21, 1940

I'm shocked, shocked to find that gambling is going on in here!
Capt Renault in movie Casablanca

The answer to that is nothing! Nada! Zero! Rien! Nichts! Neinte! Diddly squat! Zilch! [~SB^]
Repetition of same word in different languages for heightened effect.

I can just hear Muhammad saying now, "Well, I thought I should be eulogized by at least one President. And by making you last in a long, long, long, long line I guaranteed you a standing ovation." *Bill Clinton at Muhammad Ali's Memorial Service*

Mr. Maryk, you may tell the crew for me that there are four ways of doing things aboard my ship: The right way, the wrong way, the Navy way, and my way. They do things my way, and we'll get along. *Capt Queeg, in the movie The Caine Mutiny*

Maybe, maybe, Mr. President, if you visited some more places; maybe if you went to Appalachia where some people still live in sheds; maybe if you went to Lackawanna where thousands of unemployed steel workers wonder why we subsidize foreign steel. Maybe, maybe, Mr. President, if you stopped in at a shelter in Chicago and spoke to the homeless there; maybe, Mr. President, if you asked a woman who had been denied the help she needed to feed her children because you said you needed the money for a tax break for a millionaire or for a missile we couldn't afford to use. Maybe, maybe, Mr. President.
Mario Cuomo at 1984 Democratic Convention (referring to President Reagan)

6. Repetition of a Word (or Phrase) with None in Between

[Rhetorical term: Epizeuxis, pronounced ep-uh-ZOOX-sis]

When the same word (or short phrase) is repeated two or more times in immediate succession its unexpectedness catches attention and engages minds. And when repeated words are in threes, besides having the natural feel of a series, they create a sense of rhythm, making them even more attention-getting and ear-pleasing. The following examples provide an excellent base to draw ideas from as you build your personal reservoir.

Are you ready? — Are you ready? — ARE YOU READY? [VJ^] [In increasing volume]

He was late! Late, I tell you! [AN]

Hey, Hey, Hey—who do you think you are? [KR^]

His father would wait in a bright, shiny BMW to pick him up, and there I was —waiting, waiting, waiting—for my dad to pick me up. [PS^]

I learned that your mind can—and will—amaze your body if you just keep saying to yourself—It's possible. It's possible. It's possible. [OW^]

I never got a phone call from the police or the FBI during that time. Not one person. Not one! Not one! Not one! [ZH]

If you practice, you get better. If you don't, you don't. [TK]

Keep hope alive! Keep hope alive! Keep hope alive! On tomorrow night and beyond, keep hope alive! [JJ+]

Many bosses believe they know how we employees feel about them—
Wrong! Wrong! Wrong! [BW]

Never, never, never quit! [WC]

Never! Never! Never! — In a thousand lifetimes, never!

Our life is frittered away by detail ... Simplicity, simplicity, simplicity. [HDT]

Rhett, Rhett, Rhett! If you go, where shall I go? What shall I do? ... *Movie: Gone with the Wind*

When adults tell me "I have the right to own a gun," all I can hear is my right to own a gun outweighs your student's right to live. All I hear is—mine, mine, mine, mine. [EG]

Words! Words! Words! — Friends, we need much more than words!

For one second, he let go and she screamed —
She screamed so that the neighbor's, neighbor's blood froze. [DK^]

7. Repetition of a Word with a Pause in Between

Pausing between repeated words is not common, but when it does occur it catches one's ear and attention. It is another element of differentiation and well worthy of experimentation.

always—**Always**—**ALWAYS** remember that ... *[With increasing intensity]*

We talk about these grand speeches that are going to —
Change — Change — Change —
the —
World — World — World SS^ *[Double repetition]*

I was so excited to get into the real world and get a real job
I applied everywhere—
and waited —
and waited —
and waited.
Not a single phone call. ~JL^

Those words that Echo — Echo — Echo through life. JK+

Go—Go—Go—Down—Down—Down.

If you are in a job that you hate
It's not too late — Change—Your—Seat.
If you are in a relationship that's going nowhere
Don't just stay there — Change—Your—Seat.
And if your dreams are still up ahead
And you have no way of reaching them
Then please Change—Your—Seat. MQ^

I learned that your mind can—and will—
Amaze your body
If you just keep saying to yourself
It's possible—
It's possible—
It's possible. OW^
[Closing lines of WCPS speech]

8. Repetition of a Word with 1-2 Words in Between

[Rhetorical term: Diacope, pronounced die-ACK-oh-pee]

This technique has a different impact from when you have no separating words. Both approaches work; which option you choose is determined by what you are describing. Following are some excellent examples to adapt to your individual style:

Bond. James Bond. [IF]

Gus would talk and talk and talk to them—and they would nod and nod and nod right back at him. [MW]

Do I want to stand up, stand out, and stand fast—for who and what I am? Do I want to be the same or different? [MH^]

I've seen him make the same mistakes again and again and again.

No ifs—no ands—no buts. Just do it!

Nothing communicates, nothing penetrates, and nothing motivates more than a speech based on the convictions of the speaker. [LM^]

People who like people are people that people like. [RBZ]

What's the Future after the Future? [RL+]

Perpetual war for perpetual peace. [GV]

A nation has no permanent friends; no permanent enemies; only permanent interests [WM]

We were told we must always report such instances to authorities again and again. We did—time and time again. [EG]

He stood in the dark—under data-filled screens—and read to us—word for word for word for word. [KS]

In my search for the perfect partner, I discovered that perfect partners are those who keep perfecting their partnerships by choosing to pull less and bend more. [MV^]

It was not the senior citizens who took the melody out of music, the pride out of appearance, the courtesy out of driving, the romance out of love, the commitment out of marriage, the service out of patriotism. [AN]

9. Repetition of a Word Dispersed Through a Paragraph

A single word (or phrase) can also be used effectively to reinforce a thought when scattered through a paragraph in no traditional pattern as the following examples demonstrate:

Only one thought crossed my mind at the time –
What are the odds of beating the odds
And then getting beaten by the odds?
And to this day I wonder—
Did I beat the odds or not? [PM+]

... A memorable speech closing, recapping the speaker's experience of being offered a job against the odds (tough competition), and then having it withdrawn against the odds (global recession hits.)

Now this is not the end. It is not even the beginning of the end. But it is, perhaps, the end of the beginning. [WC]

A man has two reasons for doing anything: a good reason and the real reason. [~JPM]

I come careening down the stairs to see my youngest son lying on the floor amongst a slew of decapitated Greek gods. Funny sentence—not a funny scene. [KH^]

I had changed everything in my life—but nothing had changed. [LM^]

It'll be centralization all the way and, if that fails, more centralization. [RIM]

The younger generation will be replaced by a younger generation. [AN]

There is a difference between people who live in the future and people who live in the pasture. The difference is horsepower. [MM^]

What lies behind us and what lies before us is tiny compared to what lies within us. [RWE]

For an entire year, not a single one us got into trouble—not one, not once. [RJH]

Sometimes in the springtime of life
When young blood courses through vibrant veins.
Sometimes later in life
When more sluggish blood cruises through varicose veins.
My blood no longer courses—nor even cruises—it just coagulates ... [JE^]

When I was in Arkansas, I saw a saw that could out saw any saw I ever saw saw. If you happen to be in Arkansas and see a saw that can out saw the saw I saw saw I'd like to see the saw you saw saw. [AN] *[For readers who enjoy mental gymnastics.]*

10. Repetition of a Word Dispersed Through Whole Speech

Sometimes a speaker chooses a theme which revolves around a single word which is carefully threaded throughout the whole speech. It is noticeable, different, and compels attention.

An outstanding example is Darren Tay's speech titled *I See Red.* Its structure is simple: Growing up, Darren used to get annoyed ("I saw red") with family, friends, etc, who asked him stupid questions, or asked them at inconvenient times. Then, one day while at Law School, in a lecture given by a psychology professor, the students were asked what they saw on a sheet of paper that he held up. It was a large red dot. The answer was easy: the large red dot. But that was not the answer the professor was seeking. For the large red dot was surrounded by a sea of white and, as in life, we focus on the blemish (the red dot) rather than the general goodness (the large amount of surrounding whiteness).

This insight changed the way Darren saw things — he started seeing the larger area of goodness in others rather than just the blemishes. His behavior changed—from criticizing others' blemishes to praising their goodness. He closes by inviting us to do likewise. The speech smoothly flows from start to end and we are ready to accept his invitation.

What is remarkable about this 7-minute speech is the frequency of the word "red"—19 times in various ways: *red, I see red, I saw red, redness, I see a red dot, instead of seeing red, when you see red.* Such is the work of a master craftsman. Read the speech and watch Darren's well-connected delivery. [Two days later after winning this Semifinal contest Darren won the World Championship.]

I See Red
Darren Tay
Winner 2016 Semifinal World Championship of Public Speaking®

Website: www.publicspeakingacademy.com.sg
View YouTube: Darren Tay Toastmasters

I can recall vividly my high school English teacher
Would use the seven colors of the rainbow in the sky
To teach us how to describe our emotions.
If someone were to say "*I see green*"
The person is probably feeling green with envy
And hopes to emulate a role model to attain the same level of success.
If a person were to say "*I see blue*"
The person is probably feeling a sense of calmness, serenity, and tranquility.
But if someone were to say "*I see red*"—
How do you think a person is feeling?
The person is probably feeling—
[Audience response: "*Angry*"]—Absolutely!

Mr. Contest Chair, Fellow Toastmasters
Over the past years as I grew older I tended to see red most of the time.
I don't know why.
Even though I'm blessed with clothes to wear, food, a job, and an education
Something was still missing in my life — I felt dissatisfied and frustrated.

Let me paint you a picture of a typical day.
Early in the morning — at 7:00
I would be dressed in a suit and tie — holding a brief case — ready for work.
As I step out of my house I would see my neighbor Joy next door —
Watering the plants.
Joy would ask me the silliest and most obvious question—
"Hey, Darren, going to work?"
I was thinking —7:00 in the morning —
Dressed in a suit and tie—holding a brief case—
Where else could I be going?
I really felt like telling her
"Oh, no — I'm not going to work — I'm going to your house."
And once—when my car had a flat tire—Joy asked —
"Hey, Darren, flat tire?"
I felt like telling her — "Oh, no! The other three — are swollen."
So you see, my friends, at the start of a day—I saw red.

And at work I saw red as well
Because no matter how much of an effort I invested in my work
My boss would nit-pick on my performance —
Even my pronunciation and enunciation—
I suspect he was a Toastmaster—a very good grammarian!

And at home—
When I thought finally I could have peace of mind—
My mom would make me see red as well
Because my mom—
Who was learning how to use the Internet—
Would interrupt me at the worst time possible.

There was once I was busy working on a project
And my mom would ask
"Hey, Son, how do I log onto the Internet?"
I said, "Mom, just click on the Internet Explorer icon."
"Which one is the Internet Explorer icon?"
I said, "Mom, the one with the "E" & Internet Explorer at the bottom."
"Should I left-click or right-click on the mouse?"
I said, "Mom, just left-click on the mouse."
"How many times should I click?"

I said, "Mom, just click two times—double click."
"Which finger should I use to click?"
"Which finger? — It doesn't really matter which finger.
Just click on the mouse, left click, two times, double click."

So you see, my friends, at the start of a day until the end — I would see red.
And just as I was about to be distressed, dejected, depressed
In this vicious cycle of the pattern of redness
I came to see the light.
There was a turning point in my life.
This was when a psychology professor, Dr. Dan Gilbert
Came to visit my law school.
He spoke before 200 law students and — before he started —
He took out a piece of paper that looked just like this
[Holds up a sheet of paper with a large red circle on it.]
He asked all of us — "What do you see?"
We are all thinking this is not a trick question.
I see red — to be more specific — "I see a red dot."
The professor said, "Well, good, what else do you see?"
So, we law students were thinking—
Okay we need to be a bit more creative.

So, one law student raised his hand and said
"I know — it is a blemish on an otherwise pristine white piece of paper
And under chapter 393 of the Republic of Singapore Statute of Reprovision,
Section 14, Section 123B —
You can sue the manufacturer for damages."
The professor said
"Well, these are good answers
But they're wrong — not exactly wrong —
But not what I'm looking for.
You see, ladies and gentlemen
It's very easy as human beings to focus on the red.
We focus on the red first—
It's like the negative traits in others—
The blemishes in others—
The contamination in others.
It takes a lot more courage
To take a large step back
And look at the larger area of purity and strength in others.

The next time when you see red
Let us all take a larger step back
And look at the larger area of goodness—
And praise others—

And we'd have a whole new, positive outlook on life.
Determine to make a change.”

The next day when I met my neighbor Joy—
When she was watering her plants —
And she asked me the same question
"Hey, Darren, going to work?"
Instead of seeing red
I took a step back and I told my neighbor Joy
"Joy, thank you for taking an interest in my life.
You are a very nice person.
Let me buy you dinner next time."
The next day — did she ask me the same question?
She asked me the same question again
But this time around — instead of watering her plants —
She came to my house to water my plants for me.
And at work when my boss criticized my performance once more
Instead of seeing red
I took a step back—and I told my boss—
"Boss, when you give me feedback, you invest in my progress."
At the end of the year
He gave me the best employee's appraisal in the entire firm.
And at home when my Mom made me see red—
Instead of seeing red
I took a step back_and I told my mom—
"Mom, I will teach you how to use the Internet patiently
Because you have been doing that for me since I was young—
And I love you."
You all must be thinking —
Darren's mom must be thinking “Oh, so sweet.”
No   she looked at me and she said —
"Who are you? Are you my son?"
But guess what?
The next day on the dining table were all my favorite dishes.

My friends, do you see red in your life?
When you see red
Can you join me and take a step back
And look at the larger area of goodness.
My challenge to you is —
The next time you see the rainbow don't just focus on the red
Look at the beautiful spectrum of the seven colors —
Because you may just find your pot of gold at the end of the day.

11. Repetition of Words with the Same Root

[Rhetorical term: Polyptoton, pronounced puh-lip-toe-thon]

Here we focus on the repetition of words that share the same root, like *laugh* and *laughter*.

Repeating words that share the same root links them together in the listener's mind, creating a subtle rhyme effect through their connection. This form of word repetition offers speakers an immense playing field of words to choose from compared to repeating a single word as he following examples will illustrate:

And she laughed. And her laughter danced through the leaves like dappled sunlight. [RK^]

Ability has nothing to do with it. Stick-ability has everything to do with it.

Andy was perfectly imperfect [KYY]

For the first time in a long time Miss Mamo was hopeful. She went from waiting to die to dying to live. [DH+]

I dreamed a dream… *Les Miserables*

I hear the voices, and I read the front page, and I know the speculation. But I'm the decider, and I decide what is best. [GWB]

I've seen things you couldn't pay your therapist enough to help you un-see. [JA>]

In an ordinary kitchen I learned an extraordinary lesson. [MH^]

It is in pardoning that we are pardoned. [FOA]

It upsets me that something so upsetting happened.

It wasn't until I could no longer touch Grandpapa that he really touched me. [JAG]

Love is an irresistible desire to be irresistibly desired. [RF] *[Double repetition]*

Make your life a mission— not an intermission. [AHG]

NATO exists to manage the risks created by its existence. [RS>]

Not everything that counts can be counted. [DB]

Our goal is to be better than the best.

Perfection consists not in doing extraordinary things, but in doing ordinary things extraordinarily well. [AA]

Power tends to corrupt, and absolute power corrupts absolutely. [LA] *[Double]*

Sing your own special song [MC+]

That's a distinction without a difference.

The few who do are the envy of the many who don't.

The instinct of a man is to pursue everything that flies from him, and to fly from all that pursue him. [V]

The privilege of being underprivileged. [RWK]

The things you own end up owning you ... *from the movie Fight Club*

There is no end to the withering of withered flowers [TSE]

Think like a man of action, act like a man of thought. [HB+]

This isn't a bar for writers with a drinking problem — it's for drinkers with a writing problem [JJ>] *[Double]*

To love is nothing. To be loved is something. To love and be loved is everything. [AN] *[Double]*

Treat equally. Reward unequally. [RS+]

We are, by nature, imperfect. It takes no special talent to find an imperfection in another person. [LM^]

Where is the civil in our civilization? [AN]

Who audits the auditors? [RWK]

Sheriff Snodgrass caught us red-handed —red solo cups in hand [RA^]
... Imaginative repetition of red and hand in red-handed and red cup in hand

12. Repetition of a Word Whose Meaning Changes

[Rhetorical term: Antanaclasis, pronounced ant-an-uh-class-iss]

Words frequently have different meanings. Placing two such words near each other often tickles your listeners' minds, and makes them think as these examples demonstrate:

Doing the right thing is more important than doing the thing right. [PD+]

Great men are not know-it-alls—great men want to know it all.

If you aren't fired with enthusiasm, you will be fired with enthusiasm. [VL]

Leave a legacy—regardless of how you place [in the contest], let your place be in the hearts of your audience. [RJH]

Let us never negotiate out of fear. But let us never fear to negotiate. [JFK]

Management is doing things right; leadership is doing the right things. [PD+]

Only those who will risk going too far can possibly find out how far one can go. [TSE]

The greatest present is to be present when you are present with those you care about.

We must all hang together, or assuredly we shall all hang separately. [BF]

While we live, let us live. [RBE]

You don't have to be perfect to be a perfect parent.

Your argument is sound—all sound. [BF]

So what are the barriers?
I've identified three of them,
And I'll present them to you in too's—
Too afraid, too comfortable and too indifferent. [DLM]
... Creative use of word misdirection

But . . . But . . . <u>But</u>.
If we don't get off those <u>butts</u>—
We'll be forever frozen to a bucket. [MM^]
... Using the same-sounding, but differently spelled, word.

13. Repetition of Words with Similar Beginnings

The repetition of a series of words with similar beginnings is ear-catching, mind-tweaking, and helps you stand out. Consider the following as ideas on how you might include words that are both easy on the ear and easy to remember:

Always forgive; never forget. [JFK]

The world is smaller for his departure,
And we will remember him as he was—
Unwavering, undimmed, unequalled.
... *From George W. Bush's Eulogy of John McCain*

Although overworked, I was overwhelmed, overjoyed, and over-the-moon when ...

Like a superstar's, his super-sized, super-inflated, super-ego was something to experience.

I've never met such a disagreeable, discordant, disputatious, discontented, disruptive, disingenuous person—Oh, I wish he'd just disappear. [AN]

Imagine the shock one feels
When he realizes that for most of his life
He has been nothing more than the ink—
The ink inside of a pen—being guided by a bunch of
Unknown—Unnamed—Unauthorized—biographers. [DS>]

Our lives leave a trail of unfinished tasks. Unanswered letters, unvisited friends, unwritten articles, and unread books haunt quiet moments when we stop to evaluate. [CEH]

"No one will be awake at this hour." I protested. "Yes, they will," my mother replied. "And they'll want to know what happened." She was right. At every other house, it seemed, in those pre-cellphone, pre-email, pre-cable television, pre-Internet days, a light was on.

... *Carl Cannon, remembering the morning, as a kid newspaper carrier, when Robert F Kennedy was assassinated (1968)*

We travel together, passengers on a little space ship, dependent on its vulnerable reserves of air and soil; all committed for our safety to its security and peace; preserved from annihilation only by the care, the work, and, I will say, the love we give our fragile craft. We cannot maintain it half fortunate, half miserable, half confident, half despairing, half slave—to the ancient enemies of man—half free in a liberation of resources undreamed of until this day. [AS+]

... *Adlai Stevenson talking to the UN of planet earth (1965)*

14. Repetition of Words with Similar Endings

[The repetition of words with similar endings is Homoioteleuton, pronounced homo-yoto-lew-ton]

This has the same benefits as words with similar beginnings, plus an extra one—a better opportunity for rhyme, which is usually stronger in endings than beginnings. Rhyme, of course, makes remembering easier. Use this selection to suggest ideas:

And will you succeed? Yes, you will indeed — "98 and 3/4 percent guaranteed. [JW^]

Aspire to inspire before you expire!

Associating too closely with some Presidents dulled my senses to some of their excesses. [BG+]

Banks seem to believe that gain should be privatized and pain socialized.

Children still suffer from starvation, dehydration, and exploitation. [AN]

Do you want education or validation? [CV^]

Drinking allows you to do two things at once: lose inhibitions and give exhibitions.

He explained politely as I listened contritely. [MD]

He is upstanding, outstanding, and understanding.

In defeat, unbeatable; in victory, unbearable. [WC] *[said of Field Marshall Montgomery]*

Love is the quest. Marriage, the conquest. Divorce, the inquest. [HR>]

Our son set out—full of idealism, optimism and, fortunately, realism. [~CM+]

The house that I visualized and now live in is spacious, gracious, and palacious. [MVH]

The Mississippi steamboat *Delta Queen* appeals to the newly-weds and almost-deads.

They were a bunch of zeroes, heroes, and wackos. [~BF^]

Better Listening. Better Thinking. Better Speaking.
... Original Toastmasters motto. It has double strength: the repetition of Better and the "-ing" endings create a rhyme out of the sequential words, Listening, Thinking, Speaking.

15. Repetition Where the Last Word Becomes the First

[Rhetorical term is Anadiplosis, pron. ana-dee-plo-sis]

Repeating the last word of one clause or sentence to begin the next is an attention-grabber because of the seeming mental gymnastics the speaker has gone through to come up with his pretzel-like statement. This is more commonly used with a non-humorous theme. When stated in ascending or descending magnitude it achieves even greater effect. Examples:

Aboard my ship, excellent performance is standard. Standard performance is sub-standard. Sub-standard performance is not permitted to exist... *Capt Queeg in movie The Caine Mutiny*

Fear leads to anger; anger leads to hatred; hatred leads to conflict; conflict leads to suffering... *Yoda in movie Star Wars*

Five minutes early is on time; on time is late; late is unacceptable. [VL]

Watch your thoughts, for they will become actions. Watch your actions, for they'll become habits. Watch your habits for they will forge your character. Watch your character, for it will make your destiny. [MT+]

Freedom of expression, freedom of speech, is the fertile soil from which truth grows. And truth leads to freedom. Your freedom. My freedom. [BW]

If you can't fly then run, if you can't run then walk, if you can't walk then crawl, but whatever you do you have to keep moving forward. [MLK]

Once you change your philosophy, you change your thought pattern. Once you change your thought pattern, you change your attitude. Once you change your attitude, it changes your behavior pattern and then you go on into some action. [MX]

The general who became a slave. The slave who became a gladiator. The gladiator who defied an emperor. Striking story! ... *Commodus in movie The Gladiator*

The poor wish to be rich, the rich wish to be happy; the single wish to be married, and the married wish to be dead. [AL+] *[Two parallel constructions]*

This, it seemed to him, was the end, the end of a world as he had known it. [JOC]

When we drink, we get drunk. When we get drunk, we fall asleep. When we fall asleep, we commit no sin. When we commit no sin, we go to heaven. So, let's get drunk and go to heaven. [BOR]

16. Repetition in Reverse

[Rhetorical term is Chiasmus, pron. kigh-az-muss]

It's nice to be important, but it's more important to be nice [JT+] This simple reversal of a statement is a *mental speed bump*. It catches your attention and makes you think. Audiences enjoy their cleverness. Many platform speakers use this technique—and so should you. Their catchiness will help you to be appreciated and remembered.

A lawyer starts life giving $500 worth of law for $5 and ends giving $5 worth for $500.

Ask not what your country can do for you, but what you can do for your country. [JFK]

Believe what you say, say what you believe.

Carlyle wondered whether the poor are poor because they are ignorant, or ignorant because they are poor. [WD+]

Do I love you because you're beautiful? Or are you beautiful because I love you? [OH]

Eat to live, not live to eat. [S]

Freedom of speech leads to truth; truth leads to freedom [BW]

Good judgment comes from experience; experience comes from bad judgment.

He struggles in life because he is a Bebopper and doesn't plan his life, live his plan. [DS^]

Her life was full of children; her children were full of life.

I have discovered that people with money have no imagination, and people with imagination have no money. [SW>]

I meant what I said and I said what I meant. [DS+]

I'd rather be looked over than overlooked. [MW+]

I'm not in Toastmasters—Toastmasters is in me.

If we don't abolish war from this earth, one day war will abolish us from this earth. [~HST]

In peace sons bury their fathers; in war fathers bury their sons. [FB]

IRS Motto: *We've got what it takes to take what you've got.*

It is better to deserve honors and not have them, than have them and not deserve them. [MT]

It is not about the years in your life, but about the life in your years.

It's not the size of the dog in the fight that counts, it's the size of the fight in the dog. [DDE]

Kids in the backseat cause accidents. Accidents in the backseat cause kids. [AN]

Learn something about everything; and everything about something. [THH]

Mankind must put an end to war, or war will put an end to mankind. [JFK]

My job is not to represent Washington to you, but to represent you to Washington.[BO]

The absence of evidence is not the evidence of absence.

The music of our lives and the life of our music are woven into the fabric of our being. Life is music. Music is life and surely you cannot have one without the other. [DS^]

The purpose of life is a life of purpose. [RB>]

The value of marriage is not adults producing children, but children producing adults. [~PDV]

To receive a compliment from the best is the best compliment to receive. [BW]

To the world you might be one person; but to one person you might be the world. [AN]

We know what to do. Will we do what we know.

We're going through the ups and the downs and the downs and the ups.

Your audiences won't care how much you know until they know how much you care. [CR]

Gramma—Now there's a word filled with memories—
Most of them good—the rest of them— good for you! [Rubs his behind] [RK^]

17. Repetition of And, And, And

[Rhetorical term: Polysyndeton, pronounced poly-sin-dee-ton]

Repeating the word **"and"** (or any other conjunction) at the beginning of a series of consecutive clauses is uncommon but effective. As you'll see in the examples below, this technique can be used to indicate emphasis or excitement or a hurried or galloping pace or a stream of consciousness or add rhythm to your words or simply add a smile to your audiences' faces. [Did you just note the repetition of the conjunction "or"?]

"**And**" is the most common of the seven most frequently-used conjunctions which are: **for, and, nor, but, or, yet, so** (whose mnemonic is FANBOYS). Any conjunction, or variation thereof, can be used, such as "And then, And then…" Allow the following examples to germinate and grow ideas for an upcoming speech:

I wanted to be rich—so I pooled my money together.
I sat down and I came up with plans.
Plans for marketing, plans for sales and budgets.
Ah! I had a budget for income and a budget for expenses.
And I started my business as a consultant.
And I'd phone up people
And I'd knock on doors
And I'd send out faxes and post letters—
But not too many people replied.
So I put ads in the newspaper
And ads in different articles
And still not many people replied.
And this went on for many, many months—
And soon I was broke. [DN^]

That's the first time in my whole life
Someone has said that he sees something in me.
And I started working for Sam
And every day after work he used to tell me stories—
About the world, about history, about country, about philosophy—
And it was much, more interesting than what I learned in school.
And I discovered I can dream.
And I started dreaming.
After one year I went back into high school—completed my exams—
And went into college. [DH^]

What is your passion?
Is it music
Or is it car racing
Or belly dancing
Or chasing golf balls? [JA^]

As the volume of her voice gets louder—
The pitch of her voice gets higher.
And the volume gets louder—
And the pitch gets higher—
And louder—
And higher—
And louder—
And higher—
And louder—
And higher—
Until only dogs
Can hear the frequency coming from her body. [KS^]

The way I see it we have two options.
Option one—denial. Me?
Getting older? Oh—No — No — No!!!
I am not ready
For bingo
And shuffleboard
And Jeopardy
And Wheel of Fortune
And Florida
And cruises—
And Cracker Barrel. [SJ^]

I looked over at the mirror next to me
And it was as if my reflection stepped out of the mirror
And walked over to me
And looked me in the eye
And stared me in the face—
I told you I had a lot of conversations with myself ...[CV^]

The bride came over to us and said,
"Mom, Dad, we're leaving now.
Thank you for everything and we love you very much."
And as the two of them left, I could see her mother's lips quivering.
And that evening the two of us went home to an empty house.
And we were placed on the parent's inactive list.
And my role as Ivan the Terrible came to an end. [~JS^]

Let the white folks have their money and power and segregation and sarcasm and big houses and schools and lawns like carpets, and books, and mostly–mostly–let them have their whiteness. [MA*]

... *Maya Angelou* in her autobiography, *I Know Why the Caged Bird Sings*

18. Repetition of an Idea

[Three successive words used to express a single central idea is Hendiatris, pron. hen-die-a-tris]

Sometimes you wish to emphasis a point in a fresh way without repeating the same word. One ages-old way is to use *hendiatris,* which is repeating three different words that represent one idea. A well-known example comes from Marc Antony's eulogy for the slain Julius Caesar: *Friends, Romans, Countrymen, lend me your ears.*

Those three terms are all words of brotherhood, ranging from friend to nation.

Another approach is to use phrases rather than single words to express a single idea. Again, history provides us with a well-known example:

But, in a larger sense—we can not dedicate — we can not consecrate — we can not hallow — this ground.

Here, Lincoln, in his Gettysburg Address, expresses a single idea using three different phrases—the words *dedicate, consecrate,* and *hallow,* all reflecting the idea of *honoring as holy* and, accordingly, adds to the solemnity of the speech and occasion.

Experiment with and develop your own fresh three-part word/phrase packages to replace some of the well-known, older ones such as *wine, women, and song* and *sex, drugs, and rock'n'roll.* To help you start, here are some expressions over a range of topics:

America is not a blanket woven from one thread, one color, one cloth. [JJ+]

Anjali was beautiful, educated, and cultured. She was perfect for me. [VJ^]

Been there. Done that. Got the T-Shirt [JE^]

But Kennedy's serious purpose was— to acknowledge—to praise—to reinforce — the endurance and fighting spirit of the people of West Berlin. [~PKP]

Freedom of speech, as those vociferous protesters demonstrated, is life pulsating through the sinews, veins, and arteries of society. [BW]

How do I continue on in a world that can be so cold, so cruel, so unfair? [EE^]

I closed my eyes and returned to the Swami's question, *Who are you?* And in that deep silence—I heard the music of my dreams, the song of my talents, the symphony of my spirit — and I finally understood what the Swami had done. [VJ^]

I had a dead-end job, a dead-end relationship, and a dead-end life. Ladies and gentlemen, I needed help. [CV^]

I had recently turned 50. The big 5-0! Five decades! Half a century! [PB^]

I submit to you that the richest place on earth is the graveyard. Full of people who haven't acted on their dreams, and because they were too timid, too fearful, too comfortable their treasures are buried with them. [OW^]

If you take 5 minutes of silence each day I guarantee you that the other 23 hours and 55 minutes of your day will be filled with a tranquility, a serenity, a peacefulness you never knew even existed. Five minutes of silence will give you confidence. [CV^]

In the clear daylight of married life, she could see that he was vain, self-absorbed, and unreliable. [KF]

In this bidding cycle, Greenville stood on its own merits. It stood toe to toe with Raleigh and Cary. It stood arena to arena with Charlotte and Greensboro. It stood restaurant to restaurant with Jacksonville and Memphis. Greenville challenged the toughest, deepest competition [MR+]

It's time to take off the blinders *[takes off his big black eye-mask]* of disappointment, failure, and self-doubt and get back on the ride [JW^]

The future is not meant to be pot luck, blind chance, pure fate. [JE^]

The key decision-makers have done nothing; done the wrong thing; or done the right thing too late. [JM+]

The world watches with shock and disbelief as all hell breaks loose and thousands of lives are incinerated, crushed, suffocated. [JM^]

There are not enough jails, not enough policemen, not enough courts, to enforce a law not supported by the people. [HHH]

There's just three of us to tackle this problem: me, myself and I.

Within all of us is a divine ability—to see past people's weaknesses, mistakes, and shortcomings.[DJ^]

My grandmother used to say—
"Son, if you want to see a god, look no further than the person next to you."
I obviously didn't believe my grandmother
Because none of my friends could throw lightning bolts—
None of my friends had the strength of a thousand men—
And none of my friends had fought evil giants. [DH^]

19. Repetition with a Twist

A word or phrase repeated builds audience expectation for yet another. This expectation provides a great opportunity to be different by replacing what the audience is expecting with a Twist— either serious or humorous. If serious, it acts as a thought break; if humorous, as a smile break. The following examples are self-explanatory:

I remember back in 1994 my undergraduate interview
For a place to study history at Oxford University, England.
Three o'clock sharp.
Three professors on the panel —
Four glasses of sherry. [SB^]

I could tell you all the facts.
I could tell you all figures about breathing,
But the thing I cannot do for you
Is give you the answer. [KS^]

For years, I became obsessed with getting everything right.
I was the student trying for perfect grades.
I was the employee trying for the perfect job.
I was the boyfriend who was just — trying. [SB^]

And I've said, I'm —
Not good enough
Not smart enough
Not tall enough
Not rich enough
Not talented enough
I'm just "not enough." [KYY]

Now Mike and I – we were like this [fingers crossed].
When the car broke down at 3:00 in the morning
Who did I call? —Mike.
When I got married
Who planned my bachelor party?—Mike.
When I started a business and needed a partner
Who did I ask?—Mike.
And, all right, I'll admit it –
When I almost fainted giving my Icebreaker speech
Who was there to catch me?—Mike. [EF^]

Do you know what's wrong with me? —
Do you know what's wrong with you? —
Who cares! [LM^]

You see, my brother wasn't just older than me—
He was taller than me;
He was bigger than me;
He was stronger than me.
He was growing facial hair—in like the fourth grade. ~KS^

We sailed through our honeymoon.
Then differences started to emerge.
She liked outdoors—I liked indoors.
She loved swimming—I feared drowning.
She liked cooking—I liked to tell her how I missed my mama's cooking. MV^

My two all-time favorite speech twists, both humorous, come from a friend who has a wickedly witty mind, World Champion Speaker Jock Elliott. The first, from his 1994 speech based on the then-popular Doris Day song, *Que Sera, Sera*. It opens with the song's opening words. In the second, presented in 1996, Jock makes a series of five statements, each followed by the repetitive phrase, *That's called* —, followed by a different rhyming polysyllabic word, each building to the climatic last word. Read on...

When I was just a little boy
I asked my mother
"What will I be?
Will I be handsome?
Will I be rich?"
Here's what she said to me.
She said—
'No.'

All of us have a seen a member of the opposite sex naked
And not closed our eyes—
That's called ***curiosity****.*
Jimmy Carter took a fancy to someone
Who was not his to fancy—
That's called ***fantasy****.*
He talked about it on national TV—
That's called ***stupidity****.*
Then his wife heard about it—
And that's called ***catastrophe****.*
And some of us may even have taken things to their logical conclusion
As Bill Clinton did
And that's the millstone—
Called ***Lewinsky****.*

20. Repetition of a Sound

Earlier, we saw how Lance Miller continually repeated *Chi-Chink* (see *page 161*), the sound of a ticket validation machine creating differentiation and memorability. Such repeated sounds stand out because they titillate the ear and, frequently, create rhyme which increases our listening pleasure.

We look at three ways that sound can be used in a speech:

20.1 Repeat a sound

20.2 Repeat the opening sound of nearby words (Alliteration)

20.3 Repeat words that rhyme

20.1 Repeat a Sound

Rory Vaden, runner-up in the 2007 WCPS Contest, titled his 7-minute speech, *Slam*, and then used *slam* (or *slammed*) 12 more times through the speech. In addition, he used the couplet *Knock! Knock!* on five occasions preceding the door being slammed in his face. The repetition of the two complementary sounds, *knock* and *slam,* graphically described the reception Rory, when a student, regularly received as he went door-to-door selling children's books.

Another landmark repetitive sound from the annual WCPS contests came in 2013, when Pres Vasilev, in his superbly-designed 7-minute World Champion Speech, titled *Changed by a Tire* [YT+], used his voice to emit the squeaky sound of a rusty jack 22 times (spread over four occasions his car had to be raised or lowered.) The sound really added to the reality of the scene. In fact, his vocal sound was so realistic, I thought, incorrectly, a mechanical sound device was being used.

In his 1993 WCPS contest speech, Richard Spencer spoke of the hotly-held convictions that his father held on every topic which he usually let loose on. To bleep out his father's frequent cuss words, Richard used a small child's bicycle bulb horn—a horn that required a lot of squeezing in that speech.

Angela Louie opened her 2005 WCPS contest speech with a short delightful Chinese lullaby related to her daughter's birth and ended the speech with a similar soothing lilt. Various World Champion Speakers have also sung a few lines (with equal enthusiasm and varying shades of rhythm) including Arabella Bengson[86], Mark Brown[95], Jim Key[03], Randy Harvey[04], and LaShunda Rundles[08].

Individual scenes can also be enriched by injecting repeated sounds, as seen in Randy Harvey's *Lessons from Fatdad* (see *page 134*) in scenes such as this:

> *[Woof!! Owwwooo!!]* I was surrounded by a pack of black and tan hunting hounds. *[Owwwooo!!]* My heart jumped. Then so did I … [RJH]

Similarly, David Henderson, in his speech, *The Best Medicine (see page 126)* used sound effectively to add another dimension to the scene in his grandmother's hospital room. His repetitive use of the beep sound heightened the anxiety:

> Until one day Miss Mamo went "ugh" [Put his hand to his chest]
> And that machine that goes *beep, beep*
> Starts going *beep, beep, beep, beep,*
> And a nurse rushed in — And a doctor rushed in—
> And when it seemed like that machine couldn't beep any faster—
> Or Miss Mamo's face couldn't get any tighter
> Something happened — Miss Mamo relaxed — she looked peaceful.
> And that machine went *beeeeeeeeeeeeep.* [Draws a straight line with his hand]. [DH+]

20.2 Repeat the Opening Sound of Nearby Words (Alliteration)

Alliteration is when two or more nearby words have the same first letter or sound (e.g., f and ph), even though the words may not necessarily rhyme. The repeated letter or sound catches our ear, often adds to the speech's rhythm, enables easier recall, while connecting and highlighting important words. It's why companies sometimes choose alliterative names—think of *Dunkin' Donuts, Best Buy*, and *Bed Bath and Beyond.* The easy-to-say and retention feature of Alliteration makes it a favored form of repetition. Examples include:

> And he went on to make it contemptuously clear ... [TM^]

> And when at some future date the high court of history sits in judgment on us. [~JFK]

> Are we looking for the huge, high drops of disappointment or the twisting turns of ill-fated failure? [JW^]

> Better to dollop it out boldly than dribble it out in Dixie cups.

> Harry Truman was known for his courage, character, and commonsense. [SE]

> He's just a mouth with a mind.

> I have a dream that my four little children will one day live in a nation where they will be judged not by the color of their skin but the content of their character. [MLK]

> I looked up and there were red, raging eyes with fists clinched... [RJH]

> I try to avoid fat-infested food...

I was directionless, depressed, damaged… [OS^]

I was into hope and happiness. [JJ^]

I'll never forget the look on my wife's face as fear and confusion filled her eyes in the form of tears… [KS^]

In the United States today, we have more than our share of the nattering nabobs of negativism. They have formed their own 4-H Club — the hopeless, hysterical hypochondriacs of history. [SA>]

Literature is literally littered with lively legends. [MH^]

Mario Andretti she wasn't. More like Molasses Mindy! [DW]

My wish for you is that your ending days are spent sipping champagne each evening watching the sun slowly slip into the ocean.

No craft, no crew can travel safely with such vast contradictions. [AS+]

She skedaddled like a scalded cat. [RJH]

Success is not final, failure is not fatal: it is the courage to continue that counts. [WC]

The All Blacks showed the world how rugby should be played—with pride, passion, and panache. [LN]

The answer I know not.

The smart and the skilled get paid vastly more than the dumb and the dropouts, regardless of whether they come from Birmingham or Bangalore.[NF]

The Terrible Twos—that point in a child's development where that precious little toddler turns into a diabolical demon of destruction. [FM^]

They were candidates without ideas hiring consultants without convictions to run campaigns without content. [GF]

Truman's campaign cash cupboard was bare. Corporate chieftains came calling, carrying cashiers' checks. [BW]

20.3 Repeat Words that Rhyme

When repetition rhymes, your speech rocks, be it simple or soaring. *A dentist drills, fills, and bills* is a simple rhyming example. Martin Luther King Jr's speech *I Have a Dream,* is a soaring example. Think of your favorite Country & Western song—most likely threaded with a repeated phrase that creates a memorable rhyme. Country & Western songs are sometimes described as repetition, rhyme, and a story that "gets to you" — a formula that also works well in speaking. The *Iliad* and *Odyssey* had a repetitive lyrical structure allowing the bards to easily remember and sing these long epics. Churchill believed that speeches, like poems, should be pleasing to the ear. Repetition helps create an ear-pleasing rhyming effect in various ways:

Rhyme Can Draw Attention to Your Title, Such As

Make Your Life A Mission—Not an Intermission [AHG]

Success is Never Ending, Failure is Never Final [RS]

Let My Dataset Change Your Mindset [HR+]

From the Outhouse to the Penthouse [AN]

Turn Setbacks into Comebacks [BK]

Don't Motivate—Inspirate! [RM]

Turn Your Scars into Stars [RS]

If It Is to Be, It's Up to Me [RS]

Trust is a Must [RA^]

Plain Jane [LC^]

Rhyme Can Draw Attention to Your Message Phrase, Such As

If we don't show it, how will they know it? [JK^]

If they can't repeat it, they didn't get it [PF]

Be willing to go when others say no. [KRM]

Invest the time if you want to shine

If it doesn't fit, you must acquit [JC+]

Live—don't give—your speech [RJH]

Begin your day the right way [JS>]

Be the sage of the stage

Rhyme Used in Speeches Captures Attention, Such As

Tilt it left.
Tilt it right.
The kids will love it.
It's outta sight! [EH^]

Other Rhyming

As they say in Hollywood, funny is money. [JC]

Do you know what? — I know diddly-squat!

Grammie had lost her home; she had lost her husband; and now she had lost her hearing. Yet she wasn't just surviving, her spirit was thriving. [EF^]

I come to speak to you in defence of a cause as holy as the cause of liberty—the cause of humanity. [WJB]

I was 23. I thought I was bulletproof. I worried about flying—not dying. [MM^]

I'm a member of the Old Boys Network—male, pale, and stale.

If you can't resolve it, then dissolve it! [LM^]

If you're not laughing, you're not living. [JC]

Marriage is a 3-ring circus—Engagement Ring. Wedding Ring. Suffering.

Marriage is a union brought on by yearning and maintained by earning. [AN]

She was young and single—and ready to mingle.

Show your ability by showing your vulnerability. [PH+]

The blame. The pain. The shame. I wanted to commit suicide. [AN]

There is no cast for a broken heart. [HL^]

Trader Joe's — my destination for exploration.

Turn your slides from boring to soaring. [MR]

You need a check-up from the neck up. [ZZ]

In lieu of flowers, go buy a backpack
Fill it with school supplies
Let's make that visitation room
Look more like a classroom. [JA>]

The difference between a cat and a comma is one has claws at the end of its paws, and one is a pause at the end of a clause. [AN]

Aunt Vymetta was one of them that was consumed by her personal appearance. There wasn't a part of her body that hadn't been tucked, sucked, plucked, tweezed, shifted or lifted at one time or another. [KS]

5.2 Differentiate

Differentiate — or Die! [JT]

Introduction

Zig Ziglar's Conferences were always a pleasure to attend. Not just because of Zig's warm and optimistic personality but because they were different. For example, I still remember the silver pump he energetically worked to demonstrate drawing well-water to the surface, his unique bumper-sticker phrases such as *You Need a Check-up from the Neck-up,* and observations like *Too many of us live on Someday Isle.* Zig's differences made his presentations memorable.

Differences that Helped Make World Champions

I think back over the many Toastmasters World Champions of my era and what they did differently that stood out and helped them earn that prestigious trophy. Following is a selection that illustrates the creativity and preparation invested in finding a way to be both different and remembered. Each were "firsts" in the history of the contest which accentuated their differentiation:

> When introduced, the speaker runs onto the stage and speaks from in front of lectern. Until then, speakers walked out smartly and spoke from behind the lectern. [MA^ 78]
>
> Speaker appears, not in a traditional suit, but in a Texas Tuxedo. *What's that?* you ask —It's jeans and a tuxedo. As the native Texan speaker explains: many locals had (figuratively) lost their pants in the Texas Oil bust. [The contest was in Texas.] [DB^ 90]
>
> *Stuck to a Bucket* closes with the speaker summarizing how we become unhappy in life because we get stuck to a bucket of habits and — holding up a large shiny silver bucket — he urges us to let go of our ours as he lets go of his—with a big clang. [MM^ 94]
>
> Contest attendees were introduced to the Space Age in a speech that had the speaker engaging in an imaginary, but vivid, laser sword fight (with appropriate dialogue) with Darth Vader. [BR^ 98] [Interestingly, the speaker later said: *I came to the International Contest to be either first or last, not some place in-between.* In other words, his planned differentiation would either soar mightily or fail miserably. It soared.]
>
> The speaker, recalling the time when he was contemplating suicide, has a lengthy, fascinating, back-and-forth conversation with his reflection who steps out of his mirror for the dialogue. A second major differentiation occurs at the close, where, explaining the lesson he has learned stands still for a huge 12-seconds of silence. [CV^ 99]
>
> Imagine grabbing everyone's attention from the moment of introduction. This WCPS speaker stood center stage with a quiet, confident, warm smile that embraced the audience with a much-longer-than-normal, 8-second-silence followed by 5 more silent seconds as he pulls a notebook from his pocket before uttering his first word. [ET^ 00]

Seventeen seconds into his speech he falls, face-forward, onto the floor (to reinforce his point) and then addresses the Chairman, and audience, face-down from floor. [DLC 01]

This speech caught our attention with closing words unexpectedly "spoken" — in sign language. Yet we understood what was being said because a minute earlier he had signed the same message while vocalizing it. It was an appropriate, emotional, different, and memorable close. [JK^ 03]

When you have a beautiful singing voice, use it. This speaker did, perfectly, at the opening and the closing, to great effect. That you can imitate. The rest of her speech you can't, as she talks of her past, present, and future in a very personal way for she knows she is dying. She talks delicately of the life-taking *lupus* she has, in a way that encourages us to think of our mortality. [LAS 08]

The speech opens with the speaker putting a cigarette to his lips and pulling out a lighter—looks up surprised as the audience collectively and anxiously gasped in reaction. He responds by telling them they are simply reacting to words they hear about smoking. Which words are right? He asks. Which words are wrong? It was a brilliant opening mental challenge to a speech titled *The Power of Words.* [MQ^ 15]

Were you ever bullied at school? Want to grab your audience's mind with how emotionally painful it is? Here's one speaker's approach. He opens by putting on, over his suit trousers, a pair of white underpants—which is what a bully made him do at school. And he leaves them on for most of the speech. An image—and point—that will last forever. [DT^ 16]

Portraying a role that is out of character is another effective differentiator. We don't expect to see women speakers dressed fully in black, sparring (realistically) in an imaginary boxing ring. But when one does, employing the movements, antics, and language of the ring to describe being knocked down in life but climbing back up—so that she's *Still Standing* (the title), you truly notice. As did the judges. [RJS 18]

In summary, to use Nancy Duarte's term, each offered a STAR—**S**omething **T**hey'll **A**lways **R**emember—to their audience. And if we generalize about all great speakers, we find:

Speaking Stars have STARS in their Speeches

There Is No Limit to What and How You Differentiate

You can differentiate absolutely everything and anything in your speech — from the time you approach the stage until the time you leave it. To illustrate:

Burn victim and paraplegic W Mitchell sometimes opens a speech from his wheelchair, simply by raising one eyebrow. [WM+]

Kirk Carr drew 23 feet of tape from his tape measure to demonstrate the length of a Blue Whale at birth—and then left the tape on the floor during his whole speech. [KC^]

Andy Dooley opened a humorous speech with a 31-word title—*A Short But Unbelievably Intriguing Tale Of How Destiny Unexpectedly Showed Her True Colors Against The Backdrop Of Pure White Snow On A Colorado Mountaintop While All Other Conditions Remained Normal.* The speech was differentiated before Andy uttered his first word. [AD>]

In his 2009 TED Talk about ending malaria as a big killer, Bill Gates magnetizes attention by opening a jar of mosquitos and letting them loose among the audience! (They are disease-free, he explains a minute later.) Such an unexpected act made the speaker, the speech, and the message forever memorable. Gates repeated his attention-getting flair at a 2018 forum in Beijing on reducing disease and death, globally, by improving sanitation, drawing attention to the lack of toilets in developing countries by holding up a jar of human feces. Definitely different. Definitely unforgettable. [BG*]

Steve Jobs from time to time would end a speech with *Oh, just one more thing* and go on to announce a new product or feature. [SJ+]

Jo Maypole would occasionally open up her Q&A session when speaking to professional audiences with the words: *Now, it's time for me to throw out a few questions.* And she would crumple up a letter-size sheet, with a question pre-typed on it (16-20 font) for the receiver to ask, and throw it into the audience. She'd do that 3-4 times, usually with one including an amusing question. The audience loved it and often grabbed for the crumpled-up sheets thrown out. It also relaxed and loosened the audience so that other questions readily flowed. [JM*]

J. A. Gamache, comparing the struggles of man to the struggles of a chrysalis before becoming a beautiful butterfly, ends his speech with a (mechanical) butterfly suddenly settling on his shoulder. [JAG]

Phil Barth opened a speech recounting a lazy summer beach vacation. Taking his suit jacket off, he lays it on the stage floor, as one would a beach towel, sits on it, as though it was one, and then addresses the chairman sitting on his "beach towel" before carrying on with his speech. [PB^]

Ask your audience a question they should know the answer to (but often don't) differentiates, too. For example, "Quick—what building is on most nickels?" [Answer: Monticello] was the attention-getting opening of a speech on Thomas Jefferson.

Express words differently. Instead of "in one week" say in "168 hours" or "10,080 minutes." Instead of saying your age, give the audience a *mental speed bump* like "I have walked this planet three score—and more—years." And throw in fun-sounding town names, e.g., "I'm from Boring, Oregon. Want to see my High School Year Book?" Or "I think the newcomer was born in Satan's Kingdom, Vermont."

Props used with purpose can also be great differentiators. In one still-talked-about speech, Morgan McArthur [MM^] uncovered a full-size horse replica (Title: *The Difference is Horsepower*) to conclude his speech. In another, Robert Ferguson [RF>] bounded up a 10-foot stepladder for a farewell kiss with his teenage, summer-vacation girlfriend. (Her parents were sleeping on the ground floor.)

> The day before John F Kennedy's Inaugural, it snowed so heavily that 10,000 cars were stranded on Washington streets. Inauguration Day was clear, sunny, but viciously cold. You likely know that JFK's well-known spoken address was different in various ways. But so, too, was one non-verbal element — JFK spoke bareheaded in the bitter cold. That day, formal hats at Presidential Inaugurations melted into memory.

And remember that differences don't even have to be "big" to make an impact. Differences are in the details, too. Recently, for example, two small details caught my eye and told me they came from craftsmen-prepared speeches.

> One, titled *Haymaker*, came when the speaker recounted a special boxing match when he was younger. The subtle difference was he lifted the imaginary ring rope and bent over as he both entered and left the ring rather than just walking to where the imaginary ring was. He was reliving, not just giving, the scene. [KJ^]

> The other related to the death of the speaker's grandfather. It describes how she was always too busy for him, yet he kept preparing an evening meal for her. He dies unexpectedly. The following night, her mother gives her the red rice bowl in which her grandfather had placed her meal, left uneaten, the night before. That simple, highly visual, bright red bowl she now held, summed up the scene, the speaker, her memories, and the speech's memorable message. [WN^]

One simple visual detail can make a noticeable mental difference.

Closing Comments

To make an impact you don't have to be technically perfect but you do have to say or do something different. When thinking of your next speech, what do you hope the audience will remember afterwards, in addition to its message? It could be one (or more) of many things such as a: Surprise. Phrase that Stays (that might even be used during the rest of the Convention). Twist. Mnemonic. Poem. Feeling. Prop. Metaphor. Repeated sound. Or it may be your speech title; your audience participation; the way you use pauses, silence, or words; your animation and passion; how you are dressed; or how you konnect with everyone.

Steven Pressfield, in his inspirational book, *The Authentic Swing*, points out that every golfer's swing is different, uniquely his or hers. His message, to golfers and non-golfers alike, is to be yourself. As a speaker, people come to hear YOU – not a clone of Tony Robbins or Zig Ziglar or Jim Rohn. Be yourself, not the polished shadow of someone else — and share your uniquely different swing with your audiences.

In other words:

Be different and you stand out; be bland and you blend in.

5.3 Closing

If the ending isn't memorable, the talk itself may not be. [CA]

Introduction

Closing your speech is the last impression you leave with your audience of you and your message. Suggestions when considering your last impression are:

- Make or restate your message in clear, simple, memorable terms
- Point to the first action step if you are seeking action from the audience
- Close on a positive, not negative, note

Introducing Your Closing

One of the most difficult challenges when closing a speech is finding the right balance between nudging and pushing your audience to action. If too soft, nothing may happen; if too aggressive, nothing may happen. As discussed in Section 1, choosing the right words to encourage your audience to take the first action step is key. To help you further, here are more speech closings ideas:

Are we ready to play our part? For the sake of... For the sake of... For the sake of... [JM^]

But we all knew that — We all know that — We've heard that story before... [DR^]

Close your eyes. Open your minds. Fire your imaginations. Dare to dream. And ... [BR^]

Friends, look at your watch right now. Commit not to do ...... for the next 24 hours [JC>]

I learned ...... from my grandma. So, this morning, I offer you her wisdom... [~MH^]

I submit to you that...[OW^]

I want to leave you with this... [CV^]

If you care for ...... then give yourself the challenge of ...

If you forget every word I say today, it would thrill me if you remember this ... [JK^]

If you want ...... then you must do ... [*Note the call to action is optional]*

Let me challenge you to take control...

My invitation to you is ...

So the next time you feel the need to share a problem of the heart... [JS^]

Take a chance... Don't be afraid to try again... [~DLM]

The next time you hear *It can't be done,* remember... [MM^]

We have great challenges and opportunities and, with your help, we will meet them [TR]

We mustn't look back ... It's never too late to learn—to grow—to create [RF^]

We've covered a lot today. But if you remember just one thing, I want it to be this... [~NS]

Different Closing Techniques

The following shows a selection of various closing techniques. Like a departing handshake, our closing should be encouraging, warm and memorable.

Using a Call-Back to Speech Opening

Jock Elliott ***Just So Lucky***

Background

- A very conversational speech
- Spoke directly to the audience in simple terms
- Closing and Opening lines artfully tied together.

Opening

If I joined Twitter or Facebook
I could have hundreds of brand-new friends
Just like that!
[Snaps finger to indicate ease of getting friends on social networks.]
But how many of them
Would roll out of bed at 3 o'clock in the morning
And come to my aid if I needed them?
Probably not one!

Closing

Reach out now in your mind and heart and touch them.
Feel their warmth—
Feel their friendship—
Feel the ties that bind.
And if we treasure these ties—nurture these ties
We'll have all the luck we'll ever need—
And we won't need Facebook. [JE^]

Guiding Audience What to Do Next

Stuart Pink ***Brain Lifting***

Background

- Establishes that creativity is what makes man different
- Then asks why do we spend so much time exercising our bodies—body lifting?
- And why so little time on exercising our minds—brain lifting?

Closing

So—the next time you have a problem—
Do some brain lifting.
Next time you face a challenge—
Ask yourself—"What if?"
Next time you have a dream—
Ask yourself, —"What if?"
No matter what obstacles you face—
There is no wrong place.
There is no wrong time to ask — *[Audience responds] What If?* [SP^]

Quoting a Well-Known Poem

Phillip Kahn-Panni *Bloody but Unbowed*

Background

- Inspirational speech drawn from Henley's poem, *Invictus*
- Speech opening and closing lines are from the poem
- Title is repeated in the final line (making the speech "complete")

Opening

I thank whatever gods may be, for my unconquerable soul.
Those words of William Henley
Expressed one of the finest human qualities—a fighting spirit.

Closing

What matters is how you perform when it all goes wrong.
That's when you need fortitude—
And if you have it—you deserve to succeed
Because then you have backbone, grit, and a fighting spirit.
And whatever the outcome,
You'll be able to stand erect proudly and declare
Under the bludgeoning of chance,
My head is bloody but unbowed. [PKP]

Closing by Completing the Opening Story

Ryan Avery *Trust is a Must*

Background

- Opening sets the stage and leaves us hanging...
- Speech diverts and takes us back to where this all began
- Closing returns to the opening and we see how it worked out

Opening

I'm at the altar
Sweating in my wool suit.
She is glowing in her white dress.
Asks me the most important question of my life
Ryan, do you promise me? —
Before I make my commitment
I let my mind rewind like an old-school VHS tape.
And it takes me back to ...

Closing

I am at the altar
Sweating in my wool suit.
And Chelsea is glowing in her white dress.
Chelsea—I promise. [RA^]

Closing with Inclusive "Them-Me-You"

Steve Jobs ***Stanford Graduation Address***

Opening

The audience knows Jobs has terminal cancer
With humility, he explains he never graduated from college
Says he will talk of three simple stories from his life

Closing

On the back cover of the final issue [of their Whole Earth Catalog] was a photograph of an early morning country road—
The kind you might find yourself hitchhiking on if you were so adventurous.
Beneath it were the words: *Stay Hungry. Stay Foolish.*
It was their farewell message as they signed off — *Stay Hungry. Stay Foolish.*
And I have always wished that for myself.
And now, as you graduate to begin anew, I wish that for you.
Stay Hungry. Stay Foolish. [SJ+]

Adding Humor to Help Audience Recall

James Webb ***The Ride of Life***

Closing

Ladies and gentlemen, life is a tough roller-coaster ride.
This is our life, our ride.
If we get back on the ride—Look for success.
Persist through the lows and never give up.
We will transcend the highest heights
That will enable us to reach all our dreams.
Like the most famous motivator of all times—Dr. Seuss—said
"And will you succeed? —
Yes, you will indeed —98 and 3/4 percent guaranteed—"
If you get back on the ride. [JW^]

Restating Your Message

Brian Woolf ***The Greatest Thief***

Opening

Opens by suggesting there are no thieves in audience
Pauses, suggests there probably are
Explains: The greatest thief is he who withholds deserved praise

Closing

Friends, my message tonight is simple:
Let's stop stealing from our family and those around us!
Let's stop withholding praise from those who deserve it.
Let's be generous in giving it
For we must never, ever let it be said of us …
That WE were counted among life's greatest thieves. [BW]

Closing with a Dramatic Gesture

William Jennings Bryan *Cross of Gold*

Background

- One of America's most famous political speeches
- Delivered at, and wins, nomination at 1896 Democratic National Convention
- Closes with powerful cry—*You shall not crucify mankind on a cross of gold*— with a dramatic emotional gesture of both arms outstretched (as on a cross), for 5 seconds, offering himself as a sacrifice for the cause of silver (to benefit "the people.") The crowd erupts in pandemonium.

Closing

Having behind us the producing masses of this nation and the world
Supported by the commercial interests
The laboring interests and toilers everywhere
We will answer their demand for a gold standard by saying to them—
You shall not press down upon the brow of labor this crown of thorns—
You shall not crucify mankind upon a **cross of gold**. [WJB]

Closing a Bad-News Speech in a Positive Way

Winston Churchill *Blood, Toil, Tears, And Sweat*

Background

- Churchill's first speech as Prime Minister, May 13, 1940
- 8 months into World War II
- Militarily, Britain is weak, outlook is bleak,
- Tells it straight, has little to offer, but ends positively, with hope

Middle of speech

I would say to the House,
As I said to those who have joined the government—
I have nothing to offer but blood, toil, tears and sweat.
We have before us an ordeal of the most grievous kind.
We have before us many, many long months of struggle and of suffering …

Closing

Without victory, there is no survival.
Let that be realized—
No survival for the British Empire
No survival for all that the British Empire has stood for
No survival for the urge and impulse of the ages,
That mankind will move forward towards its goal.
But I take up my task with buoyancy and hope.
I feel sure that our cause will not be suffered to fail among men.
At this time I feel entitled to claim the aid of all
And I say— Come then, let us go forward together with our united strength. [WC]

Closing Comment

Thank you, dear student of the art of speaking, for arriving at this point. You have read the 5-part POKER framework for speech excellence drawn from experience, research, and observation. It is a framework of success that I wish someone had given me 40 years ago. My wish for you is that having read it, studied the comments and examples, your journey up Speech Mountain will be easier and faster.

Each speaking journey is unique. We all encounter different conditions and challenges along the way. But there is one constant in all journeys: the constant learning.

In the book's different sections, you have read the attributes and speeches exemplifying the section's key benefits. Now that you understand the characteristics of each section, it's time to review what you have learned by looking at a speech in totality.

I invite you now to read and view Manoj Vasudevan's winning 2017 World Championship of Public Speaking contest speech. If you evaluate the speech using POKER, it is best done by changing the review sequence from POKER to OKERP as the message and point is often not fully clear until the end of the speech.

To help start your analysis, I have made introductory comments at the end of the speech. Test what you have learned in this book by identifying the speech's strengths in the five different areas: Point. Opening. Konnect. Emotion. Remember,

Upon completing your analysis, you will see how much your own skill in building speeches has risen.

May your journey up Speech Mountain be an enjoyable experience.

Pull Less, Bend More
Manoj Vasudevan
Winner 2017 World Championship of Public Speaking®

www.thoughtexpressions.com *View YouTube: Manoj Vasudevan Toastmasters*

001. I was 24 years old — I had a nice job, nice car—nice hair. [Speaker is bald]
002. Still my girlfriends didn't stay for long.
003. Have you ever had problems with your relationships with others?
004. What was wrong — with them?

005. Conference Chair, ladies and gentlemen,
006. When I was 24, I was living in India.
007. I was still waiting for cupid to shoot his arrow—and find me the perfect partner.
008. Guess what? — It seems Cupid doesn't live in India.

009. So I went to another angel who had all the answers — My Mama.
010. "Mama, I can't find good girls — how will I ever marry?"
011. She said
012. "No problem—we can fix it."
013. My mama offered to introduce me to some good girls—nice Mama.
014. Soon arrangements were made
015. For my meeting with the first prospect—Sindu.
016. There she was —— Wow!!!
017. In a beautiful blue dress she looked like a star from Hollywood.
018. She looked at me—like I was George Clooney.
019. Cupid shot his arrow — and we fell in love.
020. Do you remember a time
021. When you got into a new relationship?
022. What were you expecting?
023. I imagined spending the rest of my life holding her hand,
024. Listening to music, and doing—"hot" yoga.
025. A few weeks later on the 4th of July we got married.
026. On America's Independence Day — I lost my independence.
027. We sailed through our honeymoon.
028. Then differences started to emerge.
029. She liked outdoors—I liked indoors.
030. She loved swimming—I feared drowning.
031. She liked cooking—I liked to tell her how I missed my mama's cooking.
032. Hey, I didn't want to follow her ways—and she wasn't willing to change.
033. We argued over big things, over small things, even over nothing.
034. I used logic; I used emotion; I even showed her a role model.
035. "Darling, why can't you just be perfect like — me?"
036. Within 6 months we grew apart under one roof.
037. We were two people living in solitude.
038. No holding hands, no music—only silence.
039. Looking for solutions, I asked my friend Jay.
040. He just had his divorce — he was the expert.

041. Jay said — "Man, life is short; don't suffer, separate."
042. "No, Jay, I just want to fix it."
043. "Exactly. My lawyer will fix it" — I called my Mama.

044. The next day she spoke to Sindu and me.
045. She said — "You will never find a partner who is 100% perfect.
046. You fall in love because of Cupid's arrow.
047. But what keeps you in love is Cupid's bow.
048. You see the bow and a string have a great partnership.
049. The more the string pulls back, the more the bow bends—
050. Equal is what pulls the string.
051. Still, the mighty bow bends because it cares for the partner.
052. When she pulls, you bend — When you pull, she bends.
053. If you pull too hard, your relationship can break.
054. If you want to fix it
055. Both of you need to pull less and bend more — pull less and bend more."
056. Have you ever seen anyone who pulls too hard?
057. Have you pulled too hard?

058. Since then, during arguments I became more flexible.
059. When Sindu wanted to go out, I joined her.
060. When she wanted to swim, I joined her — at the shallow end.
061. When I became nice, she became nicer.
062. Soon she started cooking better than Mama.
063. In my search for the perfect partner
064. I discovered that perfect partners
065. Are those who keep perfecting their partnerships
066. By choosing to pull less and bend more.

067. You can see problems in any relationship—
068. Within families, between friends, between colleagues,
069. Between races, cultures, nations.
070. Today it seems like our world is breaking apart, doesn't it?
071. Still when you look at this room
072. You see people from 142 different nations sitting together
073. Shoulder to shoulder — and getting along fine.
074. How is that possible?
075. Toastmasters—you are proof
076. That no matter what our differences are—
077. By choosing to pull less and bend more—
078. We can stay together.

079. Last month my wife and I celebrated our 19th anniversary.
080. Yes — that's the same wife!
081. Do you think we still argue?
082. Yes—but now even when we argue, we are still holding hands.
083. My mama is no more with us — but her words still ring in our ears
084. "Pull less and bend more."
085. Pull less and — *[waits for the audience response]* — *"Bend more."*

Pull Less, Bend More — Manoj Vasudevan Comment

Manoj's message is clear—*Pull less, bend more*—and the whole speech is artfully designed around it. The message also acts as the easy-to-visualize-and-remember action step he points us to: when we experience problems with our spouse, then *Pull less, bend more.*

The speech is about how to have a healthy interpersonal relationship using a basic formula, *Demand less, give more.* But that phrase paints no vivid picture to remember in times of need so instead Manoj uses a well-recognized, easy-to-visualize, metaphor of love: Cupid and his bow.

Let's start by examining how he structured the speech.

Speech Outline

As a young man in India—unable to find a wife.
Asks mother for help [arranged marriage].
Love strikes at first sight—wedding follows.
Differences emerge—divorce or seek wisdom?
Mother— Cupid's bow is the secret— *Pull less, bend more.*
It worked! And is still working.
Works for all relationships.
(Implied) It will work for us, too, when we next encounter the problem.

Or, in Simple Structural Terms

Universal problem.
Finds unique solution.
Reassurance (been working almost 20 years).
Assures it will work for us too.

Why Was the Speech Received So Well?

- Speaker was energetic and "alive" [see video]
- Strong entertainment element [see video]
- Engaging repetitive style and vivid vignettes held our attention
- Message was clear
- The problem was real and relevant to each audience member
- The solution pointed the way as to how we can solve our problems
- The story was personal, authentic and credible
- He related well by showing he realized he was "the problem" (put himself down)

Manoj Used Mental Speed Bumps to Help Connect with Audience

Some mental speed bumps that grabbed our attention and minimized the inclination of minds wanting to wander included:

(i) He Asked Questions of the Audience

Do you remember a time when you got into a new relationship? What were you expecting? [L.20]

Today it seems like our world is breaking apart, doesn't it? [70]

You see people from 142 different nations sitting together shoulder to shoulder and getting along fine. How is that possible? [72]

Do you think we still argue? Yes. But now even when we argue, we are still holding hands. [81]

(ii) He Used Ear-Catching Contrasts

Pull less, bend more [0]

"No, Jay, I just want to fix it."—"Exactly. My lawyer will fix it." [42]

When she wanted to swim, I joined her—at the shallow end. When I became nice, she became nicer. Soon she started cooking better than Mama. [60]

(iii) He Used Twists to Trigger Laughter and Relax the Audience

Have you ever had problems with your relationships with others? What was wrong — with them?[3]

She looked at me—like I was George Clooney [18]

I used logic; I used emotion; I even showed her a role model. "Darling, why can't you just be perfect like—me?" [34]

...Now Jot Down What You Discovered About the Five Elements

OPENING

KONNECT

KONNECT **(contd.)**

EMOTION

REMEMBER

POINT & MESSAGE

OTHER NOTES

SUPERSCRIPT INDEX

Note: If a tilde (~) precedes a listed superscript (such as [~MT]), the original quote has been slightly altered to make it shorter or clearer. Symbols after initials (eg, DB^, DB+, and DB=) are used to differentiate people with the same initials.

The term WCPS following a person's name denotes Toastmasters® World Champion of Public Speaking® (sometimes shown with the year the title was won.) Some winners use the term World Champion Speaker for the same accomplishment. A member can win the title only once. Likewise, a person's name with a 2-digit superscript indicates the year the person competed.

Many of the recent World Champions' speeches can be viewed on YouTube by entering the speaker's name followed by the word Toastmasters in the YouTube Search Box. Likewise, other speakers in the book whose name is followed by [YT+] can be viewed on YouTube by entering their name in its Search Box.

A	Aristotle
AA	Angelique Arnauld
AB^	Arabella Bengson [WCPS-86]
AB+	Aaron Broussard
AB>	Aaron Beverly
AD	Andrew Dlugan
AD^	Anita Davis
AD+	Angus Deaton
AD>	Andy Dooley
AE	Albert Einstein
AF	Anatole France
AFT	Anita Fain Taylor
AG	Alexander Gregg
AHG	Arnold H Glasgow
AL^	Angela Louie
AL+	Ann Landers
AN	Anonymous
AP	Alan Perlman
AS+	Adlai Stevenson
AT	Arnold Toynbee
AT^	Anne Taylor
B	Bible
B+	Brit
BB	Bill Bonner
BC	Bill Clinton
BC+	Brian Clark
BF	Benjamin Franklin
BF^	Brian Farison
BFS	Bishop Fulton Sheen
BG	Bill Gove
BG*	Bill Gates
BG+	Billy Graham
BH^	Bob Herndon
BHP	Brian Picot
BJ	Benjamin Disraeli
BK	Beverly Kirkhart
BM^	Bill Mintz
BO	Barack Obama
BOR	Brian O'Rourke
BR	Bob Richards
BR^	Brett Rutledge [WCPS-98]
BR+	Bertrand Russell
BS+	Bill Sands
BT	Brad Thor
BT+	Barbara Tuchman
BW	Brian Woolf
C	Cicero
CA	Chris Anderson, CEO, TED
CB	Cam Barber
CB+	Carl Buehner
CC	Carl Cannon
CEH	Charles E Hummel
CG^	Carlos Greene
CJT	C John Tupper
CM	Charlie Munger
CM+	Christopher Myers

CN^	Chakisse Newton
CO	Candace Owens
CR	Cavett Robert
CR^	Christine Robinson
CV^	Craig Valentine [WCPS-99]
DB	Dr. Denis Burkitt
DB^	David Brooks [WCPS-90]
DB+	James “Doc” Blakely
DB=	Dave Barry
DB>	Daach’ana Blaydes
DC	Dale Carnegie
DC+	Doug Casey
DDE	Dwight D. Eisenhower
DH^	Dananjaya Hettiarachchi [WCPS-14]
DH+	David Henderson [WCPS-10]
DJ^	Don Johnson [WCPS-89]
DK	Dacher Keltner
DK^	Douglas Kruger
DLC	Darren LaCroix [WCPS-01]
DLM	Dana LaMon [WCPS-92]
DMC	Gen. Douglas MacArthur
DN	David Nottage [WCPS-96]
DP	Dan Pink
DP^	Diane Parker
DP+	Dennis Prager
DR	Dave Ramsey
DR^	David Ross [WCPS-91]
DS	Doug Stevenson
DS*	Dabo Sweeney (Clemson coach)
DS^	Dwayne Smith [WCPS-02]
DS+	Dr Seuss
DS<	David Stockman
DS=	Daniel Silva
DS>	David Sanfacon
DSR	Doug Ross
DT^	Darren Tay Wen Jie [WCPS-16]
DW	Dan Weedin
DW*	Daniel Webster
DW>	Douglas Wilson
EE^	Elliott Eddy
EEC	e e cummings
EF^	Eric Feinendegen
EG	Emma Gonzalez
EH	Elbert Hubbard
EH^	Ed Hearn [WCPS-06]
EH+	Eric Hoffer
EK	Edward (Ted) Kennedy
EMS	Eisenhower Middle School, NJ
ET^	Ed Tate [WCPS-00]
FA	Fred Allen
FB	Francis Bacon
FDR	Franklin D Roosevelt
FM^	Frank Morris
FOA	Francis of Assisi
G	Goethe
GB	George Burns
GF	Gerald Ford
GJ	George Jessel
GKC	G K Chesterton
GN+	Gary North
GO	George Orwell
GP	Gregg Parr
GS	Gerry Spence
GS+	George Santayana
GS>	Gertrude Stein
GV	Gore Vidal
GW	George Will
GWB	George W. Bush
HB	Helen Blanchard
HB+	Henri Bergson
HC	Sen. Happy Chandler
HC+	Harvey Cox
HD	Harvey Diamond
HDT	Henry David Thoreau
HEF	Harry Emerson Fosdick
HHH	Hubert Humphrey
HK	Helen Keller
HK+	Herbert Korthoff
HL^	Hans Lillijord
HLB	Henry Louis Bergson
HP^	Harold Patterson [WCPS-87]
HR	Harold Russell
HR+	Hans Rosling
HR>	Helen Rowland
HST	Harry S Truman
HT	Harriet Tubman
IF	Ian Fleming
ISU	isu.edu/success/writing
JA	John Antonakis
JA^	Jonathan Abuyan
JA+	Sheriff Joe Arpaio
JA>	John Andrews

JAG J. A. Gamache

JB* Jordan Bradden

JB^ Jeremiah Bacon

JB> Jimmy Buffett

JC Judy Carter

JC+ Johnny Cochran

JC> John Chapin

JE Johnathan Edwards

JE^ Jock Elliott [WCPS-11]

JE< Jacoby Ethridge

JF Jane Fonda

JFK John F Kennedy

JG John Glenn

JG+ Jim Grant

JH Jack Hart

JJ Joseph Joubert

JJ^ James Jeffley

JJ+ Jesse Jackson

JJ> Judy Joice

JK^ Jim Key [WCPS-03]

JK+ Jamaica Kincaid

JK> Jezra Kaye

JKG John Kenneth Galbraith

JL^ Josephine Lee

JM Jon Morrow

JM* Jo Maypole

JM^ Jonah Mungoshi

JM+ John Mauldin

JN^ Jay Nodine

JO Jamie Oliver

JO^ Johan Ooi Keng Kee

JOC James Oliver Curwood

JP+ John Pilger

JPM J P Morgan

JR< Jeff Reagan

JR> Jeanne Robertson

JS John Shepherd

JS* John Steinbeck

JS^ Jerry Starke [WCPS-88]

JS+ Johnathan Swift

JS> Jeff Sanders

JT Jack Trout

JT+ John Templeton

JW John Wooten

JW^ James Webb

JW+ Joel Weldon

JWE J W Eagan

KB^ Kingi Biddle

KC Kathleen Callendar

KC^ Kirk Carr

KF Ken Follett

KH^ Katina Hunter

KJ^ Kevin Johnson

KM Kieran Meyer

KMC Kenneth McFarland

KN^ Kageni Njeru

KP Kathleen Parker

KR^ Kaishika Rodrigo

KR+ Ken Robinson

KRM Kenny Ray Morgan

KS Kelly Swanson

KS^ Kevin Stamper

KS> Kelly Sergent

KT Kevin Taylor

KYY Kwong Yue Yang

LA Lord Acton

LC Lee Child

LC^ Linus Chang

LC+ LitCharts.com

LC> Lewis Carroll

LE Lisa Evans

LG> Louis Ginsberg

LH Lou Holtz

LM^ Lance Miller [WCPS-05]

LN Liam Napier

LSR LaShunda Rundles [WCPS-08]

LT Larry Taylor

LV Laura Vanderkam

M Mistinguett

MA Maureen Abdulla

MA* Maya Angelou

MA^ Michael Aun [WCPS-78]

MA+ Mike Anthony

MAM Movie *Auntie Mame* (1958)

MB^ Mark Brown [WCPS-95]

MC Michael Caine

MC+ Mama Cass

MD Maureen Dowd

MF Mark Forsyth

MF+ Mary Fisher

MFT Martin Farquhar Tupper

MH Mitch Hedberg

MH^	Mark Hunter [WCPS-09]
MH>	Mark Haugh
MI	Molly Ivins
MJ	Sister Mary Joseph
ML^	Mario Lewis
MLK	Martin Luther King Jr
MM	Mitch Murray
MM^	Morgan McArthur [WCPS-94]
MN	Martina Navratilova
MPW	Malvery Pilgrim-Williams
MQ^	Mohammed Qahtani [WCPS-15]
MR	Mike Robertson
MR+	Manie Robinson
MR>	Mitt Romney
MS+	Michael Sansola
MS>	Mark Steyn
MT	Mark Twain
MT+	Margaret Thatcher
MV^	Manoj Vasudevan [WCPS-17]
MVH	Mark Victor Hansen
MW	Marie Woolf
MW+	Mae West
MX	Malcolm X
ND	Nancy Duarte
NF	Niall Ferguson
NG	Newt Gingrich
NK	Norman Kent
NK+	Neil Kinnock
NM	Nick Morgan
NM+	Norman Mayne
NQ	Nido Qubein
NS	Nick Skellon
OH	Oscar Hammerstein
ON	Ogden Nash
OS^	Olivia Schofield
OW	Oscar Wilde
OW^	Otis Williams Jr. [WCPS-93]
P	Plato
PB^	Phil Barth
PD+	Peter Drucker
PDV	Peter de Vries
PF	Patricia Fripp
PH^	Peter Hempenstall
PH+	Dr George (Pete) Hoffman
PH<	Patricia Hill
PH>	Patrick Hammond
PKP	Phillip Kahn-Panni
PL	Patrick Lau
PM	Pamela Meyer
PM^	Phoenix Miller
PM+	Pooja Mahajan
PS^	Palaniappa Subramaniam
PTB	P T Barnum
PV^	Pres Vasilev [WCPS-13]
PW	Pat Williams
PW+	Sen. Paul Wellstone
RA^	Ryan Avery [WCPS-12]
RA>	Reubin Askew
RB	Rick Bragg
RB+	Ron Barnett
RB>	Robert Byrne
RBE	Rhetoric.byu.edu
RBZ	Roy B Zuck
RE	Ric Elias
RF	Robert Frost
RF^	Roy Fenstermaker [WCPS-83]
RF>	Robert Ferguson
RH^	Rich Hopkins
RIM	Raul Ilargi Meijer
RJH	Randy J Harvey [WCPS-04]
RJS	Ramona J Smith [WCPS-18]
RJW	Robert James Waller
RK^	Robert Killen
RL+	Ron Lunde
RM	Rusty Mitchell
RM^	Richard Madison
RM+	Robert Mackenzie
RM>	Roy Mitchell
RP	Ron Paul
RR	Ronald Reagan
RS	Robert Schuller
RS^	Richard Spencer
RS+	Roger Stangeland
RS>	Richard Sakwa
RW	Ralph Walker
RW^	Ruth Witty
RWE	Ralph Waldo Emerson
RWK	Ralph W Ketner
S	Socrates
SA+	Scott Adams
SA>	Spiro Agnew

SB^	Simon Bucknall
SB+	Major-Gen. Smedley Butler
SD^	Sharook Darawala
SE	Sam Ervin
SH	Sam Horn
SJ	Samuel Johnson
SJ^	Sherwood Jones
SJ+	Steve Jobs
SK	Soren Kierkegaard
SK^	Sameera Khan
SK+	Sean Keener
SL	Sam Leith
SP	Spanish Proverb
SP^	Stuart Pink
SS	Steve Siemens
SS^	Simon Scriver
SS+	SpeakingSherpa.com
SS>	Simon Sinek
STC	Samuel Taylor Coleridge
SW>	Simone Weil
SWD	Sherwin W Dillard Jr
TC*	Thomas Carlyle
TC^	Todd Collins
TC<	Tom Cruise
TE	Thomas Edison
TES	Tom Smith
THAC	Tom Ah Chee
THH	Thomas Henry Huxley
TK	Timothy Koegel
TM	Thomas Montalbo
TM^	Ted Mathew
TN	Toastmasters Newsletter
TR	Tony Robbins
TS	Tom Smith
TSE	T S Eliot
V	Voltaire
VCB	vocabularly.com/dictionary
VJ^	Vikas Jhingran WCPS-07
VL	Vince Lombardi
VL+	Vladimir Lenin
VS	Various Sources
VVE	Vanessa Van Edwards
W	Wikipedia
WA+	Wale Ayeni
WC	Winston Churchill
WCF	W C Fields
WD+	Will Durant
WH	William Hazlitt
WHP	William H Peterson
WJ	Willie Jollie
WJ^	Willie Jones WCPS-97
WJB	William Jennings Bryan
WM	Whitehall maxim
WM+	W Mitchell
WN^	Wiewiek Najihah
WS	William Shakespeare
WS>	William Strong
WW+	Willie Wonka
Y	Yoda
YB	Yogi Berra
YP^	Yuri Ptschelinzew
YT+	Available on YouTube (as at Sep 2019)
ZH	Zerohedge Feb 4, 2018
ZSS	Zifang "Sherrie" Su
ZZ	Zig Ziglar
Z1	*The Speaker's Toolbox*
Z2	*The Non-Humorist's Handbook*

Selected Resources

Ackerman, Angela & Puglisi, Becca. *The Emotion Thesaurus*
Ailes, Roger. *You Are the Message*
Anderson, Chris. *TED Talks*
Barber, Cam. *What's Your Message?*
Carter, Judy. *The Message of You*
Clark, Roy Peter. *Writing Tools*
Donovan, Jeremey and Avery, Ryan. *Speaker Leader Champion*
Donovan, Jeremey. *How to Deliver a TED Talk*
Hart, Jack. *A Writer's Coach*
Harvey, Randy J. *Messages That Matter*
Horn, Sam. *Got Your Attention?*
Humes, James C. *Instant Eloquence*
Humes, James C. *Speak Like Churchill, Stand Like Lincoln*
Koegel, Timothy. *The Exceptional Presenter*
Landon, Brooks. *Building Great Sentences* (The Great Courses Series, DVD)
Leech, Thomas. *How to Prepare, Stage, & Deliver Winning Presentations*
Montalbo, Thomas. *Public Speaking Made Easy*
Murray, Donald. *Writing to Deadline*
Safire, William. *Lend Me Your Ears*
Schwartzberg, Joel. *Get to The Point!*
Stevenson, Doug. *Story Theater Method*
Olson, Ricky. *Hook 'Em With Humor*
Robertson, Jeanne. *Don't Let the Funny Stuff Get Away*
Valentine, Craig. *The Nuts and Bolts of Public Speaking*
Van Edwards, Vanessa. *Captivate*
Vasilev, Pres. *How to Master Compelling Storytelling* (available at *pressays.com*)

Excellent Books on Rhetoric (educational and entertaining)

Forsyth, Mark. *The Elements of Eloquence*
Leith, Sam. *Words Like Loaded Pistols*
Leith, Sam. *You Talking to Me?*

Excellent Free Presentations on Speaking

Ryan Avery 2013 (D-62. 1hr:48) View YouTube: Ryan Avery Toastmasters
Randy Harvey (D-61. 0:47) View YouTube: Randy Harvey Toastmasters
David Henderson (0:49) View YouTube: David Henderson Toastmasters

Excellent Free Websites for Speakers

speaklikeapro.co.uk [Editor: Nick Skellon]
sixminutes.dlugan.com [Editor: Andrew Dlugan]
LitCharts.com
RhymeBrain.com
Rhetoric.byu.edu

About the Author

Brian Woolf is a speechaholic. He loves listening to speeches, thinking about them, and giving them; and he loves reading and studying them — their makeup, their message, their music — to discover their magic.

It wasn't always so. In high school, he ardently avoided entering the annual speech contests. While at University he "bombed" with a speech at a major black-tie dinner. At 22, in his first job, he knew he needed speaking help. Toastmasters clubs were just being introduced to his native New Zealand. He joined. He learned. He gained speaking confidence ... enough to subsequently use the skills learned to graduate with Distinction from Harvard Business School with its two-year program of dialogue-based case studies. In later years, he has spoken extensively, including at conferences on five continents.

Toastmasters plays a key part in his life. Brian has been an active member in clubs in New Zealand, Ireland, and six states in the USA. Besides earning its highest award, Distinguished Toastmaster (DTM), he has won six District (State) Speech Contests — and lost many more (which is when the intensive learning occurs!) In 2003, he was one of nine finalists in Toastmasters World Championship of Public Speaking.®

Mastering communication skills has helped him not only at Toastmasters but also in the business world and as an author.

Comments and suggestions

Should you know of any quotation attributed in this book with an older pedigree, I would appreciate learning of it. Likewise, if you care to share any comments or suggestions, or have any quotations you think worthy of inclusion in a future reprint or website posting, please send them to me at:

brianwoolf@speakers-toolbox.com

Also Available at Amazon.com

Made in the
USA
Columbia, SC

81793587R00133